MISSION
CULTURE ON
THE UPPER
AMAZON

David Block

MISSION CULTURE ON THE UPPER AMAZON

Native Tradition,
Jesuit Enterprise, &
Secular Policy in Moxos,
1660-1880

University of
Nebraska Press
Lincoln and London

This book has been published with the aid of
a grant from the Hull Memorial Publication
Fund of Cornell University.
The paper in this book meets the minimum
requirements of American National Standard
for Information Sciences – Permanence of
Paper for Printed Library Materials,
ANSI Z39.48 – 1984. Library of Congress
Cataloging-in-Publication Data
Block, David, 1945–   Mission culture on
the upper Amazon : native tradition, Jesuit
enterprise, and secular policy in Moxos, 1660–
1880 / David Block. p. cm.
Includes bibliographical references and index.
ISBN 0-8032-1232-1 (alk. paper)
1. Mojo Indians – Missions.
2. Indians of South America – Bolivia –
Moxos – Missions.
3. Jesuits – Missions – Bolivia – Moxos.
4. Moxos (Bolivia) – History. 5. El Beni
(Bolivia) – History. I. Title.
F3320.2.M55B56   1994
266'.28442 – dc 20   93-24620 CIP

For Elizabeth and Tryon,
always more than in-laws

CONTENTS

Maps

Plates

Figures

Tables

ACKNOWLEDGMENTS

This book took a long, bumpy path to publication. Originally conceived as an ethnohistorical study of the early years of Spanish contact with the native people of Amazonia, its first presentation, as a Ph.D. thesis, strove to reconstruct the first two centuries of conquistador and Jesuit missionary penetration of Moxos. But the area's pre-Jesuit documentation proved insufficient to the demands of ethnohistorical research, and the early years only began to develop what was truly significant about cultural change there. What you have before you now represents an expansion of the chronology of the thesis as well as a reconceptualization of its approach to include additional materials on Moxos' European inhabitants.

Implicit in this description of the work's metamorphosis is the passage of time. The expansion of the project and the vicissitudes of my career prolonged the completion of the book for a decade. The support of a number of institutions and individuals sustained me over that time. Funds from a Dissertation Research Grant from what was then the Department of Health, Education and Welfare and a grant from the Dora Bonham Fund of the University of Texas enabled me to visit archives in Spain, Peru, and Bolivia as a graduate student. Subsequent awards from Cornell University's Latin American Studies Program, St. Louis University, and the National Endowment for the Humanities underwrote an expansion of the original research by allowing me to consult additional materials in Bolivia and Rome. Consistent in my travels was the professional, supportive attitude of archival personnel. I am especially indebted to Gunnar Mendoza and his staff at the Archivo y Biblioteca Nacional de Bolivia, who received my requests for materials for over a decade.

Since graduate school, I have worked as a librarian, charged with supporting rather than producing scholarship. This change in my professional trajectory removed some of the stimulus and most of the rewards for completing the project. Others in my position have been forced to set their research aside or to channel their energies into areas more central to the canons of librarianship. I have been fortunate in finding my supervisors — Martin Faigel, Herb Finch, and Ross Atkinson — supportive or at least willing to wink at the opportunity costs of my historical work.

I am very grateful for this financial aid and professional encouragement, but, in the long run (and it has been long), the support of family and friends has made this book possible. My parents, especially my father, consistently encouraged me to expand my thesis manuscript. A series of scholars — Jay Lehnertz (I hope you see this, Jay), Frank Safford, and Erik Van Young prominent among them — offered aid and comfort over the years. While translations to English are my own, Marcia Jebb and Cecilia Sercan of the Cornell University Library came to the rescue when my high school French and "reading knowledge" of Portuguese proved inadequate in the face of eighteenth-century texts. And members of the High Noon A.C. provided criticism and motivation amid marathon training. As the revised manuscript began to take shape, two historians here at Cornell, Tom Holloway and Dan Usner, read it with a care that reflected friendship rather than collegial responsibility.

Finally, my wife, Peggy Robinson, while never sharing my interest in mission culture, appreciated its importance to me and made sacrifices in time and energy that allowed me to work everything in.

Thank you, one and all.

LIST OF ABBREVIATIONS

ADLB   Archivo de Límites de Bolivia, La Paz

ADLP   Archivo de Límites del Perú, Lima

AGI   Archivo General de Indias, Sevilla

AGNP   Archivo General de la Nación del Perú, Lima

ANB   Archivo Nacional de Bolivia, Sucre

ADM   Archivo de Mojos

MH   Ministerio de Hacienda

MI   Ministerio del Interior

MYCH   Mojos y Chiquitos

ARSI   Archivum Romanum Societatis Iesu, Rome

BNL   Biblioteca Nacional del Perú, Lima

BPR   Biblioteca del Palacio Real, Madrid

BN   Biblioteca Nacional, Madrid

INTRODUCTION

Fleeing retribution for crimes of passion committed in Europe, Candide visits the Jesuit missions of Paraguay. Through the voice of his satirical alter ego, Voltaire expresses a fascination with these outposts of Western civilization located on the edge of El Dorado. And his sentiments resonate through generations of treatments of the tropical missionary enterprise, whose titles — *A Vanished Arcadia* and *The Lost Paradise* to mention two of the most illustrative — reflect the often millenarian character of their messages.[1] Perhaps the most accessible example of this imagery is a recent film, *The Mission,* which offers its viewers soft-focused images of tropical scenery, noble savages, heroic priests, and corrupt Europeans. The work you have before you explores the mission from another perspective, stressing process over personality and daily life over heroism. It examines the role of the encounters between Europeans and native Americans in establishing new societies.

The region of Moxos, lying on the upper Amazon in what is modern Bolivia, forms the basis of this study. Jesuits reached Moxos in the mid-seventeenth century and began missionary activities that would fundamentally change the area and its inhabitants. Here, as they did in Paraguay, missionaries and Indians established centers that became the focus of economic, social, and spiritual life for two centuries. Also as in Paraguay, these centers became the focus of rivalries between the Society of Jesus and secular governors. And as a final parallel to the Paraguayan saga, Jesuit operatives were forced to leave Moxos when the Society's fortunes declined after 1767. But the departure of the missionaries did not spell the end of the centers they had helped to establish. For in the hundred years of Jesuit presence, Moxos witnessed the evolution of new systems — biological, technological, organizational, and theological—which conditioned another century of its history. These new systems, which I will call mission culture as a shorthand reference, are the focus of this book.

Mission culture is visible in a wide range of activities and processes in the region. It signifies the emergence of a native population resistant to European diseases, a resistance gained through exposure and suffering but one that supported stable populations by the time of Jesuit exile and for a century afterwards. Mission culture also may be seen in the mixing and selection of European and Indian modes of subsistence, and in a resultant hybrid that adopted more efficient ways of performing traditional tasks. Under mission culture native people preserved much of their autonomy. Traditional leaders retained their positions and expanded their functions, and the introduction of Spanish models of government actually enlarged the political elite. Similarly, the missions ushered in a new social and economic complexity by establishing a functional hierarchy based on occupation, with those practicing European arts and industries constituting a separate group from those involved in subsistence activities. The missions became miniature urban centers populated by Indians who produced goods for their own subsistence and for Spanish markets in the highlands. While mission culture developed during the century of Jesuit presence on the savanna (1668–1767), it established a set of mores and regimens that would dominate life in Moxos until the middle of the nineteenth century.

Spanish missions have inspired scholarly study since the beginning of this century. Herbert E. Bolton's identification of the mission as a frontier institution inspired generations of scholars to investigate its development everywhere in the Americas. Much of this investigation has concentrated on the methods, motives, and messages of the missionaries or on the role the missions played in the formation of state policies. Bolton himself saw the shortcoming of this approach, decrying the monotonous sequence of "chronicles of the deeds of the Fathers" and imploring students to broaden their horizons.[2] Mission studies began to explore new ground with the publication of Magnus Mörner's monograph on the economic and political activities of the Paraguayan Jesuits.[3] A number of investigators have expanded Mörner's emphases for mission systems throughout the Americas. Current scholarship has begun to concentrate on the mission Indians, especially on their demographic histories, land tenure patterns, and social organization.[4] A concentration on the Indian populations is consistent with my own approach, and much of this new work provides a comparative context for the Moxos case.

The scholarly foundation for any work on Moxos began with Gabriel René-Moreno's assembly of the largest single corpus of primary documentation on the area. As he reviewed the manuscripts inherited by the Bolivian national archive, this Bolivian savant prepared the first history of the area, the introduction to his *Catálogo del Archivo de Mojos y Chiquitos* (1888). As the title implies, his work was intended principally as a finding aid. However, René-Moreno wrote from personal association with events then still fresh in his native city of Santa Cruz de la Sierra, located at the threshold of Moxos. Because of this background and his close reading of the documents themselves, René-Moreno was able to establish a reliable chronicle for the last half-century of the Spanish colony and to comment accurately on the demise of the Moxos centers, an event completed almost as he wrote.

A half-century would pass before Moxos again would become the subject of serious investigation. In the 1940s, José Chávez Suárez and Manuel Limpias Saucedo, both sons of the region, wrote extensive syntheses of Moxos history. Chávez Suárez's *Historia de Moxos* examined the region from its supposed contact with Incaic expeditionary forces to the end of the colonial period. He provides the first modern treatment of the Jesuit age in Moxos, and although he denies using unpublished sources, many of the lengthy passages he quotes without references are, to my knowledge, to be found nowhere else. Limpias Saucedo's *Los gobernadores de Mojos* begins with the creation of the Beni Department (1842), which included Moxos within its territory, and provides a governor-by-governor synopsis of events in the department to the beginning of the twentieth century.

For the last fifty years, foreign scholars have joined their Bolivian colleagues in investigating Moxos. Alcides Parejas Moreno's work on the Bourbon period in the missions adds valuable information on their commercial and administrative development in the eighteenth century. Studies by Rogers Becerra Casanovas and Rodolfo Pinto Parada have illuminated new facets of art and folklore in the area. Alfred Métraux's pioneering historical ethnographies, published in the *Handbook of South American Indians,* show little need of revision forty-five years after publication. William Denevan's *The Aboriginal Cultural Geography of the Llanos de Mojos of Bolivia* is without a doubt the single most important work on the region published to date. Denevan did an excellent job of summarizing extant sources to the mid-1960s and of introducing his own highly original contribution on Moxos' extensive system of human-made earthworks. He continues to deal with Moxos through his broader research on aboriginal earthworks and pre-Columbian population levels.[5] Leandro Tormo Sanz has spent much of his scholarly career investigating the historical demography of Moxos. His oeuvre is scattered in periodicals published in his native Spain and in the Americas; samples appear in the bibliography to this book. The latest contribution to the history of Moxos comes from the Catalan Josep M. Barnadas, who in editing an important chronicle written by the eighteenth-century missionary Francisco Xavier Eder wrote an extensive commentary on the Jesuit age.[6]

These scholars provide students of Moxos with a great deal of important information. Through trial and error, they have established an accurate chronology of the region's history and identified many of the principal events and personalities. In addition, these men have sketched the broad cultural contours of the native people and explored some of the important themes of their lives since Spanish contact, especially their demographic history. I readily concede that this book relies heavily on previous work for context and insight. But if my work covers traveled ground, it does so with the aid of new sources and new perspectives.

For their treatments of the age of mission culture, my predecessors relied almost exclusively on published sources dealing with the administration of the missions. These "official" accounts tend to present the aggregate rather than the discrete, and they leave many processes totally unexplored. This book has benefited from my extensive work in various archives, resulting in the discovery of previously unreported data. Moving beyond the official view involved more than new sources, however; it necessitated that I invoke the techniques of social history, examining small pieces of information on a large number of individuals to discover life events and patterns of behavior. One of my objectives in this book is to expand knowledge of daily life in the missions. What were the social and economic activities that occupied the inhabitants? How were regimens maintained and rules enforced? I was also interested in the economics of supporting a mission system. Recently we have learned a great deal about the activities of colonial religious orders, especially the Jesuits, in generating income from landed estates and other investments. Was there a link between these activities and the missionary activities of the same orders? Most important, I was interested in reconstructing the history of mission Indians. How did the native populations of Moxos react to contact with Europeans? What was life in the missions like for its native populations? This study insists on the importance of Indian action in the missions and identifies at least some of the ways in which native people asserted themselves there.

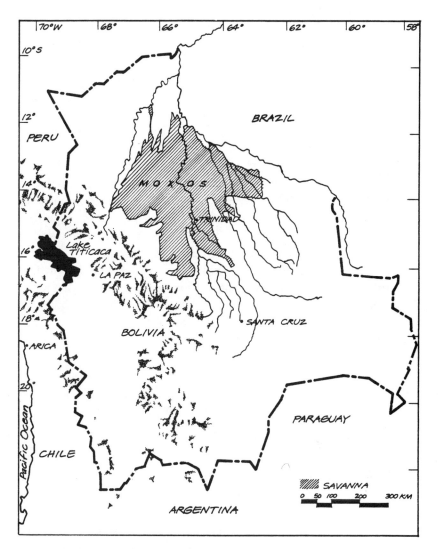

Map 1. Orientation of Moxos

Moxos is both a geographic and administrative designation. The former describes a vast savanna lying on the uppermost reaches of the Amazon river system. As an administrative jurisdiction, Moxos initially referred to the Jesuit missionary province delineated by the major river networks shown in map 1 and by several groups of river-oriented native people whose domains covered the same territory. This geocultural locus later became a governorship during the last half-century of colonial rule and the Beni Department of Bolivia. Current Bolivian usage preserves the term, using modern orthography to describe the savanna lands — *Llanos de Mojos*.

The history reconstructed in this book took place in a physical setting that was critically important to the rhythms of native life and to the direction of European contact. In addition to showing Moxos' river systems, map 1 illustrates that the area was removed from the heavily populated regions of the colonial and modern periods by two hundred kilometers of mountain passes and densely forested Andean slope. This isolation sheltered Moxos from intensive contact with the highlands before and after European arrival. On the savanna, control of the river courses, especially the central network flowing through Trinidad, determined the domination of the region. The native people of the historical period probably reached Moxos by traveling up the river systems from central Amazonia. The first Spaniards to reach the region, during a century of frustrated searches for El Dorado and subsequent slave raids, certainly used the rivers as routes for their horse- and canoe-borne entries. Moreover, the "spiritual conquest" achieved by the Jesuits derived from their use of the fluvial networks to contact the native people.

European introductions formed a second important component of mission culture. Jesuit arrival significantly altered Moxos' physical landscape. Most prominent were the mission complexes, which impressed all who saw them with their size and substance. For here at the very edge of the Spanish colony rose churches, housing, ranches, agricultural complexes, and light industrial plants, which delighted resident priests and amazed their visitors. But hidden from the visitors' eyes, and from most of the field priests' as well, was a corporate support network. Jesuit investments made in the highlands and coast of Charcas and Peru, and directed by financial managers resident in Lima, generated most of the revenues that underwrote the European component of mission culture.

The most important European introduction was biological — the Old World pathogens that spawned periodic outbreaks of smallpox, measles, influenza, and various other diseases often described only by the generic term *peste*. The Jesuits were powerless before these epidemics. They ministered to the infirm and often joined them as victims. Yet, despite their frustration, the Jesuits stayed on in Moxos, where their diligence and dedication helped to foster formation of mission culture. Chapter 5 illuminates the Jesuit component of mission culture by preparing a composite of the priests and lay brothers who served in Moxos, emphasizing their backgrounds and career patterns as well as their activities as missionaries. This chapter challenges two traditional assumptions of mission history: the essentially spiritual character of the missions' foundation and maintenance, and the inveterate paternalism of the fathers and brothers.

Try as they might, the Jesuits could never enforce their stated desire to preserve the missions as a kind of sacred reserve, free from the corrupting influences of the secular world. Despite its isolation — in fact because of it — Moxos occasionally became a theater for secular action. At the end of the Jesuit century, an advancing Portuguese presence in the South American interior brought tension and expeditionary armies to the missions. After Jesuit exile, Moxos became the object of plans intended to integrate its economy, if not its people, into the highland-oriented economies of Charcas and Bolivia. While the state played only a minor role in savanna life, it cannot be ignored. Most graphically, it was a series of policy initiatives made during the Bolivian Republic that contributed to the ultimate unraveling of mission culture.

The consistent and central focus of mission culture, and of this history, falls upon the native people of Moxos. At the time of European arrival, Moxos' Indians showed a remarkable sophistication. Despite their undeniably reduced numbers and probable political vitiation — both the result of a century of exposure to European diseases and slaving — the native people presented an attractive target for a missionary enterprise. At the time of their Jesuit contact, they still had relatively large populations, thriving agricultural and fishing operations, and organized political and religious practices. Just as important, they proved willing to receive the priests in peace.

The missions ended forever the monopoly of native cultural modes in Moxos. But they established a viable substitute for premission life-styles, one acceptable to both priests and Indians. Chapter 4 emphasizes the paramount role played by the Indians in the establishment and functioning of the missions. Far from being passive wards of the priests, the native people actively participated in all phases of mission life, sagaciously sifting and shaping European traditions to local realities. A close examination of mission life in the Jesuit period reveals a variety of social and economic patterns that formed the new cultural amalgam. Yet it is the post-Jesuit period that best illustrates the strength of mission culture.

Jesuit exile engendered an initial enthusiasm for the integration of missions into the Spanish Empire. However, the priests' successors soon discovered that mission wealth, at least in the contemporary context of the expression, was illusory. When the Spanish Crown confiscated Jesuit estates in the highlands and coast, Moxos held little that secular administrators considered valuable. The post-Jesuit period was characterized by a series of ventures designed to make the missions pay—a redirection of agriculture and skilled labor from subsistence to export, and a liquidation of mission property for quick commercial gain. This period was understandably one of native unrest. With traditional modes of production and traditional patterns of redistribution under attack in Moxos, native challenges were launched first through the judicial system and then through movements of open rebellion. As testimony to the durability of mission culture, resistance bore the stamp of Jesuit precedent. Opposition to the Spanish administration invariably harkened back to the "days of the fathers," and the native leadership consistently used tactics based on social alliances within the missions and knowledge of the Spanish legal system beyond it.

During the Bolivian Republic, a second cycle of optimistic prediction and white, that is, highland Bolivian, entry into the area began. True to the liberal spirit in which the republic was established and recognizing the need to promote its economic stability, Bolivian state functionaries redoubled the efforts of their colonial predecessors. The missions—now called towns by men who called themselves "citizens"—received their first significant influx of immigrants and a parallel impulse toward increased commercial agriculture and large-scale production of cotton textiles for the highland market during this period. Moxos also became linked with the world market for tropical products during the Republican period, first fleetingly through cinchona bark collection and then definitively and tragically in the Amazonian rubber boom.

As a chronological context for this work, I suggest that the history of Moxos falls into three distinct epochs. The first, called tropical forest culture in Donald W. Lathrap's compelling analysis, began when Arawak speakers arrived on the savanna, circa 500 A.D.[7] This initial epoch, sketched briefly in chapter 1, was characterized by the dominance of Amazonian modes of material and spiritual life. In Moxos, tropical forest culture spans a millennium of prehistory and the first century of Spanish contact.

The last great period, still ongoing, dates from the breakdown of Moxos' isolation from the rest of the world. The national laws that dissolved communal rights in the area as they created the Beni Department in 1842 swept away the legal basis for mission culture. More important, Moxos' entry into the world economic system during the Amazonian rubber boom destroyed community life by taking its members far away from the mission centers. In addition, substantial numbers of whites and mestizos arrived in the area during this period, and many natives sold their property and labor power to the newcomers. The modern period in Moxos has yet to find its historian, even though work by James C. Jones and J. Valerie Fifer provides very useful insights, and the placement of the archives of the principal Bolivian rubber firm in a public repository promises to open this period to fruitful investigation.[8] Between these two great ages lies a middle period dominated by the culture that arose in the Jesuit missions.

From a European perspective, mission culture marked the establishment and consolidation of the Jesuit system across the savanna as well as its subsequent decline under secular successors. This interpretation empha-sizes the work of the missionaries, their conversion of the Indians, the construction of the physical complexes, the organization of a native popula-tion into societies based on Iberian models, and the Jesuits' successors' attempts to integrate the missions with the politics and economies of colonial Charcas and the Bolivian Republic. According to the European view, mission culture reached its apex under Jesuit rule; it then slid steadily from 1767 to 1910, when Bolivian participation in the rubber boom re-duced the former missions to ghost towns.

The aboriginal viewpoint was substantially different. To native eyes, the missions opened Moxos to regular deliveries of metal implements, offered the several competing ethnic groups an opportunity to redress their posi-tions vis-à-vis their neighbors, and fostered a new sociopolitical structure based on Indian and Iberian models. Only inducements such as these could have convinced the native peoples of Moxos to abandon their tropical forest culture, tied as it was to centuries of subsistence and belief structures, and to enter missions established to centralize their conversion. The native view-point also offers a different perspective on the post-Jesuit period. Rather than watching a ceaseless decline in living conditions, the native people actually increased their numbers and maintained vital components of their mission culture, including native leadership. Finally, a native point of view offers a different interpretation of the events that led to indigenous margin-alization in Moxos. The four decades between 1840 and 1880 were crucial in the dissolution of mission culture. During the 1840s and 1850s, an increasing Bolivian bureaucracy and immigrant population were bent on appropriating animal resources as private property and on using the native population as a labor force for tending them. During the 1860s and 1870s, the rubber boom siphoned off mission men as tappers and haulers on the middle Amazon. Although the boom would not reach Bolivian soil for another twenty years, the missions, as the largest available labor pool on the upper Amazon, were full participants in the enterprise by the mid-1860s.

The culture described in the following pages was a transitional one, falling between the enormous age of tropical forest culture and the capitalist epoch that continues to this day. However, despite its short duration and interstitial character — falling chronologically between 1660 and 1880, cinematographically between *The Mission* and *Fitzcarraldo* — the importance of mission culture should not be underestimated. Neither aboriginal nor European, it marks off a period of sustained adjustment. Mission culture bridged Moxos' ancient and modern worlds, giving the native people a breathing space between autonomy and dependence.

I THE SETTING

Moxos lies along a geographical frontier, its head in the Andes, its body and feet in the Amazon. It is separated from the highland centers that nominally govern it by both distance and difficult terrain. This isolation and Moxos' peculiar environment, a combination of tropical forest and savanna, had as much to do with its development as did the patterns of native life or the trajectory of its European contact.

The geographical expression *Moxos,* as used in this work, subsumes some 200,000 square kilometers in what is now the Beni Department of Bolivia. Three-quarters of this extension is tropical savanna, the *llanos de Mojos* in local argot, which stretches from the last escarpments of the Andes to the Brazilian border. The remaining 50,000 square kilometers consist of forested lands in the lower Andean slopes and the northern Chiquitos Uplands.

The most prominent topographical features of the area are its bodies of water. Four large lakes — Rogagua, Rogoaguado, Yachaja, and San Luís — dot the north central savanna. They provide year-round sources of water on the open grasslands and serve as a major focus of life in the areas they drain. Three river systems, all major tributaries of the Amazon, incise Moxos' landscape. The Beni River, with headwaters near La Paz, plunges down the steep valleys or *yungas* of the eastern Andes before entering the savanna at its southwestern margin. From there it flows directly north to enter the Madre de Dios-Madeira near present-day Riberalta. A second major network, the Guaporé or Itenez, rises in the Brazilian highlands and delimits the northern boundary of Moxos. At a point near San Joaquín, the Guaporé receives the waters of a series of streams that drain the Chiquitos Uplands and eastern savanna. The Mamoré and its principal tributaries rise in the eastern Andes and form an extensive network flowing northward toward the Amazon. This third system is the most important to the history of Moxos, not only for its paramount size but also for its central location. With its main channel cutting through the heart of the savanna and its tributaries reaching eastward into the intermontane valleys, the Mamoré forms a natural link between Moxos and the Andes.

Once they reach the savanna, the rivers meander extensively. Constantly shifting channels leave a series of oxbow lakes, rich in marine resources, scattered along the floodplains. These abandoned riverbeds join the active networks again each year during the wet season, which extends from October to March and peaks in December and January. Although rains are heaviest near the mountains, they are extensive throughout the region. Over the ten-year period between 1960 and 1970, an average of 1480.4 millimeters (58.2 inches) of rain fell at Trinidad on the central Mamoré, less than half the average annual precipitation of Todos Santos, located near the Andean slopes.[1]

Copious rains coupled with the savanna's low stream gradients result in extensive seasonal flooding. As rains increase in October and November, rivers rise quickly. By December most streams have left their banks; by January much of the savanna resembles a vast lake. In an "average" year, the seasonal floods cover roughly one-third of Moxos. Exceptionally heavy rains, such as those of 1990–91, inundate all but the highest elevations. In March flood conditions abate; in April isolated pools of standing water fill with stranded fish and their predators. Little precipitation occurs in May through October, and by mid-August near-drought conditions usually obtain. During these months only the rivers and perennial lakes offer dependable sources of water.

The oscillation between flood and drought limits the kinds of vegetation that thrive in Moxos. Open lands support grasses and occasional stands of palm and tajibo (*Tabebuia suberosa*). Only water-resistant grasses and sedges can survive in the lowest-lying areas. But even slight relief from the savanna floor affords lush tree growth, including stands of cedar, balsa, mahogany, and Brazil nut. The river systems support true gallery forests populated by trees typical of the Amazon basin. A manuscript prepared for the Spanish Crown in 1789 lists eighty-six separate tree species and describes their uses for building material, handicraft, and a variety of medicinal purposes.[2]

Moxos is the habitat for a variety of game animals. Monkeys, including the howler and spider species, inhabit the forested regions. The grasslands

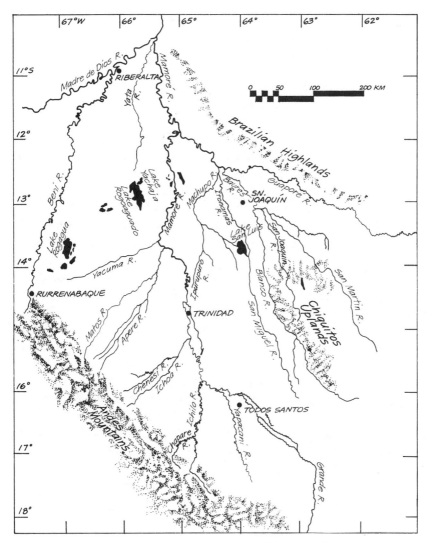

Map 2. Moxos

support several varieties of deer, armadillo, and some of the richest bird life in South America. Moxos' rivers and lakes are home to two species of cayman, manatee, and freshwater dolphins as well as important food fish such as the pacú (*Huleus setiger*), suribí (*Pseudopasystoma fasciatum*), and dorado (*Salminus*).

At first glance Moxos' natural landscape seems uniform. Contemporary charts and field surveys show huge areas of grassland broken only by bodies of water. However, infrared satellite imagery reveals a complex blend of savanna and forest that can be divided into three discrete niches. Areas of gallery forest in the north and along the Andean foothills comprise roughly 25 percent of Moxos' surface. These wooded zones are rich in timber, tropical mammals, and plant life and are receptive to swidden cultivation. Open savanna, some 60 percent of the land area, offers the least palatable conditions for human habitation. Floods and typical claypan soils create serious obstacles to cultivation, and the annual drought wilts the succulent grasses that nourish game and livestock. Riverfront lands, *várzea* in their better-known Portuguese-language equivalent, comprise the remaining 15 percent of Moxos and provide the optimum settlement sites. Rivers form the most viable means of communication, the routes for trade or warfare. In addition, rivers provide optimum agricultural sites. The continuous flow of water deposits silt along the riverbanks, which increases soil fertility and forms a series of natural levees less subject to the annual floods. The subsistence potential of the riverfront is enhanced further by the presence of abundant aquatic fauna.

As William Denevan has shown, this mix of grasslands, forests, rivers, and lakes makes Moxos' natural environment different from other areas in the sub-Andean tropics.[3] A part of this difference stems from the changes that constantly alter the landscape: rivers regularly alter their courses, sediment deposited on the floodplains moves with the waters, and the flood-drought cycle recurs annually. Yet within this ecological framework of change, a basic model for the relationship between the land and its peoples emerges. The river courses define the most desirable settlement sites. Their waters concentrate resources for transportation, subsistence, and flood relief. From prehistory to the present, Moxos' human populations have gravitated toward its river systems.

PREHISTORY

The prehistoric record supports an Amazonian origin for Moxos' major native peoples. Linguistic studies of Arawak posit a savanna peopled by a series of migrations moving up the tributaries of the Amazon. These demographic pulses may have begun as early as 3000 B.C. and certainly reached the savanna by 500 B.C. According to this model, successive waves of migrants opened new territory to Arawak occupation and displaced those groups that previously had occupied lands on the migration routes.[4]

Archaeological documentation for Moxos' prehistory is based largely on the excavations conducted on the central savanna by Baron Erland Nordenskiöld in the early twentieth century.[5] Nordenskiöld worked on three large mounds located some one hundred kilometers southeast of Trinidad. He recovered refuse and pottery in at least two distinct strata. The lower strata, tentatively dated 500 A.D. by Gordon Willey, contained ceramic artifacts related to those of the Yampará style found on the eastern slopes of the Andes.[6] Artifacts from the upper strata suggest a culture dominated by Amazonian modes of subsistence in the years immediately preceding European contact. The objects recovered include grooved platters used in manioc processing as well as a number of other ceramic forms adorned with purplish-brown paint and featuring tripodal bases. Willey dates the upper strata between 1000 and 1100 A.D.[7] A more recent work, which surveys artifacts recovered from the Beni River drainage, insists that this region comprised a prehistoric culture different from that of the central savanna, a suggestion in part supported by the historical evidence to follow.[8]

Work on the cultural geography of the savanna focuses attention on another set of remains from ancient Moxos. Mounds, causeways, and drained fields appear in several locations, especially the regions west of the Mamoré between the Apere River and Lake Rogoaguado. Drained fields, the most pervasive of the earthworks, blanket large expanses of savanna. Denevan calculates the extension of such fields at a maximum of 50,000 acres and demonstrates their increased agricultural potential in areas perpetually flooded in the rainy season.[9] He further suggests that the people who used these structures probably met at least the first Europeans to reach Moxos. However, more recent studies of the earthworks, using a combination of stylistic analysis and carbon 14 techniques, date the last of these structures no later than the thirteenth century, leaving the identity of their builders in doubt.[10]

The prehistoric record remains incomplete, but a combination of linguistic and archaeological evidence establishes two important points. First, Moxos culture was Amazonian in origin. While contacts with the highlands were a regular feature of savanna life, the evidence supports Donald Lathrap's thesis that a dynamic culture moved out of a central Amazonian hearth on the river networks. As this chapter will show, the distribution of Moxos' historical peoples corresponds closely to the implications of this migratory model: dominant groups occupy the riverfronts and weaker peoples live on the open grasslands. Second, this Amazonian culture was remarkably sophisticated. The prehistoric inhabitants of Moxos brought with them a prosperous agriculture based on manioc cultivation. At some point they augmented the agricultural potential of the savanna lands by constructing and using raised fields.

Colonial Spaniards, no strangers to linguistic and cultural diversity in their own land, seemed genuinely confused by what they discovered in Moxos. The earliest chronicles of European contact with the savanna bristle with names for its native people. As late as 1674, existing documents list twenty-one "nations" inhabiting the area of the upper Mamoré alone.[11] The confusion extends to the name Moxos itself. After the fall of the Inca state, aspiring conquistadores sought a fabulously rich land ruled by the Gran Moxo. This important variant of the El Dorado legend, centered on an axis between Cuzco and Charcas, inspired a number of entries into the upper Amazon. Putting aside El Dorado, the eighteenth-century linguist Lorenzo Hervás y Panduro offers his readers an explanation for the name based on a classic piece of bilingual misunderstanding.

> This name [Moxos], according to an opinion more than a little popular in Peru, was given to the nation and to its language because the first Moxo that the Spaniards saw, when asked by one of them what his nation was, replied "*ñuca muha*," or "I mange," that is, "I have the mange," and the Spaniards, thinking that the word *muha* was the name of his people, called it Moxa or Moha, a word that, in its pronunciation, is similar to the word *muha*.[12]

Only the arrival of Jesuit missionaries in the last quarter of the seventeenth century begins to focus the fuzzy picture left by early Spanish accounts.

Groups of Native People

While Jesuit records also underscore Moxos' linguistic diversity, they distinguish six major peoples from the thirty-odd they identify. The Jesuits' implicit hierarchy of native peoples was based on their knowledge of the Indians' population size, political power, and resource base. In this scheme the Moxo and Baure head a list that includes the Kayubaba, Canisiana, Mobima, Itonama, and twenty-six other groups shown on map 3.

The Arawak-speaking people whom the Jesuits would denominate Moxo were the first major group contacted in the initial missionary thrust of the 1660s. The Baure, another group of Arawak speakers, controlled the rivers

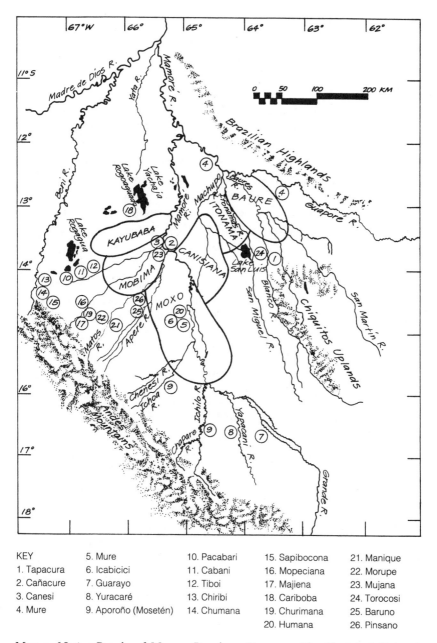

KEY

1. Tapacura	5. Mure	10. Pacabari	15. Sapibocona	21. Manique
2. Cañacure	6. Icabicici	11. Cabani	16. Mopeciana	22. Morupe
3. Canesi	7. Guarayo	12. Tiboi	17. Majiena	23. Mujana
4. Mure	8. Yuracaré	13. Chiribi	18. Cariboba	24. Torocosi
	9. Aporoño (Mosetén)	14. Chumana	19. Churimana	25. Baruno
			20. Humana	26. Pinsano

Map 3. Native People of Moxos. Based on Denevan, *The Aboriginal Cultural Geography of the Llanos de Mojos of Bolivia*, p.41.

of the far eastern savanna, the adjoining forest, and at least a portion of the north central region near Lake San Luís, at the time of the contact by members of the Society. The Jesuits considered the Baure the most "civilized" of the native populations and placed great emphasis on their conversion.

Occupying a second rung in the Jesuit hierarchy were four peoples: the Kayubaba, Canisiana, Mobima, and Itonama. The location of the Canisiana on prime riverfront property north of the Moxo, coupled with eighteenth-century descriptions of their aggressive behavior, offer evidence for including this group among the most powerful of the savanna tribes. However, missionary accounts emphasize the importance of hunting to Canisiana subsistence and the absence of woven cottons among them.[13] Perhaps, in keeping with traditional patterns of population dynamics, these people represented the arrival of new, more aggressive migrants to the central savanna.

The Kayubaba also present typological difficulties. One early missionary reported these people living in several large villages. His account stirred considerable excitement because it mentioned a Kayubaba chief, Paititi, a name associated with El Dorado.[14] However, this letter stands alone in its description of the premission Kayubaba; later documents do not support the contention of either large populations or sophisticated political structures among them.

The Itonama and Mobima inhabited minor rivers and open savanna at the time of their contact with Jesuit missionaries. The Itonama, denizens of the marshy area between the Mamoré and the lake that bears their name, were described in a missionary history as the "most backward people in all the land."[15] With their homeland on the seasonally flooded savanna of the far west, the Mobima practiced an agriculture subject to frequent failure. To escape inundation, these Indians concentrated near the Beni River, where occasional hills afford relief from the annual deluge.

In addition to these five clearly delineated groups, Jesuit documents mention a number of peoples whose place in the native world and whose fate in the mission system can only be surmised. The circled numbers in map 3 give the reader an idea of the variety and distribution of these Indians at the time of their mention in Jesuit sources.

At least three of these peoples — the Tapacura, Cañacure, and Canesí — were casualties of their encounter with Europeans. The Tapacura, allies of the Spaniards, lost many of their number in an ill-starred conquest expedition in 1617. They were eventually absorbed by the Spanish settlement of Santa Cruz de la Sierra. Both the Cañacure and Canesi were decimated as slaves in a "just war" when Spaniards entered the savanna in support of these peoples' traditional enemies. Jesuit mission strategy further clouds the identity of these "minor" peoples. Under resettlement programs sponsored by the Jesuits, Chapacura from near the Guaporé River were withdrawn to missions on the middle Mamoré with the onset of Portuguese threats against the northern stations in the 1740s. Missionaries of the western savanna removed Cosseremono people from their homelands to a new mission on the Río Matos to prevent recurring difficulties between this group and its enemies living across the Beni River.[16]

But if the exact fate of these minor peoples remains hidden, the general implications for Europeans working on the savanna are clear. Communication with the multilinguistic and often competitive groups would be complicated. Missionaries would have to learn several languages or the Indians would have to adopt a lingua franca. Perhaps more seriously, any attempts to create a new order of larger social and economic units ran the risk of stirring up hostilities among traditional rivals.

Demography

The native people of Moxos suffered a precipitous decline in population as a consequence of their contact with Europeans. The earliest accounts of the savanna uniformly describe large populations. For example, testimony given by members of the Spanish force that entered southeastern Moxos in 1617 describes a densely settled region. Addressing the Royal Audiencia of Charcas, Juan de Limpias reported that he counted eleven settlements with some 720 dwellings, ninety cook sheds, and nine drinking houses within a three-league march.[17] While Limpias's account hardly represents a modern household census, it suggests a population density approaching 2.5 inhabitants per square kilometer, using figures of five inhabitants per dwelling and 825 square kilometers (nine square leagues). The substance, if not the detail, of Limpias's estimates is corroborated by other accounts, such as that of the Jesuit Jerónimo de Andión, who visited the central savanna with a Spanish expedition in 1595–96. The priest reported large populations who received their uninvited guests hospitably and supplied them with food and forage until floodwaters covered their gardens and the native pastures.[18]

In his monograph on the cultural geography of Moxos, William Denevan emphasizes the essential reliability of these early descriptions and uses a combination of historical sources, archaeological evidence, and models of carrying capacity to support an estimated population of some 100,000 for 1690, the beginning of the Jesuit age. A more recent statement on the subject estimates the population of Moxos before European arrival at 350,000.[19] I am willing to accept Denevan's estimates as reasonable approximations for the pre-Columbian era. A recent surface survey of the central savanna suggests a prehistorical village configuration strikingly similar to that described in 1617, another piece of evidence supporting large aboriginal populations, even Denevan's 350,000 estimate.[20] I also accept Denevan's contention of drastic population decline. Extant documents describe Indians dying in frightening numbers, both from disease and the pervasive effects of conquest and slavery. However, Denevan's chronology, the timing of the sharpest drop in the population, and the date of its nadir seem anachronistic. I suggest a sharper decline from pre-Columbian levels, an interpretation based on accounts produced by the first sustained Jesuit penetration of the region in the late 1670s.

In 1679 three Jesuit fathers, Pedro Marbán, Cipriano Barace, and Clemente Ygarza, reconnoitered the upper Mamoré with an eye to converting its native people. The results of this trip, published by Leandro Tormo Sanz, offer detailed information enabling scholars to reconstruct the area's aboriginal population at the beginning of the Jesuit century. Writing to their provincial in Lima, the travelers carefully noted the location and number of inhabitants in each village they visited as well as the names the native people used to identify themselves. Map 4 depicts the villages visited by the priests.

The travelers counted a total of thirty-six hundred Indians living along the length of their journey, roughly 2° latitude or 160 kilometers. To estimate the total area surveyed, map 4 fits a right triangle over the villages described in the report. The area of the figure is 17,600 kilometers, which combines with the recorded native population to yield a density of 0.21 persons per square kilometer, less than one-tenth that reported some sixty years earlier.

Before these calculations can be used as the basis for an estimate of native population density in 1679, they must be adjusted to conform to the contexts of the document and to the limitations of plane geometry imposed by the map. Evidence supplied by the priests themselves suggests that their count underestimates the total population of the territory they visited. In their conclusion, Marbán, Barace, and Ygarza admitted they were unable to

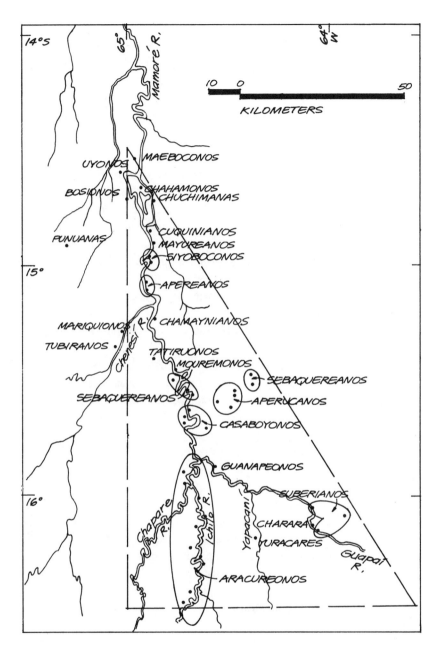

Map 4. The Upper Mamoré, 1679. Based on Tormo Sanz, "Situación y población de los Mojos en 1679," p.159.

Table 1: Aboriginal Population of Moxos, ca.1679

Ecological Zone	Area (km²)	Density (pop/km²)	Population
Riverfront	30,000	0.315–0.42	9,450–12,600
Forest	50,000	0.158–0.21	7,900–10,500
Open Savanna	120,000	0.08–0.11	9,600–13,200
		TOTAL	26,950–36,300

visit all the villages described to them by native informants. As the large white spaces on map 4 show, the priests simply bypassed the areas of the Chenesí, Chapare, and Yapacaní rivers. Thus table 1 shows a range of populations based on two interpolations. First, it inflates the initially calculated density by factors of 50 and 100 percent to account for people not seen by the Jesuits. Second, following earlier suggestions about the relative habitability of forest, riverfront, and open savanna, the table deflates the calculated density, which is based primarily on riverfront sites, by factors of two and four to account for the presumably smaller populations of the interfluvial zones. The figures in table 1 represent an estimate of the aboriginal population of Moxos in 1679.

Mission Indian demography, presented in chapter 4, favors accepting the high end of this range, some 35,000 Indians, as the native population at the beginning of the Jesuit century. I believe that this figure represents a nadir population for the native people of Moxos. I suggest further that during the first century of Spanish contact (ca. 1560–1660), the area's native population decreased at least 65 percent.

Material Culture

The diverse linguistic groups of Moxos showed remarkably uniform cultural practices at the time of Jesuit contact. All the major peoples displayed features common to what Julian Steward and Louis Faron have called tropical forest chiefdoms: surplus agriculture, developed patterns of trade and warfare, political and religious specialists, and a belief system with a hierarchy of deities.[21] It is worth stressing, however, that uniformity does not imply a lack of cultural sophistication as a recent work on the development of twentieth-century lowland Bolivia has asserted.[22] Rather, the native peoples displayed a remarkably rich culture and proved themselves well adapted to conditions that Europeans found anything but inviting.

Even the descriptions of the native peoples stressed uniformity. A nineteenth-century visitor to the savanna described them thus:

Their craniums are large and a bit elongated at the posterior. Their faces, less full and smaller than those of the Chiquito [a group to the south of Moxos], are a bit oblong; their cheekbones are slightly rounded; their noses are short, flattened without being too large; their mouths medium-sized, with large lips; their eyes are generally small and hooded; their ears are small; their eyebrows are narrow and arched; their chins are rounded; their beards are black, a bit bushy, appearing late and covering only their chins and lower lips, and even there they are not curly; their hair is black, long, thick, and straight.[23]

The only substantial variability reported by this observer was in the height of the different peoples: the Mobima, Moxo, Canisiana, and Kayubaba averaged 5'2" and the Itonama a quarter inch shorter.

As Europeans came into contact with the native people, they began to document their well-adapted life-styles. Descriptions of the annual floods portray the savanna people as practically amphibious. Early observers of the upper Mamoré described Indians who "lived in their canoes," and the first vocabulary of Moxo Arawak is filled with watery words, including seven separate expressions for river, describing various sizes, colors, and textures.[24] The same reports that chronicled the disastrous Spanish encounters with floodwaters marveled at the amphibious character of savanna culture. When rising waters covered their village plazas, the Indians built elevated barbecues, covered them with earth, and resumed their normal cooking. They traveled freely over the flooded savanna, navigating their canoes over what Europeans viewed as an uncharted ocean. They slept by merely hitching their hammock cords higher on the poles that supported them — quite a revelation to Spaniards with bedrolls.[25]

Subsistence depended primarily on agriculture. The native people of Moxos excelled at meeting their immediate needs and producing a surplus that they could barter with their neighbors or store against future scarcity. Farmers of the central savanna cultivated the riverfronts, planting crops typical of tropical forest horticulture. Sweet and bitter manioc provided the dietary staple, with cuttings planted ubiquitously and continuously to provide an ongoing harvest. Peanuts, yams, beans, squash, and peppers supplemented the primary cultivars.[26] The Moxo also grew maize, but they limited its consumption to celebrations and fermentation for alcoholic beverages. The Baure raised the same plant inventory but in swidden fashion. They used stone axes to girdle trees and fire both to clear underbrush and to reduce wood pulp to ash for fertilizing their plots.

To supplement the ample carbohydrates gained from their cultivated plants, the Indians added other vegetable material from gathering and animal protein from hunting and fishing activities. Palms furnished fruit and nuts, as did several other species of trees, including the almond and Brazil nut. The Indians also gathered turtle, cayman, and rhea eggs, worms and grubs, wild honey, and freshwater mollusks. Among the Moxo, Baure, and Canisiana, fishing was a more important pursuit than hunting. The major river courses and flooded lands teemed with edible species of all sizes, which the Indians took with bows and arrows, hooks, weirs, and poisons. For peoples living away from the rivers, hunting quarry such as deer, tapir, peccary, and wild fowl took primacy over fishing.

Economic activities also included trade with people living outside Moxos. The presence of artifacts such as polished stone axes and quartz plugs in excavated savanna sites provides clear evidence of contact with the highlands. Early European accounts tell of silver ornaments worn by the Moxo, which they surely obtained from Andean sources.[27] However, scholars have debated the nature and intensity of these contacts since Nordenskiöld published his first surveys in the 1910s. A recent examination of certain archaeological sites on the central Andean slopes makes a convincing case for an ancient and continuous contact between the savanna and the highland regions bordering Lake Titicaca. Pointing to natural open corridors in the dense tropical vegetation stretching from the lake to Moxos via Apolobamba and to the remnants of road networks and fortified sites along this route, Thierry Saignes suggests this as a natural route for penetration by the Incas and possibly by forces of Tiahuanaco as well.[28]

Additional ethnohistorical evidence shows that the Moxo established links with Andean civilizations through intermediaries who lived along the upper reaches of the Mamoré tributaries. Here Jesuit missionaries discovered a flourishing trade network in which products of the savanna were exchanged for those of the highlands. The Moxo offered cotton cloth, feather work, and manioc flour as their major exports and received highland manufactured goods — metal, stone ax heads — and salt in return.[29] Patterns of contact likely were governed by the ebb and flow of Andean politics. During expansive periods, direct links involving trade, and perhaps tribute as well, ordered relationships. The decline of Andean civilizations resulted in trade relations mediated by people living on the slopes.

Descriptions of native technology mention well-developed skills in subsistence implements and handicraft items. The tool inventory consisted of subsistence implements: axes for clearing agricultural land; scrapers, presses, and pots for processing manioc; ceramic vessels for storing and cooking food; hooks, nets, and fish traps; and canoes, bows, and arrows, multipurpose implements used for transportation, hunting and fishing, and warfare. Early descriptions of savanna pottery, coupled with examples of the pieces published by Nordenskiöld, offer eloquent proof of the rich ceramic traditions of Moxos. Clays from the central and northern savanna were suitable for the primary techniques employed — coiling and molding. Once shaped, ceramic vessels were hardened by open firing, making "smoke smudged, brownish black, or mottled buff surface vessels."[30] In addition, the Moxo and Baure — and perhaps other groups as well — excelled at fashioning natural fibers into useful items. They platted and twilled grass, reeds, and palm leaves into baskets, mats, manioc presses, and sieves. Cotton and feather weaving achieved special importance among the savanna peoples. Lengths of cotton cloth, fashioned by women, became a form of specie in the trade between the Indians and the Spanish centers. European visitors reserved their highest praise for native feather work. On his 1595 trip to the middle Mamoré, Father Andión saw what he called a feather painting of "bold hues and curious designs."[31] The principal sources disagree as to whether the Indians actually "wove" the feathers, but whether they were woven or sewn to a backing, plumage taken from the bodies of tropical fowl decorated luxury goods, such as headdresses, used in festive occasions.

Social, Spatial, and Political Organization

Missionary sources, true to a European worldview, identify the nuclear family as the essential social unit in Moxos. Husband, wife, and children became a statistical and descriptive touchstone. However, the native people saw society differently. Their world extended social relationships well beyond the nuclear family into a web of blood and fictive kin.

The missionaries themselves recognized that the Indians clustered into what they called "*grandes familias*," multifamily groups sharing a communal dwelling and domestic chores.[32] Early reports also reveal the existence of mythical ancestors from whom male villagers drew their sense of identity and often their names, clearly signifying the patrilineal lineage patterns typical of Amazonia.[33] An eighteenth-century priest's observation that native brides entered their husbands' homes carrying their "beds" over their shoulders clearly alludes to patrilocal residence rules.[34] Native language further reinforces the importance of extranuclear kinship in Moxos. Father Marbán's *Arte y vocabulario de la lengua Moxa* contains over thirty familial expressions, including separate terms for male and female lines and for cross-cousins. These extended families formed the building blocks of social and economic life in aboriginal Moxos, allowing the native people to develop the productive units whose agricultural and craft goods so impressed European visitors. These family groupings created a sense of place and order that proved vital even in the face of repeated attempts to introduce European norms.

At the time of their contact by the Jesuits, the native people of Moxos lived in small village units. In their 1679 report, Fathers Marbán, Barace, and Ygarza describe small settlements of one to two hundred people distributed along the riverbanks like beads strung loosely on a series of filaments. Moxo villages featured a central plaza, containing a communal structure the missionaries called a drinking house (*bebedero*) as well as residences and kitchens occupied by extended family groups. An important variant of this pattern appeared among the Baure, whose villages bore a distinctively martial countenance. Baure dwellings were surrounded by a palisade of sharpened logs and a deep moat crossed by a removable causeway.[35]

A second group of villages, identical to the first in architecture, took shape on the open savanna. Here springs or river meanders furnished year-round aquatic resources. Many of these villages apparently retained access to river resources through kin who lived along the fluvial network. An early Jesuit report notes that Arawak speakers maintained villages on the east bank of the Mamoré and beside lakes in the open country "behind" the river. Communication between the riverfront and satellite sites was potentially enhanced by raised-earth causeways radiating from the river networks.[36] However, the extent to which these open savanna villages represent permanent settlement sites remains unclear. Riverfront lands were extensively occupied and jealously guarded from the incursions of neighbors. Yet evidence from historical and modern documents shows a peripatetic settlement pattern and recurring village fission resulting from demographic or political events. Perhaps the inland sites represented settlements of village fragments that later retained contact with the riverfront sites and eventually rejoined their former neighbors. In 1682 Antonio de Orellana, a Jesuit missionary, described the breakup of a Moxo village after its site had been inundated by flooding. Half of the village remained on the river while the other half eventually founded a new settlement on the open savanna.[37] Such commentaries point definitively to a mobile life-style that was not amenable to fixed mission centers.

Despite occasional reports of large confederations, the people of Moxos probably recognized no polity larger than the individual village. Each settlement had an elite of political and religious specialists, who had varying degrees of power and privilege. The Moxo chiefs, *achichaco*, held their offices more by deeds than by descent. They functioned primarily as harmonizers and advisors rather than rulers. Their privileges of office consisted primarily of the respect the holder received from his villagers. Baure chiefs, or *aramas*, assumed greater powers. The arama decided whether his village would go to war, handed out punishment to those who transgressed local customs, and supervised the cultivation of manioc used in the preparation of alcoholic beverages. A missionary who spent some twenty years among the Baure described their chiefs as supported by village labor and succeeded by male heirs.[38]

While they curried favor with the chiefs, Jesuit missionaries sought to marginalize the village spiritual leadership. Men and women whom the priests called *hechiceros* (shamans) functioned as healers of the sick and as intermediaries with village deities. As healers, the hechiceros used ritual and a knowledge of medicinal plants to aid their patients; as intermediaries, they interacted with a plethora of deities, each of whom had different attributes and functions. The most important gods were those who looked after each village. Because these divine patrons were thought to reside in particular local landmarks, they served as strong barriers to the relocation of Indians fearful of losing their protection in a different part of Moxos.

The native societies the Jesuits encountered in Moxos presented an array of opportunities and challenges to men intent on introducing patterns of European culture. Moxos' native people were readily accessible to travelers moving downriver from Spanish settlements to the west because of their relatively large numbers and riverfront locus. Moreover, the Indians' political organization and robust subsistence practices made them attractive targets for spiritual conquest. However, the plethora of native languages and the local deity-based belief system, coupled with the forbidding nature of the region—both its distance from Spanish centers and its tropical climate—offered challenges to even the most determined invaders.

SECULAR CONQUEST

Although the Jesuit missionaries were the first Europeans to establish ongoing contact with the savanna peoples, their arrival in Moxos followed a full century of intermittent forays by would-be conquistadores. The first Europeans to reach the area sought the kingdom of the Gran Moxo, a legendary monarch who ruled over heavily populated lands rich in precious metals. In search of this chimera, expeditions penetrated the heart of South America from both sides of the continent. Spaniards based in Cuzco launched three major thrusts toward Moxos between 1536 and 1567; and lesser parties left Cochabamba and La Paz during the same period. Although none of the Andean-based bands actually reached the savanna, these early operations established the Viceroyalty of Peru's legal claim to the realm of the Gran Moxo, wherever it might prove to lie.[39]

Despite its Peruvian jurisdiction, Moxos was first explored by the impetus of expeditions mounted from the Atlantic coast of South America. The early history of this region revolved around the settlement of Asuncion, founded in 1540 some one thousand miles up the Río de la Plata. In search of the sources of tales their Indian allies had told them, Spaniards launched a series of forays radiating north and east from their city. One of these campaigns trekked north to the Xarayes marshes before entering the Chaco on their way to the "rich lands" to the west. In 1547 members of the expedition encountered a group of Spanish-speaking Indians camped on the banks of the Guapay (Grande) River, the vanguard of settlements reaching out from the Pacific coast. Frustrated in their plans to travel farther west in search of riches, the members of the expedition returned to Asuncion after dispatching several of their number to cross the Andes and meet with Crown administrators in Lima. But the ambassadors, who entered Peru at the time of Gonzalo Pizarro's rebellion, found royal representatives preoccupied with mounting forces to restore order. With their claims unrecognized, the party retraced their steps to Asuncion. One of their number, however, a young Estremeduran named Nuflo de Chávez, would lead men from the Río de la Plata region across the continent again.

In 1548 Chávez had returned to Asuncion, where he served for a time in activities centered on the eastern interior of South America. Then, in 1557, he organized a party intent on recrossing the Chaco in search of conquests. Chávez and his troop followed the same route he had explored a decade earlier, but they encountered difficulties with Indian resistance and heavy rains. Finally, in 1559, Chávez founded Nueva Asuncion, the first in a series of towns on the tropical plains between the Chaco and Andean escarpments. This initial settlement was moved farther west in 1561 and there rechristened Santa Cruz de la Sierra.[40]

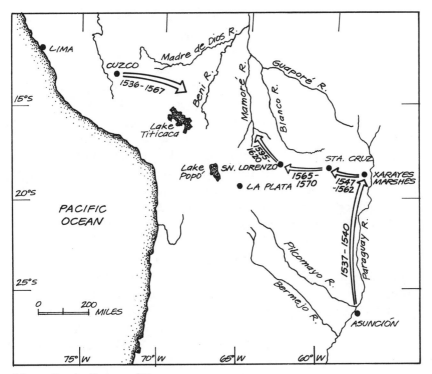

Map 5. Secular Routes of Conquest, 1536–1620

From the date of its foundation, Santa Cruz became the center of Spanish activities directed toward Moxos. The town developed a conquest ethos, first as a staging area for the exploration of "rich lands" reputed to lie at the center of the continent. Then, as the vision of El Dorado dimmed, institutions born to foster conquest became the sinews of a settled society. This conquest or frontier background underlay not only the history and development of the city but also its patterns of contact with Moxos' native people.[41]

Between the time it was founded and the onset of the Jesuit missions, Santa Cruz spawned literally dozens of expeditions bound for Moxos. The final location of the city, near the banks of the Río Grande, placed its inhabitants at the headwaters of a river route to the Mamoré and the heart of the savanna. The rhythm of Santa Cruz-directed conquest showed two distinct waves. The first lasted for a decade beginning with the appointment of Lorenzo Suárez de Figueroa as governor of Santa Cruz in 1592. Suárez de Figueroa's 1595 expedition onto the savanna, financed in Peru and chronicled by the Jesuit priest Jerónimo de Andión, marked the first well-documented Spanish entry into the upper Mamoré. Rather than traveling by water, the three hundred-member party entered the savanna on horse-back, a tragic error. Surprised by the annual floods, the expeditionaries spent two months marooned by rising waters. The Arawak-speaking na-tives, who initially had given the Spaniards provisions, canoed away to high ground with the onset of heavy rains. To avert starvation, the Spaniards slaughtered their mounts, many of which had died from lack of fodder, and finally consumed the leather trunks that held their baggage.[42] Suárez de Figueroa's successor, Juan de Mendoza, continued this practice of the great expedition, again with disastrous consequences. The 150 troops who en-tered the upper Mamoré in 1602 were decimated by desertion, disease, and losses to Indian resistance.[43]

The failure of these expeditions to discover the Gran Moxo permanently ended the practice of using large levies raised and financed in the highlands. When Spaniards entered the savanna again, fifteen years after Mendoza's fiasco, they did so using the resources of Santa Cruz. Gone were the large forces as well as the heavy reliance on horsepower and large supply trains. The groups that left Santa Cruz and explored the southeastern savanna in the late 1610s resembled the conquest bands Mario Góngora has described in his studies of early Panama. These bands were composed of tough, independent men who united as partners so as to gain through division of the proceeds of their expeditions.[44]

This transformation in Santa Cruz's expeditionary orientation had pro-found implications for Moxos' native peoples, for now they had become the quarry rather than merely those interrogated for directions to the Gran Moxo. Neither the chronology nor the trajectory of slaving in Moxos can be delineated with precision. However, the following outline captures its essence. Taking slaves was part and parcel of the Santa Cruz economy from the end of the sixteenth century. The contracts (*capitulaciones*) granted by the region's earliest governors included the rights to make expeditions — "to gather people for service" in the words of one document — a point that cruceños claimed in perpetuity as a means of support on the frontier.[45] By the second decade of the seventeenth century, savanna people began to enter the Santa Cruz labor force. A list of encomiendas in the city, prepared in 1617, enumerates nearly 20 percent of the tributaries as members of the

Moxo, Tubaiono, and Umano groups. In addition, a series of contemporary documents lists native prisoners as part of the booty taken by expeditions to the savanna.[46] Slaving intensified when cruceños enlisted native intermediaries, first the Chiriguano who inhabited the Andean foothills, then the savanna people themselves.

The clearest surviving account of a Santa Cruz slave raid into Moxos describes just such a Spanish-native alliance. An expedition, on the point of entering the savanna, made a last-minute route change when contacted by a Spanish-speaking Arawak Indian living on the upper Mamoré. This former bondsman carried a message from several Moxo caciques requesting help from the expeditionaries against their traditional enemies. The cruceño force then entered the upper Mamoré. Guided by Moxo scouts, they attacked Cañacure and Mazareono villages. The 285 captives brought back to Santa Cruz were divided into shares, ranging from fourteen apiece for the absentee governor and the leader of the expedition to one for Patico, the native interpreter.[47]

The onset of regular slaving shattered the native status quo. Capture and removal of large numbers of native people reduced productive capacities and disrupted social structures in the savanna villages. Just as disruptive was the introduction of European diseases to native people who lacked resistance to them. Contemporary critiques of the Santa Cruz frontier invariably coupled slaving and disease in descriptions of the depopulation of the region.[48] In addition, the introduction of Spanish arms resulted in a shift in the aboriginal balance of power on the savanna. Arawaks, in the manner described above, encouraged Spanish entries to overwhelm their traditional rivals. As these alliances matured, Arawaks became agents in the slave trade, taking prisoners for sale to Spaniards in much the same way as did the Indians of the middle Amazon studied by David Sweet.[49] Jesuit entry into the savanna in the late seventeenth century diminished but did not end the taking of slaves from the area. Despite the priests' protests, raids such as the one that occurred in 1667 characterized secular Spanish relations with Moxos' native peoples well into the eighteenth century.

This, then, was the pattern of the European penetration of Moxos before the onset of mission culture: a long series of entries and retreats, a period of contact rather than conquest. After fifty years of exploration from distant bases, Spanish entry into Moxos radiated from the peripatetic settlement of

Santa Cruz de la Sierra. From this base, expeditions entered the savanna, first as naive conquistadores, then as seasoned slavers. But both waves departed the savanna as quickly as they entered it. The conquest of Moxos was left to a third wave of Europeans, who had gained their initial experience in the area as members of the cruceño slave bands. These men sought a new El Dorado. Rather than for gold, they came for souls.

II THE JESUIT CENTURY

As enthusiasm for pursuit of the Gran Moxo waned, European contact with Moxos entered a new phase. Beginning in the mid-seventeenth century, members of the Society of Jesus began a period of residence among the native peoples that ended only with Jesuit exile in 1767. Like the conquistadores who preceded them, the Jesuits entered Moxos from Santa Cruz. But similarities with the conquest bands end here. The Jesuit enterprise replaced rapid, violent thrusts into Moxos with a permanent institution, the mission station, which served as the focus of new relations between Europeans and the region's Indian populations.

The Society of Jesus, founded in 1534, followed other major missionary orders into the Americas. Lima welcomed its first Jesuits in 1568, a full thirty years after the arrival of the Dominicans, Mercedarians, Franciscans, and Augustinians.[1] As a latecomer, the Society was forced to seek areas other religious orders had abandoned or left unclaimed. Following a route of expansion southward from the viceregal capital, Jesuits established colleges in Cuzco (1571), Potosí (1576), and La Paz (1580). Then, in 1587, two Jesuit fathers, Diego Samaniego and Diego Martínez, reached the southeastern frontier of Peru, establishing a residence in Santa Cruz de la Sierra. By 1590 the residence held four priests, the two founders, Angelo Monitola, and Jerónimo de Andión.

The Jesuits exercised a dual role in Santa Cruz. In the absence of secular clergy, they administered the sacraments to the Spanish population. However, the priests had come to the area to minister to its Indian communities. Thus, as soon as they arrived, Samaniego and Martínez began to learn Chané, Guarani, and Gorotoqui, the primary native languages of the Santa Cruz area, and to visit the villages that still surrounded the city in the 1590s.

33

Annual letters from the early seventeenth century show that the Jesuits constantly expanded their visits into the Santa Cruz countryside. In 1603 Father Andrés Ortiz Ortuño described six circuits walked by priests living in the city. Six years later the superior of the residence detailed an expanded itinerary that added regular visits among the Chiquito to the east.[2] These accounts all emphasize preaching, tending the sick, and baptizing the moribund rather than establishing permanent missions.

The first Jesuits reached Moxos as auxiliaries to the Santa Cruz conquest bands of the late sixteenth century. As early as 1592, Father Samaniego wrote that members of the Society were held in such esteem that "the Governor does not make an entry without taking one of us along."[3] Father Andión participated in the last of Suárez de Figueroa's expeditions in 1595. As chaplain, he lived a common soldier's life, traveling on foot, living on short rations, and struggling for survival against the rising waters of the rainy season. He makes no mention of preaching to the Indians of the savanna. Accounts of later expeditions show that the Jesuits served as priests to the conquistadores well into the seventeenth century.[4] Then, with the decline of great expeditions to Moxos, the Jesuits returned to Santa Cruz and their itinerant preaching among the Gorotoqui and Chané.

When the priests entered Moxos again, they did so independent of secular forces. In the early seventeenth century, intermittent contact between the Moxo Arawaks and Santa Cruz was mediated by hispanized Indians. Contacts became more frequent by mid-century when the Moxo began to deal directly with their Spanish neighbors, trading handicrafts and agricultural products for European manufactures. Soon thereafter, the Spaniards found themselves invited into Moxo territory as allies against traditional rivals. A Jesuit brother, Juan de Soto, accompanied such a Spanish party in 1667 as surgeon.

Soto's version of his participation emphasizes a missionary intent. Upon his arrival in the principal Moxo village, Soto begged the chief to let him preach to the Indians. Permission received, the brother began a sermon in halting Arawak in which he carefully distinguished his own nonviolent approach from the approach of his countrymen. He ended his soliloquy by urging the Indians to cooperate with the Spaniards, "who although terrible to their enemies are very courteous and kind to their friends."[5] The presence of an armed Spanish force in the Indians' midst must have given the brother's words a special emphasis.

This trip convinced Soto that the Moxo presented an attractive opportunity for conversion. When he returned to Santa Cruz, he presented his superior with an account of the expedition and a plea to push for further contact with the Moxo. Soto's appeal evidently impressed Jesuit authorities, for they authorized a trip to La Plata where Brother Soto put his findings before the judges of the Audiencia. Although his appeal for Crown support was unsuccessful, Soto did not abandon his commitment to Moxos. In 1668 he led two priests of his order, José Bermudo and Julián de Aller, back to the upper Mamoré. This first Jesuit entry proved short-lived. The priests and brother failed to attract Moxo converts and abandoned the area when the Indians began to threaten their safety. Soto never returned to the Mamoré. He died in Santa Cruz trying to organize a second expedition. But even though Soto failed to realize the establishment of missions in Moxos, he transmitted his enthusiasm for the enterprise to others.

Soto's death brings down the curtain on what might be called the charismatic phase, to use Weberian terminology, in Moxos' missionary history.[6] Up to this point, the Jesuits had acted without the support of and largely ungoverned by their superiors. These early missionaries recall the men one church historian has called "holy vagabonds" in other geographical contexts:[7] Fray Marcos de Niza in the Pueblos, Eusebio Kino in the Southwest, and Father Samuel Fritz in the Amazon established a tradition of the mission as a largely solitary and idiosyncratic enterprise. While Moxos history features its Allers, Andións, and Sotos in the early years, the establishment of its permanent missions resulted from a rational-legal impulse, an effort sanctioned, organized, and supported by central authorities.

In 1674 Santa Cruz-based Jesuits began a second series of entries. Brother José del Castillo, a Spaniard who recently had arrived in Peru, convinced a group of Indian traders to allow him to accompany them when they returned to the savanna. Castillo visited the same region of the Mamoré that Soto and his party had seen six years earlier. He reestablished contact with the native people and tried to convince them to invite other Jesuits into the area. Castillo relied less on preaching to gain the Indians' acceptance than had his predecessors. Along with his Bible and missal, Castillo carried a considerable quantity of trade goods "to ripen their [the Indians'] goodwill."[8] The truck helped to convince the Arawaks to allow Castillo's fellow missionaries into their territory. On Saint Peter's Day of 1675, Fathers Pedro Marbán and Cipriano Barace left Santa Cruz to join their brother on the Mamoré.

The new fathers entered the savanna charged by their provincial with preparing a comprehensive survey of Moxos. The resulting document provides a valuable account of native society at the onset of the mission period. More important, however, the form of the report—a series of responses to the provincial's questions—illustrates the Jesuit view of a regulated enterprise. The provincial asked his priests to determine: (1) "the disposition of the towns of the province, their number and the people that are in them"; (2) "if the province has one or a number [of] languages"; (3) "if the climate is salubrious"; (4) "if the province has neighboring nations, what are their names and how many people are there?"; (5) "the disposition of these Indians to receive the Holy Word."[9]

The Society of Jesus, operating through its Peruvian leadership, made conscious decisions about the suitability of an area by evaluating its landscape and culture, before committing men and matériel. In Moxos' case, this initial survey was followed by two subsequent *visitas* later in the 1670s, both designed to reevaluate the original survey. These careful calculations clash with the picture of the missionary freelance, but they reflect the realities of establishing and maintaining an effective mission system on the edge of the Spanish Empire.

Although the native people admitted Europeans to their lands, they approached these visitors cautiously. Two generations of continuous slaving had left a strong legacy of distrust for foreigners. The Jesuits moved freely among the Indians but encountered little enthusiasm for conversion or congregation among them. Despite this lack of cooperation, their efforts were not in vain. For six months the three missionaries lived in the principal Moxo village, gaining the confidence of the native people and learning to survive in an alien environment.

The Jesuits' early encounters with the native people were hampered by their lack of facility in local languages and the rigors of life in the tropics. Despite Father Aller's brief studies of Arawak in 1668, the missionaries found their language skills woefully inadequate for meaningful communication. When Father Marbán arrived on the Mamoré, he began to assemble the grammar and vocabulary lists that ultimately would become the *Arte y vocabulario de la lengua Moxa* (Lima, 1701); before this systematic compilation, however, linguistic progress proved slow. The priests also suffered under the hardships imposed by the Moxos climate. Accustomed to the temperate weather of Spain and the South American highlands and Pacific coast, these men complained bitterly about the humidity and the clouds of insects that characterized life in Moxos. Their complaints increased when they contracted a tropical illness, probably yellow fever, which sapped their strength and severely limited their activities.[10]

In their first two years of residence, the Jesuits reaped few rewards for their suffering. Their base remained a single village of Moxo Arawak; their clothes rotted in the sun and humidity; their health deteriorated. Yet they persevered. Unlike all Europeans before them, Castillo, Marbán, and Barace remained on the Mamoré. Their residence gave them a chance to learn the local language, to make contact with the principal Moxo settlements, and to accustom the native people to a peaceful European presence in their territory.

In 1678 the trio received an unexpected visitor when the provincial sent Father Luís Sotelo from Lima to investigate the state of the Moxos enterprise. The reasons for the visit are unclear. One chronicler claims that the provincial's action grew out of complaints by one of the missionaries that further work among the Moxo was in vain.[11] But Sotelo's instructions apparently included an order that a congregated settlement be established or the Mamoré area be abandoned as a mission field. Under this ultimatum, the missionaries managed to settle six hundred Indians at a village on the river. Jesuit sources attribute this resettlement to native volition. Convinced that further resistance to congregation would lead to loss of the Jesuits and their trade goods, the Indians consented to enter a nuclear settlement.[12] Satisfied, Sotelo returned to Lima, although soon after his departure most of the Indians returned to their traditional villages.

The Society's leaders continued to order reports from the missions. In 1679 Hernando Cabrero called upon Marbán to make a detailed survey of the population of Moxos; a year later a new provincial sent Martín de Leturra, superior of the Santa Cruz residence, to inspect conditions in the nascent missions. Finally the missionaries managed to convince their leaders that the Moxos enterprise would yield a bounteous harvest of souls for Christianity, and Lima committed itself to providing men and supplies.

In 1682 the work of seven years bore its first fruit in the foundation of Nuestra Señora de Loreto, a consolidated village or reduction, on the site of the Moxo Arawak village that had served the missionaries as a base camp. On March 25 Marbán, aided by Fathers José de Vega and Antonio de Orellana, brought together the inhabitants of three Arawak villages and conducted a mass baptism of some five hundred people. These events undoubtedly were hastened by events extraneous to the Jesuits' efforts. In 1681 cruceños mounted a large-scale expedition that took captives on the upper Mamoré. The approach of the dreaded slave raid convinced the Arawaks that their only "salvation" lay with the Jesuits.[13]

Loreto provided the Jesuits with a base for further penetration of the savanna. After 1682 the missionaries no longer followed the old conquest routes from Santa Cruz; instead, they used the Loreto site as a staging area for expeditions into Moxos. The first period of expansion, covering the years 1683–1700, concentrated on the upper Mamoré and the western savanna. Then, between 1700 and 1715, missionaries pushed their stations down the Mamoré to its confluence with the Guaporé and into the forested regions of the northeast inhabited by the Baure and Tapacura peoples. The year 1720 marked the end of the epoch of mission expansion. The Jesuits continued their efforts to attract new converts and managed to establish minor stations along the Guaporé and near Santa Cruz. But, as table 2 shows, eighteen of the twenty-four foundations in Moxos occurred during the first four decades of the Jesuit century.

The second mission site resulted from the efforts of Cipriano Barace, one of the founding fathers of 1674. After four years of proselytizing among the Arawak speakers north of Loreto, Barace founded a site he called Santísima Trinidad on the northern limit of their territory. Barace's aggressive congregation of Indians to his mission soon made the population of Trinidad larger than that of Loreto. In fact, one Jesuit chronicler claims that it was the growth of Trinidad that finally convinced the Jesuit hierarchy to reinforce the original complement of missionaries.[14] By 1688 the missionary roster lists eleven priests and a lay brother active in Moxos.

Once committed to the Moxos missions, the Province of Peru quickly responded to pleas for operatives. The Society's catalogs show that between 1690 and 1696 thirteen priests and three brothers made their way to the savanna stations. These additions to the field staff ushered in a period of rapid expansion to the north and west of the Loreto-Trinidad axis. Along the Mamoré, Fathers Juan de Montenegro and Agustín Zapata founded San Javier in 1691; six years later, Father Lorenzo Legarda established San Pedro among the Canisiana. The first mission west of the Mamoré was established among the Cañacure and Punuana in 1689 by Brother Alvaro de Mendoza and Fathers Antonio de Orellana and Juan de Espejo. This site, named San Ignacio for the founder of the Society of Jesus, became a jump-off point for the exploration of the area between the Mamoré and Beni rivers. Between 1691 and 1700, priests operating out of San Ignacio founded

Table 2: Mission Foundations, 1682–1744

Date of Foundation	Mission	Location
1682	Loreto	Upper Mamoré
1687	Trinidad	Upper Mamoré
1689	San Ignacio	Apere River
1691	San Javier	Upper Mamoré
1691	San José (abandoned 1752)	Southwestern savanna
1693	San Borja	Southwestern savanna
1696	San Miguel (I) (abandoned ?)	Southwestern savanna
1697	San Pedro	Upper Mamoré
1698	San Luís (abandoned 1758)	Southwestern savanna
1703	San Pablo (abandoned ca.1710)	Western savanna
1705	Santa Rosa (I) (abandoned 1740)	Upper Mamoré
1708	Concepción	Blanco River
1709	Exaltación	Lower Mamoré
1709	San Joaquín	Baures River
1710	San Juan Baptista (abandoned 1718)	Eastern savanna
1710	Reyes	Beni River
1717	San Martín	San Martín River
1719	Santa Ana	Yacuma River
1720	Magdalena	Itonamas River
1723	Desposorios	Santa Cruz region
1725	San Miguel (II) (abandoned 1762)	Guaporé River
1730	Patrocinio (abandoned 1741)	Upper Mamoré
1740	San Nicholás	Baures River
1743	Santa Rosa (II) (abandoned 1751)	Guaporé River
1744	San Simón y Judás	San Martin River

San José (1691), San Francisco de Borja (1693), and San Luís (1698) in the polyglot regions of the western savanna.

Two events marked the end of this initial period of mission growth. The first began outside Moxos when the Moysuti, a tropical forest people living on the Andean slope southwest of San Ignacio, burned their mission and forced their Dominican mentors to flee. The revolt closed routes from Moxos to the highlands up the Beni River and spread to the western Jesuit stations. In San Borja, Indian neophytes, emboldened by the Moysutis'

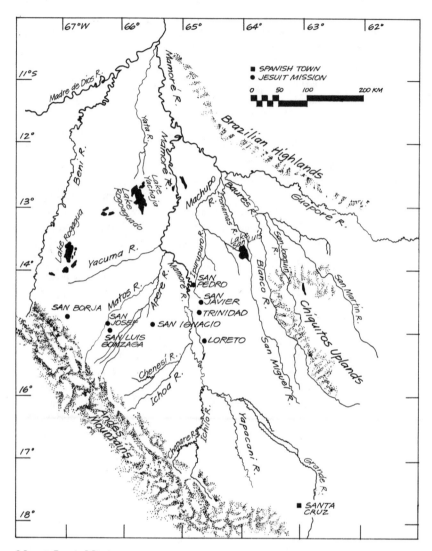

Map 6. Jesuit Missions, ca. 1700

revolt and angered by what they considered inadequate supplies of iron tools, forced the missionaries to flee across the savanna in the middle of the rainy season. Despite the efforts of the priests of San Ignacio, the uprising continued until the rains abated and a troop from Santa Cruz accompanied the Jesuits back to their outpost on the Beni.[15] Ironically, the upheaval, which temporarily displaced the Jesuits from the western savanna, resulted in their undisputed hegemony over the area after 1697. In 1695 Franciscans, advancing southeast from their Apolobamba missions, and Dominicans, penetrating the eastern Andean slopes from La Paz, rivaled Jesuit influence in the Beni valley. However, the death of a Franciscan priest at Santa Buenaventura de Chiruguas and the Dominicans' departure after the Moysutis' revolt left the area open to the Jesuits with their return to San Borja.[16]

The second event was the arrival of Jesuit officials to inspect missionary progress. In 1700 Diego Francisco Altamirano reached the savanna in his official role as *visitador,* a position that combined observation and on-the-spot decision making. Altamirano had come to Peru in 1695 after a career that spanned nearly half a century in Paraguay, Spain, and Nueva Granada. As provincial of Paraguay (1677–81), he had conducted an inspection of the province and its missions to the Guarani.[17] Although he was a septuagenarian when he arrived in Lima, Altamirano served his order as visitador and again launched a provincewide tour. He personally surveyed all the missionary stations in Moxos before returning to Loreto, where he convened a conference designed to discuss the state of the missions and establish a blueprint for their expansion. The conclusions of the meeting, recorded in Altamirano's own history of the province, clearly set out a missionary model that would direct the priests and brothers in their work with the native people of Moxos.

Altamirano placed great importance on the physical state of the missions. He decreed that wetland rice, European garden vegetables, and sugarcane be planted to supplement the native plant inventory. He decided that each mission should have cattle and oxen for beef and traction, chickens for meat and eggs. Altamirano also decided that Indians living in the missions should receive training in such European skills as carpentry, masonry, and blacksmithing. Finally, he ordered that each mission set aside land for the common cultivation of cane, rice, and cotton for export to Peru. No detail seemed too trivial to escape the visitor's attention. Noting that the missionaries had contracted local women to cook for them, Altamirano advised that, even though this practice was understandable, it would be preferable to "hire male cooks who could be free to exercise their vocation within the house, which would allow the selection of boys capable of learning and would permit the priests to dress them better than their fellows and with this [Europeanization] permit a brother to quickly teach them housekeeping skills."[18]

The visitor next turned his attention to governance with the homily that "political life results in Christian life."[19] To introduce political life in the missions, Altamirano prescribed the cabildo form of local government. Following both Spanish patterns and those of the Paraguayan missions, he called for the neophytes to elect leaders annually at each station. With the guidance of the priest, these officials would enforce the laws of the community and punish those who transgressed them.

Altamirano also sponsored a proposal for establishing the Arawak language of the Moxos as a lingua franca for the entire system, another practice reminiscent of the Paraguayan reductions, to facilitate communication between the priests and their charges. The visitor gave Father Marbán the responsibility for preparing a Moxo grammar, vocabulary, catechism, and confession for use by the missionaries. For Indians who spoke a language other than Arawak, Altamirano proposed the publication of simple lessons directed at the children of each station. Once the young had learned the new language, they could teach it to their parents.[20]

The visitor's blueprint was straightforward: bring the native people together, provide for their material needs, teach them a common language, and educate them in European arts, offices, and religion. In short, Altamirano proposed the creation of a European world in Moxos. Under this model, Europeans set the rules and Indians followed them. However, Altamirano's scheme was fatally flawed, as eighteenth-century missionaries soon would discover. First, it assumed Indian acquiescence in a European reconstruction of their world, a condition that never existed. As I argue throughout this book, the Indians of Moxos had a well-developed culture at the time of the Jesuit encounter and were very selective in their acceptance of things European. Second, Altamirano's view of Moxos was incomplete. The mission world in 1700 occupied only the Arawak core on the Mamoré. This homogeneous region proved a poor predictor of the realities of mission expansion into the multicultural zones lying to the north, east, and west of the Mamoré. The uprising at San Borja in 1696–97 should have signaled the difficulties inherent in congregating the numerous ethnic groups lying outside the Arawak core. Yet the directives that emerged from the Loreto conference stressed standardization of mission life-styles around a European inspiration, aims untenable in the missions founded after 1700. Chapter 4 will reopen the discussion of the inadequacy of this approach for describing Indian life in the missions.

During the eighteenth century, missions were founded among two of the most populous peoples of Moxos. From San Ignacio, missionaries pushed out into the northwestern regions drained by the Maniquí and Yacuma rivers. In 1702, Father Ignacio Fernández established Los Santos Reyes near the point at which the Beni River emerges from the last Andean foothills. The principal group initially settled at Reyes was Mobima. However, early accounts of the mission name twenty-five other "nations" gathered there, some of whom spoke Quechua.[21] Five years later, near the confluence of the Yacuma and Mamoré rivers, Father Martín de Espinosa gathered a large number of Mobima to a mission he called Santa Rosa, the first of two stations to bear this name in the Jesuit century.

The second major area of expansion after 1700 was the northeast, a zone of forest growth and smaller rivers draining toward the Guaporé. Immediately following the Loreto meetings, Father Cipriano Barace began a series of expeditions into the area northeast of Trinidad. Through his contact with the Guarayo, Barace learned of the existence of a numerous and "civilized" people to the north. On his visit to their territory, Barace discovered that these people called themselves Baure. The missionary found them amenable to the suggestion that he establish a station on their lands. However, on a subsequent expedition, Barace earned the enmity of a powerful shaman who lured the priest into an ambush by separating him from his escort of neophytes. On September 16, 1703, the Moxos enterprise lost its first Jesuit to martyrdom.[22]

In retaliation, the Jesuits called upon the governor of Santa Cruz for an armed campaign against the Baure. Never one to refuse what amounted to a Jesuit-sanctioned slaving expedition, Governor Benito Rivera y Quiroga dispatched a force of one thousand armed hispanized Indians and "a good number of Spanish soldiers" to Baure country. The Baure paid dearly for Barace's murder, as the governor's force hanged several Indians thought to have participated in the killing and took some 250 captives back to Santa Cruz.[23]

Following this punitive expedition, the Jesuits returned to the northeast of Moxos. Father Lorenzo Legarda entered Baure country from Trinidad in the company of twenty mounted neophytes armed for battle. Legarda's precautions proved justified, for the first Baure village his company encountered was anything but chastised by Rivera y Quiroga's campaign. Indian warriors attacked the Jesuit force, and only their horses carried the day. Although Legarda's band was forced to retreat, they captured one prisoner, who was carried back to Trinidad for training as an interpreter. After hearing Legarda's report of continued Baure resistance, the missions' superior, Antonio de Orellana, personally organized a second entry consisting of two priests, twenty neophytes, and the Baure interpreter. This time the Jesuits entered the field carrying large quantities of trade goods and forty-five head of cattle. The prospect of European supplies proved more convincing than the sword. The foundation of Baure missions at Concepción in 1708 and at San Joaquín a year later resulted directly from this second expedition.[24]

With the Baure missions begun, only the Kayubaba and Itonama remained outside the Jesuit system, and, within a decade, both of these peoples became the occupants of new stations established on the northern savanna. In 1709, Father Antonio de Garriga founded the mission of Exaltación among the Kayubaba on the lower Mamoré. Ten years later, Father Gabriel Ruiz reached the Itonama heartland of the Machupo River and congregated a number of villages into a station he christened Magdalena. This would be the last major foundation of the Jesuit century. Although a few of the sites shown on map 7 were established after 1720, by this date the Jesuits had extended their system across the entire expanse of Moxos. In less than forty years, all but a few of the native people had abandoned their small villages for the Jesuit-sponsored settlements.

The quarter-century between 1720 and 1745 marks the apogee of the Jesuit missionary period. Mission culture became fully developed during these years, as the following thematic chapters describe. This quarter-century was characterized by large, settled population clusters spread across all of Moxos. Although the Jesuits continued their search for converts, they found no major groups after 1720. Parish work rather than conversion typified mission activities. The mature missions fostered Indian skills in European letters and European technologies. Nature also favored the period as normal rains, abundant harvests, and good health blessed the Jesuits and their charges.

Missionary correspondence of the mid-eighteenth century describes a period of consolidation. Many of the stations erected or remodeled their community structures. In 1729 fire destroyed the churches at both San José and San Luís. Yet the missionaries reported that instead of discouragement, the fires "kindled a healthy rivalry between the neophytes to see which would rebuild first."[25] The huge church built at San Pedro in 1740 capped the achievements of Jesuit architecture and native craftsmen. As we shall see in a subsequent chapter, corporate investments in Charcas and Peru

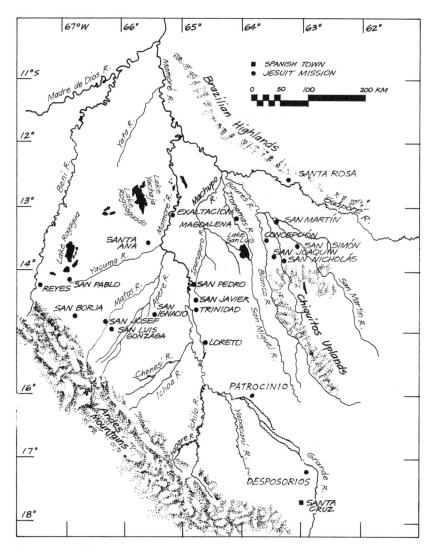

Map 7. Jesuit Missions, ca. 1740

funded mission construction as well as providing the trade goods that underwrote the Jesuit system in Moxos.

Daily life in the missions also assumed a settled quality during this time. In their writings, the missionaries evoked images of harmony and light, of worship and good music. Their discourse reflects a European church rather than a frontier redoubt. The Annual Letter of 1731 describes mission industry that produced agricultural products and Indian handicrafts prized in Santa Cruz and in the highlands; the 1746 epistle speaks of religious celebrations featuring "piety that would be the envy of any European congregation."[26]

Yet even as they sounded the praises of their neophytes, the missionary correspondents could not fully suppress their misgivings. The letter that described the friendly rivalry between San José and San Luís to rebuild their churches also expressed a fear that the fires that had consumed the original structures had been set, a sign of smoldering rebellion bursting forth. Another missionary, resident in San Borja, wondered aloud how long traditional enemies would respect the imposed *Pax Jesuitica*.[27] And several priests expressed a pessimistic view of the fate of a system plagued by low reproductive rates and few new immigrants, "a drying up of the population."[28] These conflicting themes underscore that the nature of the mission period was one of creative tension between Europeans and native Americans. The middle eighteenth century was the high point of the Jesuit century, but it was not a golden age.

The steady growth and development of the missions came to an end with the onset of a struggle between the Iberian kingdoms over their boundaries in South America, beginning in the mid-1740s, and the flood and pandemic of 1750–51. Flooding is a fact of life on the savanna. The aboriginal people lived in harmony with the annual ebb and flow of water, but mission life, stressing permanent settlements and large-scale architecture, suffered greatly because of flood erosion. The rainy season of 1750–51 brought the most extensive inundations since 1723, when flood waters had forced the relocation of several mission sites. The 1750 flood struck especially hard on the upper Mamoré, destroying crops and herds, undermining the foundation of San Ignacio's church, and forcing the relocation of both San Javier and Loreto. The priests conducted their rounds in canoes. The neophytes' activities were completely disrupted, and several of the missions experienced serious food shortages. The flood also contaminated local drinking water and carried contagion, probably typhoid, through a neophyte population already weakened by short rations. The entire system was affected, but San José, San Miguel, and Santa Rosa suffered the most significant losses.[29] While serious, floods and epidemics were cyclical phenomena in mission history. Developments in mid-eighteenth-century Europe brought Moxos a series of unparalleled events.

Much of the Iberian rivalry in South America took place in the heartland of the continent. In the eighteenth century, Jesuit missions, following the arc of the Andes from the Venezuelan llanos to the pampas of Argentina, formed the eastern frontier of the Spanish Empire. Counterposed to the missions was a series of Portuguese settlements founded by a group of restless explorer-entrepreneurs, the famous *bandeirantes*.

The westward expansion of the Portuguese Empire in Brazil forms one of the most celebrated chapters in Latin American colonial history. In the seventeenth and eighteenth centuries, the city of São Paulo sent out a series of expeditions organized around charismatic leaders whose flags (*bandeiras*) served as emblems for leaders and followers alike. These bandeirantes pushed into the heart of South America in search of precious metals, gems, and slaves. Spanish silver discoveries in Charcas attracted leaders such as Antonio Rapôso Tavares to the Andes as early as the 1630s. Tavares's arrival on the eastern flank of its jurisdiction sent a shudder through the Audiencia of Charcas, even at a time when the kingdoms of Spain and Portugal were ostensibly united. In reaction, Juan de Lizarazu, president of the Audiencia, proposed that a series of Spanish centers be founded in the Moxos region to deter further Portuguese incursions.

Portuguese activity east of Santa Cruz intensified with the establishment of Spanish Jesuit missions among the Chiquito Indians at the end of the seventeenth century and the Portuguese discovery of gold fields on the Cuiabá River of western Mato Grosso in 1718. Congregations of Indians in the nearby missions proved an easy mark for Cuiabá-based slave bands, provoking calls for secular defense of the stations and the training of neophytes in tactics of self-defense.[30] Subsequent Portuguese exploration of the Cuiabá region made new gold strikes on the headwaters of the Guaporé. Exploration of these deposits and the creation of the Captaincy of Mato Grosso in 1748 placed a Portuguese presence within easy reach of the Moxos missions.

As the Jesuits anxiously watched this steady advance of Brazilian settlements toward their northeastern frontier, they began to receive a series of uninvited visitors, who crossed the Guaporé to enter the very heart of the mission system. Some of these interlopers came alone or in twos and threes in attempts to make commercial contact with the missions. One such merchant-explorer was Francisco Rodrigues da Costa; in 1747 he entered the Mamoré network from Mato Grosso and traded salt to the missionaries of Exaltación for wax and cotton cloth.[31] Others came in large expeditions organized to reconnoiter areas west of the Guaporé.

In 1723 a force of 130 armed men reached Exaltación on the lower Mamoré. This expedition, which had been mustered the year before in Pará (modern-day Belem) by Francisco de Mello Palheta, entered Moxos after a sixteen hundred-mile odyssey up the Amazon and Madeira rivers. While in Exaltación, Palheta wrote to the Spanish governor of Santa Cruz, claiming that he only intended to search for the sources of the western tributaries of the Amazon. However, using documents compiled in Pará, a Brazilian historian, Basilio de Magalhães, has concluded that the eighteenth-century governor of that city, João da Maia da Gama, charged Palheta to look for river routes between the Atlantic and Charcas.[32]

Twenty years after Palheta's departure, another Portuguese expedition, this one from the gold fields of Cuiabá, entered the northern missions. After visiting the Santa Rosa station, the expeditionary force split into two units. One traveled up the Baures River to make contact with the missions there; the second group, commanded by Manoel Felix de Lima, visited San Martín and Magdalena. The Portuguese attempted to establish affinities with the Jesuits, taking sacraments from the missionary priest and making gifts to the church. But their request for permission to push farther up the Mamoré was rejected by the superior in San Pedro. After trading for supplies, Manoel Felix led his expedition back down the Mamoré and continued his journey northeastward all the way to the mouth of the Amazon.[33]

The Jesuits responded to the arrival of these expeditions with cautious opposition. Palheta and Manoel Felix received courteous welcomes in the stations they visited; both the leaders and their men were provided with food and fellowship. However, when the Portuguese requested permission to continue further upstream, the Jesuits balked. Moxos was the beginning of Spanish territory, and the missionaries enforced the Crown's insistence on halting foreigners at its frontier. Manoel Felix relates that despite outward courtesy, the Jesuits refused his queries for information on lands to the west and actually shadowed his movements within the missions.

Although the interlopers returned to Brazil at their bidding, the Jesuits did not forget that they had come. They petitioned the Council of the Indies for the rights to introduce firearms to the missions and to train the neophytes in their use. Rebuffed in Madrid, the Jesuits went about organizing the missions' defenses on their own, training bodies of archers and posting sentries along the Guaporé. These precautions were to prove futile in the face of escalating tensions between European powers.

David Davidson has pointed out that before 1750 European exploration and settlement of the center of South America were carried out by groups only indirectly responsible to the Iberian monarchies. Although they advanced the territorial claims of their sovereigns, both the Spanish missionaries and the Portuguese bandeirantes operated as what Davidson calls "freelances," moving where opportunities rather than Crown policies directed them. The unofficial character of Iberian expansion thus produced an informal truce along the frontier, despite growing tensions between Madrid and Lisbon in the 1740s.[34]

The truce broke down when America could no longer ignore European events. The major source of contention in South America was the boundary between the empires, a north-south line that bisects three-quarters of the continent. A first phase in the growing Luso-Spanish rivalry was defused with the signing of the Treaty of Madrid in 1750. This agreement attempted to legally define the limits of empires in South America, settle pending disputes, and prevent their recurrence. The primary focus of the discussion was the boundary between the south of Brazil and the Río de la Plata. However, the treaty also delimited the interior, defining the Guaporé as the line dividing Charcas from Mato Grosso. In article 14, Spain ceded to Portugal any mission sites on the right bank of the river (effectively Santa Rosa, founded 1743) while offering the neophytes the option of following the Jesuits to the left bank.

The Treaty of Madrid proved fragile, reflecting a personal agreement between the Iberian monarchs rather than a mutually acceptable solution to the boundary question. It broke down with Charles III's ascension to the Spanish throne and the onset of the Marques de Pombal's ministry in Lisbon. Immediately after assuming power, Pombal moved to replace freelance activities on the Brazilian frontier with institutions clearly tied to the state. Portuguese troops were sent to Brazil in the 1750s, arriving in Mato Grosso in 1752. Also under Pombal's directives, the Portuguese began to shore up their western boundaries. Using information gathered during three decades of exploration on the Guaporé, the first captain general of Mato Grosso, Antônio Rolim de Moura, explored the river's course from its headwaters to the Mamoré. Then, in 1756, Moura established two positions on the middle Guaporé, one of which occupied the former Jesuit site of Santa Rosa opposite the mouth of the Itonamas River. News of the impending abrogation of the Madrid accords brought Moura back to the area, and in 1759 he fortified the Santa Rosa site, now renamed Nossa Senhora da Conceição.[35]

A second round of negotiations between the Iberian monarchs annulled the Madrid agreements and replaced them with the Treaty of El Prado, signed in 1760. This compact removed the western boundary line established a decade earlier but put nothing finite in its place. The signing of the Treaty of El Prado and the entry of Spain and Portugal on opposite sides in the Seven Years War set the stage for conflict along the Guaporé.

The Portuguese struck first. From their position at Conceição, Portuguese troops, newly reinforced by Moura from Mato Grosso, began to menace the northeastern missions. In the wake of this show of force, the Jesuits withdrew from their relocated Santa Rosa station and moved both missionaries and neophytes to San Pedro. At the same time, they informed Spanish authorities of Portuguese movements and asked for help in countering them.[36]

News of war in Europe moved the Spanish to action. In November 1761, the Audiencia of Charcas ordered Governor Alonso de Verdugo to gather all his available forces in Santa Cruz for an entry into Moxos. In January Verdugo dispatched 160 men with instructions to raise a fort facing Portuguese positions on the Guaporé. Four months later Verdugo followed his vanguard with 450 men, only 270 of them armed. By the time this force reached the missions, Spanish and Portuguese troops had clashed, and the Portuguese had expanded the front by burning the San Miguel mission and taking its two priests and a number of its neophytes captive. Then, as the governor drilled his army at San Pedro, the Portuguese fell upon the Spanish vanguard. A combined force of Spanish troops and mission neophytes repelled the attack and forced the Portuguese back across the Guaporé. One of the Spanish defenders later would relate that the Portuguese crossed the river at night in hopes of surprising their adversaries but that the Spanish forces fought intrepidly, killing more than seventy of the attackers, including the Portuguese corporal who led the action.[37] Although it seemed that these actions would serve as the opening shots in a protracted combat, they were to mark both the beginning and the end of the fighting.

The Spanish effort suffered because of the effects tropical conditions had on troops raised in the highlands. Disease and desertion had trimmed Verdugo's levies from 610 to 303 by the time they reached San Pedro. And although the governor rushed his army to the Guaporé after the initial Portuguese attacks, he never engaged the enemy in combat. Verdugo wrote to the viceroy in Lima that he honored Portuguese requests for a truce in the wake of news of the singing of the Treaty of Paris in 1763. However, an account written seven years after the events of the conflict revealed that Verdugo doubted his troops' morale. After two months on the Guaporé, the governor returned to Santa Cruz, leaving behind a skeleton force to observe Portuguese movements. He died trying to raise a second army.[38]

A three-year stalemate followed Verdugo's departure from the savanna. In 1763 Moura retired from Mato Grosso the victor. He had advanced to the Guaporé, fortified Portuguese positions on the river, and remained in the field as his rival retired. Moura's service earned him a hero's welcome from his commanders, a knighthood, and eventually the office of viceroy of Brazil. João Pedro da Câmara, Moura's successor, arrived in Mato Grosso in 1764 and strengthened the Conceição position with artillery he had transported up the Amazon-Madeira-Guaporé route from Pará. Câmara also began to patrol the river with armed canoes based at the fort.[39]

Spanish preparations for a second expedition reopened hostilities on the Guaporé. In 1766 the newly arrived viceroy of Peru instructed the president of Charcas to raise an army. Recognizing that lack of equipment had plagued the expedition of 1762, Manuel de Amat y Juni ent sent abundant war matériel to support the proposed campaign. At the same time he ordered the Jesuit superior of Moxos to lay in provisions for the army.[40] Juan de Pestaña complied, first assembling troops in Charcas and Potosí and marching them to Santa Cruz, then entering Moxos after the rains of 1766. Acclimation to tropical conditions exacted a terrible toll on the ranks of this second expedition as well. Upon reaching San Pedro, the army surgeon reported two hundred men too sick to fight, thirty-one of whom were near death.[41] As they did in 1762, the Spaniards pushed forward to the front only to retire without engaging the enemy. Like Verdugo, Pestaña found that savanna conditions reduced his troops' combat readiness past the point of predictable performance. An early beginning of the rainy season signaled the president's departure from the Guaporé and his return to Charcas. The Spaniards preserved a military presence in Moxos in the form of a token force that shuffled between the stations along the northern frontier. These troops, commanded after 1766 by Colonel Antonio Aymerich y Villajuana, were to perform their final service to the Crown by executing the orders for Jesuit expulsion in 1767.

The Spanish campaigns of 1763 and 1766 had a grave impact on the missions. The northern stations bore the brunt of supply operations and furnished laborers for the erection of battlements and the hauling of cargo. Mission crops and herds fed the soldiers, often resulting in the Indians' privation. On the orders of the viceroy, the neophytes sowed extra fields of maize, rice, peanuts, and beans, but the duration of the conflict proved more than normal harvests and existing stores could support. The mission supplies were depleted by the soldiers' demands. Although the northern missions bore most of the burden, stations well removed from the front also supported the war effort. The expeditionary force requisitioned mounts from all the stations, and neophytes from San Pedro and Santa Ana quartered reserves and men too ill to serve on active duty.

Extant Indian testimony highlights the stress of the 1760s. Neophytes' accounts of the Jesuit century emphasized four types of events: the work of particularly influential priests, floods, disease outbreaks, and the Portuguese war. In later years, the Indians of San Pedro remembered the 1760s as a time in which they served the expeditionary force "to the neglect of everything else."[42] Spanish sources verify the stress of the war years. An officer who served under Pestaña recalled that the burdens of the conflict disrupted even the cultivation and harvesting of crops in the missions.[43] Two years after Pestaña's departure, he requested that the Royal Hacienda send rations to the missions to relieve starvation among the Indians.

Not surprisingly, given the influx of large numbers of European soldiers and the stress occasioned by providing for their support, the war years correspond with the outbreak of epidemic disease in the missions. The arrival of the first expeditionary army to the northern savanna marked an outbreak of smallpox among the Baure neophytes. Verdugo blamed the Portuguese for the contagion, suggesting that they had used biological warfare.[44] The governor's own troops seem a more likely vector, since many of them were sick and all of them were in daily contact with the mission Indians. Whatever its origin, however, disease ravaged the northern missions in 1763–64.

As the events of the second expedition reverberated in Moxos, the missions suffered another shock. According to a royal decree dated February 27, 1767, the Society of Jesus was to be suppressed in Spanish domains.

The order that reached Lima on August 20 informed the viceroy of an empirewide date of September 4, 1767 for placing the Jesuits under detention. While Amat proved unable to comply with this date for closing Jesuit positions on the frontier of the Viceroyalty, he forwarded the order to the commander of the Spanish expeditionary force in Magdalena. The year 1767 marked the end of a century of Jesuit presence in Moxos.

After he received the viceregal messenger at his headquarters, Colonel Aymerich hastily gathered his troops and moved up the Mamoré to Loreto. Here he planned to direct the Jesuit exodus. At the same time, Colonel Joaquín Espinosa assembled a force of militia and volunteers in Santa Cruz, and departed for the savanna. The union of these two Spanish forces at Loreto began the execution of exile.

Reinforced, Aymerich felt strong enough to carry out the royal decree. First he dispatched Espinosa and one hundred soldiers to publish the exile in the Baures stations and to escort the area's missionaries back to Loreto. At the same time, Aymerich wrote to the governor of Mato Grosso, requesting passage on the Guaporé for the boats that would evacuate the Jesuits from the northern missions.[45] Then he set out for San Pedro to present the Jesuit superior with a copy of the order of exile. The superior accepted Aymerich's news without protest and dispatched messengers to the missionaries on the Mamoré and western savanna, informing them of the new status quo and instructing them to assemble in San Pedro for transport.

Spanish authorities feared violent Indian opposition to the priests' removal, a recurrence of the so-called Guarani War of 1750–51, which followed the Portuguese takeover of several Paraguayan missions under the provisions of the Treaty of Madrid. However, events proved these apprehensions unfounded. The only turmoil accompanying the exile occurred when Espinosa's force departed from Santa Cruz. Indian neophytes grew restless as garbled versions of the reasons behind the Spanish entry moved downriver ahead of the troops. But the Jesuits calmed their charges, promising them that the missions were in no danger. On October 11, 1767, three priests arrived in Loreto and presented themselves to Aymerich; this event marked the beginning of a flow of missionaries that was to continue for seven months.

The Jesuit evacuation from Moxos was complicated by the distances involved and by the onset of the rainy season of 1767–68. The most difficult missions to reach were those of the western savanna. A Spanish officer and a crew of Indian boatmen spent two months making the journey from San Pedro to San Borja, eventually crossing the flooded savanna by canoe.[46] The priests and brothers left Loreto for Santa Cruz in four flotillas between October 1767 and May 1768. The last departure held several aged Jesuits deemed too infirm to accompany their companions earlier.

The Crown had ordered that the exiles be dispatched to Spain with all possible haste. Spanish officials in La Plata and Santa Cruz complied by sending the Moxos missionaries and their Chiquitos counterparts to the Pacific coast for transport to Lima. From Santa Cruz the Jesuits traveled under military guard to Cochabamba, Oruro, Tacna, and the port of Arica. Records show that this long journey took a heavy toll on the priests and brothers. Of the twenty-four Moxos Jesuits who left Santa Cruz, only fourteen actually arrived in Lima for deportation to Europe. Forty percent of these survivors of the rigors of life in the tropical world died crossing the mountains and deserts that separated Moxos from the coast.[47]

The Moxos Jesuits were lodged in Lima's San Juan de Dios Hospital as they waited for transportation to Europe. At the end of December 1768, the former missionaries joined their counterparts from Mainas and Chile aboard a ship destined for Panama. The party then crossed the isthmus and proceeded to Cartagena, where Father Joseph Reysner, the veteran priest of the Loreto mission, died. The Jesuits finally reached Spain in August 1769, after a stop in Havana.[48]

Missionary exile would mark the end of the Jesuit century but not the end of mission culture. The missions survived the Jesuits' departure on the strength of institutions that had grown out of the period between 1667 and 1767. Indeed, visitors to the area reported vibrant communities on the Jesuit sites well into the nineteenth century. As events following the exile were to prove, the Jesuits facilitated mission culture, but they were not responsible for it. That responsibility lay with the Indian inhabitants of Moxos — men, women, and children who had emerged forever from their aboriginal modes of living without totally immersing themselves in the European world.

III THE MISSIONS

The Jesuit centers pinpointed on maps 6 and 7 were the focus of mission culture on the savanna. Here the missionaries and Indian neophytes established complexes that supported relatively large populations in substantial prosperity. The significance of these original stations is perhaps best illustrated by examining modern maps of the Bolivian Republic, for the names and locations of the Beni Department's principal settlements harken back to Jesuit times, a fact Bolivians now often fail to recognize.

In these enclaves, the Jesuits and Indians labored to raise cities in the wilderness. Although the settlements began modestly, by the early eighteenth century they had become so large and elaborate that they dazzled visitors to Moxos. Contemporary reactions to the missions mixed marvel with envy. While recognizing the missionaries' accomplishments, Spanish officials could not help being struck by the clash between the palpable wealth of the missions and the hardscrabble realities of the nearest secular settlements. This contrast ultimately led to unsubstantiated charges that the Jesuits had discovered mines and had exploited native labor.

In reality, Moxos' impressive complexes may be attributed to two factors. First, the native people, governed by their own leaders and largely by aboriginal patterns of work, provided a willing labor supply during the Jesuit century. Second, the missionaries and their religious corporation furnished a European-based infrastructure based on technical expertise and large infusions of capital raised in the economy of Spanish Peru.

THE PHYSICAL COMPLEX

Under the dual strain of neglect and tropical decay, the physical structures of the missions have disappeared, the buildings dropping again to the level

55

plain from which they once rose. With a total absence of published archaeology, all that remains of the extensive complexes are the descriptions left behind by Jesuit priests and the occasional European visitor. Ubiquitous in the surviving accounts of the stations is the image of miraculous accomplishment. For, at the very edge of the Spanish Empire, hundreds of miles from the nearest secular outpost, there existed settlements of remarkable size and complexity.

When the Portuguese adventurer Manoel Felix de Lima visited Magdalena in 1742, he and his small troop went ashore and passed two weeks waiting for permission to venture farther into Spanish territory. His account of the mission preserves an eyewitness view of the Jesuit system at its apex.

> The whole settlement was inclosed within a square wall, which being probably of clay, like the Church, was covered to preserve it from the weather; and this covering projected so far that there was a dry walk at all times around the Reduction. The great square, according to the usual style of these Jesuit establishments, had a cross in the centre; but in other aspects the ground plan appears to have been traced by some whimsical architect for in whatever direction the houses were seen, they appeared in regular order, like chequeres of a chess-board; and the country was laid out in regular order with white paths of sand. A considerable space was inclosed within the walls, so as to afford room for folds and gardens; and the settlement bore the marks of civilization; there were shops for the weavers, carpenters, and carvers, an *engenho* [mill], where rum as well as sugar was made; public kitchens and stocks for the enforcement of wholesome discipline.[1]

Manoel Felix's account of Magdalena is echoed by the writing of an insider, the missionary priest Francisco Xavier Eder. While Eder never names the mission he describes in his chronicle, biographical information suggests that he wrote of San Martín in the Baure region of the savanna. Eder depicts a model community. The main plaza, which formed the center of the mission, measured seventy paces square and featured a small chapel at each corner. Four streets emptying into the plaza marked the major axes for a grid dividing the settlement into neat blocks of dwellings.[2] These European descriptions, stressing the Renaissance approach to town planning evident in the missions, obscure the importance of aboriginal modes. The Jesuits relied on native experience in siting the missions. Following the

Indians' knowledge of local topography, they were careful to locate their centers in areas providing access to riverine resources while affording as much flood relief as possible. In some cases flooding was alleviated by earth moving, but these operations proved both labor intensive and only partially successful.[3]

The countryside also bore the mark of the mission system. Cultivated fields and pastures lay interspersed around the mission core, the agricultural plots occupying the natural levees along the river courses. Manoel Felix described fields that stretched a considerable distance up and down the San Miguel River from Magdalena, and Indian testimony from the immediate post-Jesuit period broadens the Portuguese interloper's account. Neophytes from San Pedro claimed that they maintained cacao groves two days' distance from their residential center on the Mamoré. The Indians of Magdalena described a series of concentric bands surrounding their mission, the first dedicated to cotton and citrus, the second to subsistence crops, the third to cacao, and the outer band to pasturage. A similar pattern emerges from an 1830 sketch of Mission Concepción rendered by a French traveler.[4]

This extensive network of agriculture and pasturage is the physical manifestation of changes in Moxos, which transformed dispersed aboriginal settlements into a series of large complexes dedicated to the exploitation of savanna resources in the mission period. As they were in the aboriginal mode, most of the missions' economic activities were devoted to subsistence production. Traditional food crops — manioc, yams, and maize — continued to occupy most of the elevated riverfront lands. Under the Jesuit regime, these plants shared space with European introductions, especially cotton, cacao, and sugarcane. Rice, a fourth important European staple, was actually planted with some success on the seasonally flooded savanna, which effectively placed additional land under cultivation.[5]

Stock raising was particularly suited to the savanna and became a mainstay of the mission economy soon after European domestic animals were introduced to Moxos in the 1680s. Eighteenth-century missions held herds of cattle, horses, and mules, which furnished both meat and power. Cattle multiplied rapidly in a semiferal state as they roamed the open grasslands. At the time of Jesuit exile, the missions of Trinidad claimed some 7,000 head of cattle, 4,000 horses, and 70 mules. This was not an exceptional holding as demonstrated in table 3, drawn from the inventories taken by Crown functionaries as they ushered the Jesuits from Moxos.

Table 3: Mission Livestock, ca.1767

Mission	Cattle	Sheep/Goats	Horses	Mules
Loreto	7,000	400	7,000	—
Trinidad	7,000	—	4,000	70
San Javier	5,000	140	593	13
Santa Ana	1,100	100	400	—
Exaltación	2,200	—	730	—
Magdalena	400	—	1,000	—
San Ignacio	9,600	300	179	—
Reyes	4,580	—	1,305	—
San Borja	3,600	—	2,600	14
San Nicolás	2,550	—	240	—
San Simón	1,000	—	150	—
San Martín	1,800	—	170	9
San Joaquín	1,300	—	660	—
Concepción	2,600	200	560	60
San Judás	1,515	—	58	—
TOTALS	48,245	1,140	19,645	166

Sources: "Inventario de los bienes pertenecientes a la iglesia y a la comunidad de los pueblos de San Borja, San Nicolas, San Simon, San Martin y la Concepcion, 1768," Concepcion, 15/11/1768, ANB, ADM, Mojos 1, ff.172–201v, and "Ymbentarios de los bienes de Loreto, Trinidad, San Javier, San Pedro, Santa Ana, Exaltacion, Magdalena, San Ygnacio, y Reyes," Loreto, 4/X/1767, ANB, Mojos 1, ff.7–68.

In addition to the herds owned by individual missions, the Jesuits maintained commonly held livestock in a huge area of wetlands at the headwaters of the Machupo River, east of Loreto. These animals furnished a strategic reserve. They were allowed to roam freely until they were needed to replenish an existing herd or stock that of a newly established mission. On both the Machupo range and the mission spreads, Indian vaqueros tended the animals, moving them from area to area as pastures became exhausted or floodwaters rose.

While the introduction of European animals and cultigens undoubtedly increased the subsistence potential of the savanna peoples, there is evidence that the demands of mission culture strained Moxos' natural resources. Concentrating thousands of people into single settlements led to more intensive agricultural development near the missions rather than the shifting cultivation practiced before the 1680s. While existing documents provide no long-term production data, this change in cultivation patterns certainly implies that soil fertility gradually diminished in these plots. The historical record does show that activities of the Jesuit century reduced the materials available for gathering. By the second decade of the eighteenth century, intramission rivalries growing out of the Indians' desire to extract forest products from lands that had belonged to them in premission days threatened the thirty-year *Pax Jesuitica*. The ordinance that settled the dispute clearly addresses a dwindling natural resource base. Antonio de Garriga's delineation of the boundaries of each station, beyond which its inhabitants could not "occupy lands, cut palms, take wax or balsam, straw or calaba oil (*aceite de Maria*)," is a definite indication that the missions had begun to affect the ecology of Moxos.[6]

A residential, industrial, and religious complex stood at the center of each mission. These central mission buildings were of remarkable scale and detail, despite the severe limitations imposed by the local store of construction materials. The primary impediment to mission construction was the fact that the central savanna lacked stone, a medium essential to stable foundations and support structures. But Jesuit architects adapted their techniques to incorporate adobe and wattle and daub, the principles of native construction, and to use locally available materials in structural design.

According to one source, the neophytes' dwellings measured some 40 by 75 feet, or 3,000 square feet of floor space with a roof peak 30 feet high.[7] The floors of these buildings were raised to protect their contents from flooding. Their walls were made of adobe bricks stacked on the raised floors and covered by an overhanging thatched roof supported by four square-cut timbers. The missionaries' quarters were larger and more commodious than those occupied by the Indians. Alcide Dessalines d'Orbigny's sketch of Concepción has the priests' residence attached to the back of the church, joining a patio in Mediterranean style, and Rubén Vargas Ugarte's reproduction of an early twentieth-century photograph of Trinidad shows a gracefully arched brick building labeled "Casa de los Padres."[8] All dwellings received a coating of stucco, inside and out, and were fitted with locally made doors and window frames as a final touch.

Most of the missions' cottage industries were located at the central station. From the inception of the system, neophytes practiced a variety of arts and offices for the production of utilitarian and ornamental objects. By the first decade of the eighteenth century, mission artisans had reached a high level of sophistication, requiring specialized tools and their own workrooms. Manoel Felix located shops for weavers, carpenters, and carvers as well as a sugar mill within the walls of Magdalena. Orbigny sketched workshops in a building joined to the Concepción church. However, to gain an idea of the variety and number of "industrial" enterprises present in the missions, consider the following summary extracted from lists made by Crown officials at the time of the Jesuit expulsion in 1767.

Eleven of the stations held carpentry shops, three with attached foundries. Four missions, all on the Mamoré and Beni rivers, held weaving operations. The Trinidad operation was the largest, with seven looms set up to weave lengths of cotton cloth. Fourteen missions had sugar operations, ranging from simple wooden crushers at San Simón and San Nicolás to the two bronze-fitted mills and refining facilities at Trinidad. Several of these installations also stored cane by-products such as loaves of sugar, syrup, and alcohol. All of the missions held quantities of tallow, some in raw state, some fashioned into candles.[9]

The church was invariably the most impressive structure in the mission. Even in the early years of the Jesuit century, these buildings were large in scale. Writing in 1696, Father Agustín Zapata described his newly built church at San Ignacio as measuring 30 paces (approximately 60 feet) by 90 paces. As the missions grew in inhabitants and wealth, so did their churches. By the middle of the eighteenth century, these buildings had reached great proportions, so that Zapata's entire church would have fit into the sanctuary of the structure raised at the mission capital of San Pedro in 1740.[10]

Characteristic of the Moxos enterprises, church construction blended native and European skills. The size of the structures necessitated the use of engineering techniques that exceeded aboriginal experience. Jesuit architect-builders such as Zapata, Antonio de Orellana, and the lay brother Jorge Ligardo pioneered the techniques that made monumental-scale construction possible on the savanna. But if the mission churches were European in scale and style, they were also heavily influenced by local conditions.

European design depended on aboriginal execution. Millions of adobe bricks and thousands of feet of planking, all fashioned by neophytes, formed the walls and roof supports. The basic superstructure of the churches consisted of heavy timbers not found in the central savanna. To supply this vital material, Indian crews felled huge hardwoods in the sub-Andean forests of the upper Mamoré and floated them downstream to the mission sites. In the

Plate 1. Church at Mission San Ramón, 1859. *Source:* Archivo Nacional de Bolivia, Sucre. Album Mercado, f.74. Reprinted with permission.

eighteenth century, the Jesuit superiors established a forest reserve for preserving stands of *ychinicco* trees, prized for their size and their resistance to decay.[11] With materials in place, construction began with a labor force drawn from both the local population and residents of neighboring missions. Workers first established a superstructure by burying tree trunks in a rectangular pattern, defining the church nave. With this framework in place, they attached roof supports and a thatch cover. Last came the adobe walls, which in this design bore no load and could be erected as a simple shell for weatherproofing rather than for support.[12]

Although the disappearance of the Moxos churches prevents precise analysis of their design and function, surviving documents — including the mid-nineteenth-century drawings of the buildings at Concepción, San Ramón, and Magdalena reproduced here as plates 1, 2, and 3 — give readers an idea of how they looked in their prime. Clear in all three illustrations is the juxtaposition of the churches with two-storied structures, denoted *colegios* by the artist. As Orbigny's sketch of Concepción shows, these buildings housed the priests and the mission industrial complex. In both a physical and symbolic sense, this juxtaposition of the sacred and the

Plate 2. Church at Mission Concepción, 1859. *Source:* Archivo Nacional de Bolivia, Sucre. Album Mercado, f.84. Reprinted with permission.

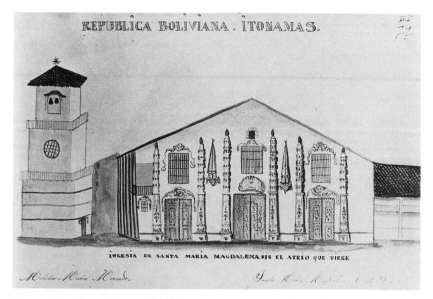

Plate 3. Church at Mission Magdalena, 1859. *Source:* Archivo Nacional de Bolivia, Sucre. Album Mercado, f.77. Reprinted with permission.

62   *The Missions*

productive was significant, for it illustrates the essence of mission culture, a union of religious and economic elements.

The major architectural feature common to Moxos churches was the prominent, overhanging roof. At Concepción and San Ramón, the roof structures covered a large frontal atrium and overhung the sides of the buildings as well. A note on the Magdalena drawing makes clear that the artist took out the frontal atrium, presumably to better illustrate the church's ornate facade. This exaggerated roofline and the timber superstructure used in Moxos are logical architectural features in areas where sunlight and rainfall are intense and where stone is absent.

Mario Buschiazzo observes a similarity between Moxos church architecture and better-known Jesuit buildings in Paraguay and the Chiquitos region west of Santa Cruz. He regards the use of tree-trunk superstructures and roof overhangs as the major feature of a style begun in church building and later extended to secular architecture in tropical regions of Bolivia, Paraguay, and Argentina.[13]

Church decoration was as impressive as scale. The facades shown in plates 1–3 show decorative reliefs resembling candelabras with candles. The meaning of such reliefs has not been explained. They may be an exterior reflection of the prominently carved posts and beams of the churches' interiors, or they may represent the tapers so prominent in church liturgy. The level of detail on these reliefs ranges from the unadorned shapes at San Ramón to the ornate patterns and paintings at Magdalena. While the differences in decoration may reflect nineteenth-century events, it is important to note that the level of detail in these three church facades parallels the relative prosperity of their missions in the Jesuit age, suggesting that intra-mission competition may have led to the most ornate building.

European visitors to the missions reserved their highest praise for church interiors. Manoel Felix wrote that the Magdalena sanctuary featured three richly decorated shrines, ornately carved and gilded beams, and pulpits featuring images of birds and foliage. Nineteenth-century accounts reveal the presence of fresco paintings. One fresco on the wall of the church at Exaltación showed a map of the mission system; another in Trinidad pictured a three-headed Trinity.[14] Jesuit descriptions, understandably, do not dwell on opulence. However, in a letter describing the work of his neophytes, one missionary reveals his pride in the contents of San Javier, which included a sacristy, a set of formal chairs, and a statue of San Francisco Javier (the mission's patron), all carved in Peru. The church doors, pulpit, and a four-vara-long chest used for storing sacred ornaments showed the touch of skilled artisans resident in the missions by the end of the seventeenth century.[15]

These qualitative descriptions were quantified at the end of the Jesuit century, when the Crown ordered an inventory of all mission property. The documents, as monotonous as they are revealing, record mission wealth in striking detail.[16] Precious metals, fashioned into ornaments, totaled some 9,500 pounds of silver and 101 ounces of gold. But weight only begins to describe this treasure. The variety and craftsmanship of church ornaments were nothing short of astonishing.

A frontier station such as San Joaquín held 448 marks, 2 ounces (some 225 pounds) of silver. Much of this mission's plate had been removed to San Pedro during the 1750s to protect it from the threat of seizure by the Portuguese. However, the inventories list a silver monstrance gilded with gold and encrusted with gemstones, three gilded chalices embellished with fine incising and with angels and flower-shaped bases, a large processional cross, three wooden sculptures of Christ decorated with silver, and a Virgin replete with silver crowns, gold jewelry, and precious stones.

The most luxuriant display of wealth was guarded at San Pedro, capital of the system at the time of the expulsion. Here the list of silver effects included thirty-eight entries of 260 separate items totaling 1,791 pounds. Along with a full complement of sacred items, images, and serving pieces appear: a large silver box in the shape of a pelican; ten chalices, several gilded with gold; eighty-nine silver candelabras; an ivory crucifix decorated with a golden crown and wooden cross covered with silver; nine silver crosses; eight silver staffs; two silver washstands with silver legs; and two large silver lamps, one hanging above the altar, the other above a shrine to the Virgin.

The inventories record additional European goods in the priests' quarters, adorning churches, or resting in storerooms. Altogether, the missions held 5,398 books. Much of this collection consisted of sacred titles — sermons, theology, and religious history. However, the mission libraries also featured a variety of works of secular history, including those of many major Spanish chroniclers of the Indies, literary classics, and an assortment of books on applied disciplines such as law, agriculture, and medicine.[17] Musical instruments were also widely distributed in the missions. The ensembles ranged from four woodwind instruments and a single harp at San Nicolás to the near orchestral complement of flutes, clarinets, violins, violas, oboes, bassoons, organs, and monochords at San Pedro. Rich cloth — brocades, taffeta, velvet, linen, damask, and gold braid — headed a list of additional mission possessions, which also included paintings, rochets, mirrors, and elaborately carved statues, retables, and chests.

These physical objects made a statement. To Europeans they represented the importance and centrality of the church in society. To native people the message was different. The monumental architecture of the mission churches and the ostentatious display of precious metals and rich cloth underlined the superiority of the European religious system. In what Valerie Fraser has called the architecture of conquest, these symbols of power signified Christianity triumphing over native religion.[18]

MISSION SUPPORT

To support the mission complex, the Society of Jesus developed a variety of resources. The missions themselves became both farms and factories, but despite impressive efforts, they never covered expenses with their own labor. The metal implements that revolutionized material life on the savanna and the sumptuous goods dedicated to religious purposes required large outlays of cash. The purchase of these items was financed largely from an investment strategy developed and maintained in the viceregal capital. Only by mixing Crown contributions with investments made in the secular economy did the Jesuits make the Moxos missions flourish.

The Moxos enterprise proved expensive from its inception. Immediately following his elevation to superior in 1698, Pedro Marbán addressed the most pressing problem confronting him. In a letter to Madrid, he petitioned the Crown for a grant on behalf of the missionary effort, stating that 100,000 pesos had been expended from Jesuit coffers to date. This sum had provided Moxos with "missionaries, tools, livestock, and other things."[19] Of the four items cited by Marbán, the first two, missionaries and tools, had taken the lion's share of the total outlay.

Missionaries' expenses consisted principally of their transportation and maintenance en route to Moxos and a salary for their services to the kingdom. The tools Marbán mentioned in his letter comprised an essential part of the missions' budgets. Iron tools had become the principal incentive for attracting the native people to the savanna stations. Their importance had not been lost on Marbán, a veteran of thirty years' service in the area at the time he assumed the superiorship. Nor did time diminish demand, for

Table 4: Disbursements from Moxos Accounts, June 1747–May 1751

Amount of Expense (pesos of 8 reales)	Nature of Expense
12,590 pesos, 3 reales	goods sent to missions (iron tools, tobacco, knives, beads, paper)
1,303 pesos, 6½ reales	vestments for missionaries and Indian assistants
2,603 pesos, 2 reales	per diem for two specialists and two priests sent to Europe
15,476 pesos, 2 reales	"transfer for costs of missions" (5,176 pesos, 2 reales to Panama, balance to Spain)
TOTAL 30,773 pesos, 5½ reales	

Source: "Resumen de la procuraduría de las misiones de Moxos, 1747–1751," Lima, 16/IV/1752, ADLP, Limites con Bolivia, no.432.

the accounts of the mid-eighteenth-century consistently feature the shipment of large quantities of tools and truck to the missions. In 1736 port officials in Cádiz cleared a cargo bound for Moxos via Panama, including "266 cases of books reviewed by the Inquisition, prizes for the Indian students, a considerable multitude of images and sacred metals, beads, knives, axes, scabbards, files, needles, fishhooks, and other trifles for the attraction and concentration of the gentiles and neophytes."[20] The shipment was valued at over twenty thousand pesos.

A more detailed account of mission outlays emerges from the data collected by an in-house audit of the Province of Peru conducted between 1747 and 1751. In the years covered by this accounting, the Moxos operation consisted of twenty-one stations and some fifty priests and brothers.

Supplies destined for the needs of Europeans and Indians resident in the missions, those expenses enumerated in the two initial entries of table 4, totaled 13,894 pesos, 1½ reales over the period of the audit, or some 3,473 pesos per annum. The per diem payment refers to the missions' assessment for expenses incurred by the province's representative to the 1748 General Congregation in Rome. Item four, the largest single entry, appears with no more explanation than the quoted words. It is likely that representatives of the Moxos system used the opportunity of traveling to the triennial General Congregation to make large purchases of European manufactured goods on behalf of the missions, as was also the practice among Paraguayan

Table 5: Royal Contributions to Moxos Missionaries, 1698–1716

Date	Amount (pesos of 8 reales)	Source
1698	8,500	500 from Viceroy of Peru 8,000 from Royal Treasury at Potosí
1699	8,000	Royal Treasury at Potosí
1711	8,000	Royal Treasury at Lima
1716	9,200	Royal Treasury at Potosí and Oruro

Sources: Antonio Astrain, *Historia de la Compañía de Jesús en la asistencia de España*, 7 vols. (Madrid: Administración de Razón y Fé, 1902–25), 6:73; Diego Francisco Altamirano, *Historia de la misión de los Mojos* (La Paz: Imprenta "El Comercio," 1891), 71, 90; "Carta de Francisco de Paredes a SM," Lima, 17/XII/1699, AGI, Lima 407; and "Real Cedula 1716," Buen Retiro, 12/X/1716, ADLP, Limites con Bolivia, no.309.

Jesuits.[21] This suggests that some supplies sent to the missions were purchased abroad to avoid Lima merchants' traditionally steep markups.

The Province of Peru covered its expenses for the missions from three major sources: contributions from the Crown, mission exports, and investments made in the Peruvian economy on behalf of Moxos. Under the terms of a papal agreement (Patronato Real), the Spanish monarchs assumed responsibility for spreading Catholicism in the Indies. Records for the eighteenth century show that by this date royal treasuries paid expenses for outfitting, transporting, and feeding missionaries bound from Cádiz to Moxos. The outlays for four shipments of men and their effects made between 1723 and 1747 totaled 16,290 pesos, 7 reales, or 198 pesos, 7 reales per man.[22] In addition to allowances for their passage and maintenance aboard ship, the Crown provided the missionaries with funds from its colonial coffers to support the American leg of their journeys and a periodic stipend known as the *sínodo*. Table 5 presents a summary of such disbursements made to Moxos missionaries.

The contributions of 1698 and 1699 resulted directly from Marbán's appeal of 1698. These sums were earmarked for vestments and sacred ornaments for new missions. The final sum, based on a Royal Cédula published in 1716, provided an annual stipend of two hundred pesos for each priest resident in the missions. This grant corresponded to the Crown support received by other missionary orders and was apparently in effect for the rest of the Jesuit century. However, as was the case for other missions in the Empire, royal contributions were regularly authorized but irregularly paid.[23]

To meet the expenses of the Moxos enterprise, the Society of Jesus supplemented monies it received from the Crown. The missions provided part of their own support, supplying subsistence to the Europeans and Indians and a number of products for export. Accounts written by the Jesuits and by visitors to the stations describe stores of sugar and cane alcohol, lengths of cotton cloth, chests of cacao, tubs of tallow, and sacks of beeswax. The holdings of museums in Bolivia and North America add furniture, musical instruments, and liturgical textiles to the list of mission exports.

This export operation sent mission products to other parts of the Jesuit corporation and into the secular economy as well. In 1767 the mission Santa Ana owed Doña Michalea Gutierrez of Santa Cruz 86 *arrobas* (2,150 pounds) of tallow in payment for a quantity of llama-wool sacks delivered to the mission the year before. In turn, Santa Ana held credits for 500 pesos in cash from the Jesuit college at La Plata, 50 arrobas of tallow from Reyes for an unspecified quantity of beeswax, and 600 pesos in cash from the San Pedro mission.[24] A more comprehensive view of mission exports emerges from the San Pedro accounts, shown as a balance sheet in table 6.

The set of transactions recorded for Santa Ana and San Pedro describe a complex network of mission trade. The stations exported tropical products and manufactures, and received an assortment of goods in return. Moxos apparently utilized the Jesuit system of colleges to place many of its exports. However, mission products also entered Spanish market centers, especially those of Santa Cruz and Cochabamba, without corporate intermediaries.

Mission trade for gain was also a feature of the North American frontier. In California and Texas, missions profited by providing the secular economy with foodstuffs and manufactures. But, in both these cases, the trade centered on nearby towns and presidios, not on the long-distance exchanges carried on by Moxos. Also in contrast to North American models, Moxos' trade involved large sums of specie. The established notion of a cash-poor frontier, and recent studies showing that California and Texas missionary trade was based exclusively on barter and bills of credit (*libranzas*), stand against the entries in table 6 as well as the presence of large sums of cash (over ten thousand pesos) at the time of the Jesuit exile.[25]

By 1747 mission commerce justified the presence of a resident financial specialist or *procurador*, Estevan Troconis. This lay brother served as a systemwide business manager: he supervised the shipment of products and money to and from Moxos, and acted as liaison between the missions and

Table 6: Mission San Pedro Balance Sheet, 1767

Debits	Credits
170 knives to Loreto for carrying Spanish war matériel	800 pesos from the Jesuit college of Cochabamba
600 pesos in coin to Santa Ana	3,000 pesos in coin from college of Cuzco for investment in *obraje* (textile shop) of Pichuichuro
50 pesos in coin to San Borja for cloth	
200 pesos to Loreto for 12-man canoe	Unspecified sum of money from college of Lima
Unspecified sum to Basilio Duran of Santa Cruz for 12 mules	Trunk of colored wool from mission storehouse at Pailas
Unspecified sum to Francisco Aviles of Cochabamba for purchase of mirrors	Load of trade goods from college of La Plata
Unspecified sum to Francisco Cortes of Santa Cruz for hooks and buttons	

Source: "Ynventarios de los bienes de Loreto, Trinidad, San Javier, San Pedro, Santa Ana, Exaltacion, Magdalena, San Ygnacio, y Reyes," 1767, ANB, ADM, Mojos 1, ff.29–31.

the central administration in Lima. Troconis provided the central administration of mission financial affairs so typical of the Jesuit approach, replacing a financial system in which each resident priest made decisions on debts, production, and marketing.

Surviving records are insufficient to chart comprehensively the volume and value of mission exports. But it is clear from descriptive accounts and from the inventories of 1767 that the missions produced more than their subsistence. The export trade, directed through the Jesuit commercial network and the secular market system, was an important factor in Moxos' support.

The final source of Moxos' maintenance was a series of investments made in the secular economy by Jesuit money managers in Lima. The Jesuit administrative structure made special provision for its financial affairs. The spiritual leader of each district, in this case a provincial residing in Lima, was aided by a number of economic specialists, each holding the title of procurador. Although the procuradores were nominally subordinate to the provincial in economic matters, they operated with considerable latitude in making purchases and soliciting credit on behalf of their corporation.

The Society of Jesus, like its counterparts in the secular and religious Church, based its revenues on what Nicholas Cushner has called a "gift economy."[26] In the Society's early years in Peru, the provincial actually sent lay brothers out to the Spanish population of the viceroyalty with begging bowls. However, by the time the Society entered Moxos, Jesuit finances had evolved into a system of assets management, with each college, residence, or mission holding specifically designated sums for its operation.

From their inception, the Moxos missions succeeded in attracting bequests from benefactors in Peru. In 1683 and 1703 the procurador of the Jesuit college at Cochabamba acknowledged the receipt of two gifts totaling 6,700 pesos. The first, in the amount of 2,700 pesos, came from two members of the laity, Don Juan de Barro Nuebo and Doña Ana de la Cruz. The second gift resulted from a bequest in the will of the cathedral chancel of Cochabamba who endowed the missions with the sum of 4,000 pesos. These donations, which entered Jesuit accounts unconditionally, were lent at 5 percent annual interest to Juan Risco for improvements on his estate at Omereque in the Cochabamba valley.[27] Then in 1704 Don Gabriel Encinas deeded his vineyard, Callejas la Baja, to the missions. Again the college at Cochabamba represented Moxos' interests, receiving title to the estate and assigning one of its lay brothers to its management. Jesuit operation of Callejas continued until 1707, when the procurador of the college realized 3,000 pesos for its sale.[28]

The missions' most lavish benefactor, General Juan de Murga, began his patronage in 1698 by establishing a fund designed to furnish Moxos with manufactured goods and to transport them from Sevilla to Cochabamba. This fund provided 500 pesos per year, the interest on 12,500 pesos invested in the general's own haciendas near Lima. At his death in 1725, Murga bequeathed one-half his assets to Father Antonio de Garriga on behalf of the missions in return for the Jesuit's promise for perpetual prayers for his soul. Murga's descendants challenged the bequest with a lawsuit, accusing Garriga of extracting a deathbed testament. But the Jesuits retained their own counsel, and at least partially parried the thrusts of their accusers, for in 1729 Garriga received 41,272 pesos, 6 reales from the general's estate.[29]

Money that entered Moxos' accounts did not stand idle. The Society of Jesus in Peru committed part of the missions' assets into interest-bearing loans, a pattern typical of Church investment throughout the Indies. To finance the missionary enterprise, ecclesiastics played the role of banker, lending money obtained from Crown and local sources to landowners and receiving mortgages (*censos*) against real property as security.[30] Jesuit commitment to censo investment spanned the seventeenth and early eighteenth centuries under arrangements similar to those made with Juan Risco for his Cochabamba estate.

Proceeds from these censos increased gradually during the first decade of the eighteenth century. Provincial accounts show that the missions received interest totaling 870 pesos in 1700, 1,850 pesos each year from 1703 to 1706, and 2,400 pesos in 1710. However, this last year marked the end of Moxos' total reliance on the mortgage market. In subsequent years, a new financial strategy was implemented, which accounts for the dramatic rise in mission income in the years before 1767.

The Jesuits never abandoned the gift economy. General Murga's bequest reached mission coffers in 1729; three years later the Jesuit priest Gabriel de España established a pious work (*obra pía*) with a 12,500-peso bequest to Moxos. However, much of the missions' increased revenues resulted from events independent of its patrons' generosity. Unlike the secular Church or their coreligionists, the Jesuits decided to purchase and manage agricultural estates. In Peru this decision coincided with the recovery of coastal agriculture from the aftermath of the catastrophic earthquake of 1687. While the effects of a general upswing on the agricultural economy of Spanish Peru remain beyond the bounds of this study, the topic of Jesuit investment in land on behalf of Moxos will be examined in some detail below.

As early as 1719, the missions held interests in a series of properties in the temperate region between Cochabamba and Santa Cruz. The most important of these holdings were the haciendas of Chalguani and La Habana shown on map 8. Chalguani, a vineyard run by a Jesuit administrator and cultivated by black slave laborers, produced wine destined for the missions. The production of the estate declined over the course of the eighteenth century, as detailed by a report written by an internal audit. According to the report, Chalguani had accumulated a debt of over 1,000 pesos for the period 1748–51 after turning a marginal profit in the previous triennium.[31] The same source describes La Habana as a supplier of grain to Moxos and to the slaves working in Chalguani. The missions also owned or held interest in several lesser properties in the region, including Palca, San Nicolás de Omereque, San Isidro, Jesús y María, Pampas del Tigre, and

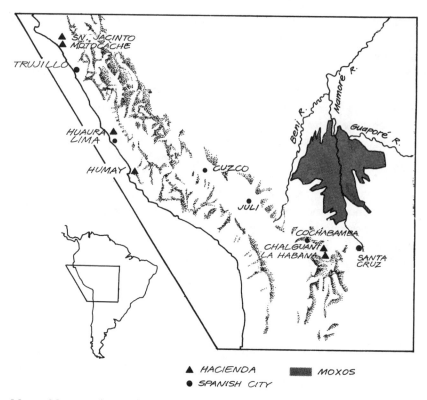

▲ HACIENDA
● SPANISH CITY
▓ MOXOS

Map 8. Moxos and Its Supporting Estates

Cuesta Negra, the last three of which were managed by Jesuit administrator Carlos Hirscko.[32] These haciendas apparently never earned large sums of money for the missions, but they augmented their contributions by providing wine and grains, which could not be produced on the savanna.

Most of the cash that supported Moxos' expenditures came from investments made on the coast of Peru and managed from Lima by the Jesuit Nicolás de Figueroa. At the time he was appointed to oversee mission finances in 1707, Father Figueroa held the position of procurador to the Jesuit Colegio Máximo de San Pablo in Lima. In this capacity he purchased the haciendas of San Jacinto and San Antonio de Motocache, located in the Saña valley north of Trujillo (map 8). The former owners of both properties had suffered greatly from the agricultural stagnation of the late 1600s and had entered the eighteenth century heavily indebted. On May 7, 1709,

Figueroa obtained the title to San Jacinto for 17,500 pesos cash and the assumption of an additional 9,000 pesos in obligations to creditors. Later the same year, the owner of Motocache deeded his property to the Jesuits in exchange for their promise to pay some 16,000 pesos in accumulated debts.[33]

These transactions mark the first signs of a special relationship maintained between Moxos and the Lima college. By a provincial decree, signed the same year as Figueroa made his purchases, revenues earned by San Jacinto and Motocache were to benefit the missions while the actual titles of the estates fell to San Pablo. Under this arrangement San Pablo provided funds to purchase the haciendas and appointed managers for their continued operation. Thus, even though Jesuit constitutions stipulate separate management of each provincial unit, mission records describe a pattern in which San Pablo subsidized Moxos with capital and administrative talent.

The histories of San Jacinto and Motocache in the first decades of the eighteenth century provide glimpses of Jesuit investment strategies and show how they benefited the missions. Inventories conducted at San Jacinto before it was purchased show that it was a large sugar estate with 127 *fanegadas* (some 81 hectares) of irrigated cane fields, two mills, a refining complex, and 101 slaves. San Jacinto's debts apparently had not affected its physical plant, for the first Jesuit manager, Father Diego de Cárdenas, reported that its land, buildings, and slaves were in excellent condition. Cárdenas advised his superiors that he would continue the milling and refining operations as they functioned on his arrival.[34]

The inventory of Motocache describes a less valuable property. Also a sugar estate, Motocache comprised a small plot of land 272 *brazas* by 149 *brazas* (approximately 13 hectares), two mills, a few rickety buildings, and a labor force of twenty-four slaves, only seven of whom were adult males. The new owners apparently considered Motocache a marginal sugar producer, for soon after it was purchased, they ordered its sugar mills dismantled.[35] Then, in 1710, the manager reported that he had begun to plow under all unharvested cane. Concomitant with changes to the land, the procurador of Moxos began work that would lead to the ultimate transformation of the property.

Between 1710 and 1713, Figueroa raised a total of 41,039 pesos in censos from throughout the viceroyalty. This money found its way to Motocache in the form of fourteen male slaves, sixty thousand vinestocks, and materials for the construction of winepresses and vats. By 1713 hacienda records note the first sales of wine, and seven years later Motocache boasted both a large storage facility and its own pottery works for the manufacture of jugs and bottles.[36]

The management of San Jacinto and Motocache illustrate the flexible investment outlook of Jesuit financial administrators. At San Jacinto, sugar production continued unabated under Jesuit ownership. Surviving records suggest that the property required no additional capital outlays for profitable operation. Despite a fuzzy picture of production, sales, and expenses, the same records clearly document that San Jacinto consistently turned a profit for its owners. Between January 1709 and October 1710, Figueroa acknowledged the receipt of 1,358 pesos as Moxos' share of sugar sales.[37]

During the period when Motocache was being transformed from a sugar estate into a winery, it produced no profits as its vines matured and its slaves constructed the necessary infrastructure. But by a financial sleight of hand, Figueroa arranged for the missions to receive income from the property by investing 13,239 pesos of mission capital at 5 percent annual return. Eight years later, Moxos' investment in the hacienda's debt totaled 33,957 pesos for an annual yield of 1,697 pesos, 6 reales.[38] This interest, essentially guaranteed by the college of San Pablo, was paid in twice-yearly installments whether Motocache's bottom line appeared in red or black ink. Thus, under Figueroa's application of the terms of the donation of 1709, the missions stood to gain doubly from this property. As owner, Moxos held first claim to profits from wine production, as creditor, it took an annual return at interest.

In fact, however, the missions never reaped this dual return from Motocache. When in the 1720s wine sales began to redeem the mortgages contracted in the previous decade, Figueroa shuffled Moxos' investment portfolio. Rather than using hacienda profits to gradually diminish the portion of Motocache's debt held by investors outside the Society of Jesus, he contracted five new mortgages for 23,100 pesos in April, May, and June of 1725. At the same time, Figueroa reduced the missions' position in Motocache's debt by redeeming 33,757 pesos, all of which he placed at 5 percent interest on the sugar hacienda of Huarura, owned by San Pablo.[39]

Previous studies of the Spanish colonial economy have pointed to similar investment patterns by the Society of Jesus. In Mexico, Colombia, and Peru historians describe what John Lynch has called a particularly "Jesuit" strategy in the development of commercial agriculture to supply the Potosí mines.[40] According to Lynch, the Jesuits "tended to buy neglected haciendas and develop them, rounding off their boundaries, building sugar mills, investing in Negro slave labor, and making the whole into an efficient unit of production."[41] Figueroa's operation of San Jacinto and Motocache on behalf of the missions offers a variation on the theme Lynch develops. While Motocache was rescued from neglect, San Jacinto operated successfully on its pre-Jesuit foundations. These two cases demonstrate an investment policy governed more by the procurador's appraisal of potential returns than by a propensity toward certain types of property.

In 1739 Figueroa shuffled the mission portfolio a second time. With permission from his provincial, he arranged to purchase a large vineyard called Humay or Umay in the Pisco valley, some 250 kilometers south of Lima (map 8). Moxos was to hold title to this property and to use its own assets to compensate the former owners, the ubiquitous college of San Pablo. Figueroa set the purchase price at 80,000 pesos, 5,403 pesos (15 percent) down and the balance to be paid from "another sum held by the said missions at redeemable censo from the hacienda of Huarura."[42]

Precisely what these investments meant to the missions' operating budgets is unclear. Neither aggregates of Moxos' total income nor the data for a systematic reconstruction of mission revenues can be extracted from surviving documents. Jesuit accounts show censos growing from 2,550 pesos in 1710 to 5,500 pesos in 1754, and that Humay, from the date of its purchase until 1754, made annual contributions averaging 5,475 pesos. But even these brief series stand alone. For a single year, 1748, a cluster of accounts, presented in the following table, reflects the magnitude of income at the missions' disposal by mid-century.

Not enumerated in the table is the annual Crown contribution to the missions, which would add another 9,400 pesos to the total, based on the formula of 200 pesos per priest established in 1716. Thus mission income from all sources totaled 20,928 pesos in 1748. This sum represents a handsome amount for its time and place. Consider that in the same period the Bishopric of Santa Cruz de la Sierra, which supported the bishop, a cathedral chapter, and parish work among inhabitants of the city, had an income of 17,314 pesos.[43] But more significant than the amount itself, table 7 shows that Jesuit investments on behalf of Moxos supplemented the royal stipend, the only support received by some missionary orders, by some 120 percent.

Moxos' resources are also impressive within the context of the Jesuit province. A recent monograph on the Jesuit economic system in Peru concludes that by the end of the seventeenth century the Society of Jesus

Table 7: Mission Income from Investments, 1748

Amount (pesos of 8 reales)	Source
5,450	Profits from Humay
967	Combined profits from San Jacinto and Motocache
770	Profits from Chalguani
4,341	Interest on censos
TOTAL 11,188	

Source: Francisco de Larreta, "Estado temporal de la Provincia del Perú," *Revista de archivos y bibliotecas nacionales* [Lima] 3, no.5 (1900):100; "Libro de la hacienda de San Jacinto," San Jacinto, 18/V/1748, AGNP, Compañia de Jesús, Censos, legajo 9, f.114v; "Visita del P. Leonardo de Baldivia a las haciendas de Challuani y Habana," Lima, 9/1751, AGNP, Compañía de Jesús, Varios, legajo 120; and "Catalogus Rerum Provincia Peruanae Societatis Iesu," 1748, ARSI, Peru 9, f.306v.

had changed its emphasis from rural mission work to educational work in the Spanish urban centers.[44] The Moxos evidence does not overturn this assertion from the perspective of the province as a whole; these missions stood alone alongside Peru's eighteen Jesuit colleges and residences. But the large investments made in maintaining the Moxos enterprise (its expenditures were on a par with all but the largest Peruvian colleges) and the continuous subsidies offered by the Society's directors offer indisputable evidence that these missions were viewed as a very important part of Jesuit activities in Peru.

The Jesuits occupy an important niche in the economic history of the Spanish colony. Their prominence stems from three basic factors. First, the Jesuits enjoyed undeniable economic success, especially in the context of the religious realm in which they operated. Growing directly out of their success came a second factor, envy from both secular and ecclesiastical functionaries. This envy became the basis for a series of polemics, creating what might be called the Jesuit Black Legend, a characterization of the order centering on arrogance, elitism, and materialism. The third reason for Jesuit prominence in colonial historiography is the practical matter of access to documentation. With the expulsion of 1767, Jesuit archives became the property of the Spanish state and its Republican successors. Our knowledge of Jesuit holdings, especially their agricultural property, bears a direct relationship to those records that are part of public archives and those records, especially secular agricultural property, that have tended to remain in private hands. Only the first of these factors stands the test of objective investigation, and even here studies to date have emphasized the sources rather than the uses of Jesuit funds. The Moxos evidence throws some new light on the economic means used by Jesuit managers and on how the proceeds of entrepreneurial activity at the core eventually settled on the missionary enterprise on the frontier.

Recent studies of Jesuit agricultural operations in Peru emphasize the essential status-quo nature of these enterprises. They were neither larger nor better managed nor more profitable than their competition, principally estates of the secular elite.[45] In fact, the Jesuits seemed to lack both the ability and the will to dominate the market at the expense of their rivals.

But if the Jesuits operated as ordinary factors in the agricultural economy, their methods were extraordinary when compared with those of other religious bodies: they managed their own estates rather than hiring secular managers, and they created positions for financial managers within their corporation. A separate study of San Pedro's procuradores would be necessary to establish even the broad contours of Jesuit financial strategies in Peru. Nevertheless, Nicolás de Figueroa's activities provide the basis for asserting that these strategies were both complex and focused. The Moxos missions were in a sense an end for which Figueroa furnished the means. He followed strategies familiar to modern investment managers — buying low and selling high, using capital to enhance the value of real assets, maintaining a diversified portfolio, moving funds from one area to another. But nowhere is there the suggestion that these essentially capitalistic activities were done in the name of gathering wealth for its own sake. The realities of mission support siphoned off capital from the center of Spanish Peru for use on the frontier. Whether this was a wise use of scarce resources may be questioned. With hindsight it could be argued that the purchase of knives and church ornaments for an area so tangential to the interests of Peru was a waste of money. But the raison d'être of the missions — their conversion, social integrative, and defense functions on a central area of the Luso-Spanish frontier — was very much in keeping with the religious and secular policies of both the Society of Jesus and the Spanish Crown.

IV MISSION INDIANS: GENTILES AND NEOPHYTES

The Jesuits' stated purpose for the development of the mission system in Moxos was nothing less than to transform those ignorant of laws and government into communities that reflected European conceptions of orderly society.[1] Such a metamorphosis, in the missionaries' argot, entailed the transformation of Indians from gentiles into neophytes. The inadvertent release of new pathogens and the systematic introduction of European ritual, political, and economic systems produced significant changes in Moxos' tropical forest culture. But adopting the missionaries' terminology does not imply accepting their view of cultural change, for the Indians played an active role in the formation of distinctive mission cultural patterns. In Moxos, mission culture often preserved and enriched native modes rather than transforming them.

DEMOGRAPHY

The most dramatic change of the Jesuit age was biological. Spanish entry into Moxos in the sixteenth century initiated a cycle of population decline, and the concentration of formerly dispersed peoples into large settlements increased their vulnerability to the lethal effects of Old World diseases. Studies of the demographic disaster that followed European contact with nuclear America offer a model for Moxos population history. Sherburne Cook and Woodrow Borah, identifying trends in Mexico and South America, delineate a three-stage process: an initial sharp decline in the number of native peoples, a period of stabilization, and finally a gradual recovery.[2]

Because the following reconstruction of Moxos' native population begins a century after the region's initial contact with Spanish intruders, it is

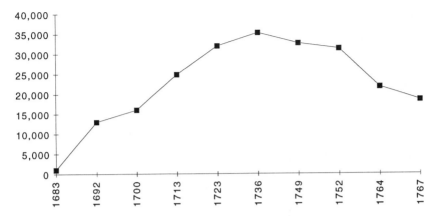

Figure 1. Mission Populations, 1683–1767. *Source:* Appendix.

not truly compatible with the Cook and Borah archetype. Nevertheless, this and other "mission variants" are likely to offer the most reliable data bases for examining the biological effects of European expansion on native populations outside the core areas of Latin America.

The aggregated population statistics, fully documented in the appendix, appear above as a time series.

The slopes of increase and decline in figure 1 follow the events narrated in chapter 2. As the mission system expanded, the Jesuits attracted gentile Indians to existing stations and established new settlements where the native populations appeared dense enough to justify the effort. Work among the Arawak of the upper and middle Mamoré swelled the missions in the late seventeenth and early eighteenth centuries. Then contact with the Kayubaba in the 1700s and with the Baure and Itonama in the 1710s brought the last of the major savanna peoples under mission aegis. The year 1720 conveniently marks the end of the growth era.

The next quarter-century comprised a period of demographic stability in which the mission populations oscillated around a figure of thirty-three thousand inhabitants. Stability ended in the mid-1740s, and the succeeding decline showed three distinct phases. A slow decrease occurred between 1745 and 1749. This trend then was accentuated by the effects of a combination of natural and biological disasters occurring in 1750 and 1751 as well as the events of the Luso-Spanish struggle over the limits of empire in the South American interior. Finally, the last three years of the Jesuit century show an attenuated decrease in mission populations. An examination of extant demographic statistics for the Jesuit century will bring these trends into sharper focus.

The initial increases in mission populations resulted from the Jesuits expanding their system into new areas, not from growth within the neophyte cohort. A crude measure of the new entrants appears in Jesuit census counts, which separate the baptized, and therefore presumably more established mission residents, from the nonbaptized, that is, the recently arrived. Of the twenty-one detailed counts compiled between 1683 and 1767, nine contain a distinction between baptized and nonbaptized people.

Seventeenth-century censuses show high percentages of the population as yet unbaptized: 37 percent in 1691 and 40 percent in 1692. However, by the 1710s, the size of this segment had declined both absolutely and proportionally, to 20 percent in 1713 and 11 percent in 1736. The diminution continued through the remaining Jesuit years, reaching the single digits in 1749 and less than 1 percent of the population in 1764. Population decreased in the years following 1745, a trend represented in the mission censuses by a parallel decline in new entrants. That the period of stable populations, 1720–45, was also characterized by declining numbers of nonbaptized Indians may be attributed to two factors. First, the reduction of the last major Indian groups during the 1710s freed the missionaries to give greater attention to conversion activities, thus reducing the time Indians would have spent in an unbaptized state. Second, this quarter-century was remarkably free of the epidemic outbreaks that diminished mission populations in both the earlier and later years of the Jesuit century, thus extending the lives of Indians baptized during this period.

Cook's study of the California missions shows a similar pattern based on more solid evidence than that extant for Moxos. The California documents show high immigration for the early mission period and correspondingly high death rates. Cook concludes that the missions' survival was utterly dependent on wholesale gentile attraction to offset the effects of declining populations among resident neophytes.[3]

Moxos censuses also describe a declining resident population. With fewer new converts, the neophytes' numbers more closely reflected internal dynamics, that is, their ability to reproduce themselves from a population pool unaffected by migration. Table 8, which provides information on eighteenth-century mission family units, introduces other factors significant in mission Indian population decline after 1745.

One of the major conclusions to be drawn from the table is that sex ratios

Table 8: Mission Family Sizes, 1720–64

Year	Couples	Male children	Female children	Child/Couple
1720	7,293	5,127	4,703	1.8
1736	7,526	6,321	6,357	1.5
1749	7,611	6,357	5,600	1.8
1752	7,688	6,525	5,757	1.5
1764	5,479	4,429	4,017	1.6

Source: Appendix.

for the entire period are seriously skewed toward male offspring. Female children range from a high of 47.8 percent in 1736 to a low of 45.0 percent in 1720, and averaging 46.8 percent for the five censuses. Whether the imbalance resulted from a continuance of native traditions of infanticide or from recording inconsistencies, such as a greater missionary concern with male children, is unclear. However, despite the inconsistency of such statistics with modern demographic models, the predominance of male children is characteristic of the colonial years. And such a long-term imbalance in sex ratios eventually would produce a scarcity of females and seriously impair the ability of mission populations to reproduce themselves.

In fact, the table documents low rates of reproduction. In the five censuses summarized here, the number of children per couple never reached 2.0, the minimum ratio necessary for population maintenance. The large numbers of offspring characteristic of modern agricultural and fishing peoples suggest that the missionary period marked a departure from the aboriginal status quo in Moxos.[4] However, premission tradition likely played a role in limiting the number of offspring as well, since infanticide, especially in the case of twins and female children, was practiced by many of the savanna peoples. One contemporary witness, Francisco Xavier Eder, specifically commented on the low reproductive rates of mission Indian women, citing long nursing periods and self-induced abortions as contributing factors.[5] This combination of aboriginal and neophyte practices was reflected in Jesuit censuses, which consistently enumerated children as comprising less than one-third of the mission populations. Even if we include the total number of neophytes enumerated as single, on the assumption that they represented a very young segment of the population, this raises the number of mission children to levels needed to replace their parents only for the 1736 count. A shortage of females and long-term low rates of neophyte reproduction made the missions ripe for population decline after 1720.

Comparative data from other mission enterprises support the Moxos evidence. Jane Rausch's studies of the Llanos region of colonial Nueva Granada show a low birthrate characteristic of the Jesuit missions there. She attributes this trend to the Indian women's reluctance to bring children into a system that they had been forced to enter.[6] In her work on the Franciscan missions of San Antonio, Mardith Schuetz concludes that Indians showed a lower birthrate in the missions than they had in the wild due to widespread abortion and infanticide.[7] Cook's study of the California missions also describes low birthrates, but attributes them to a diminishing number of females in the populations.[8]

Not all missionary data confirm below-replacement levels of Indian offspring, however. Despite her contention of a lowered birthrate, Schuetz shows that eighteenth-century San Antonio parish records document nearly 2.5 children per couple in the missions.[9] And, although he supplies no statistics to support his claim, David Owens attributes the Paraguayan missions' recovery from seventeenth-century Paulista slaving depredations to vegetative growth within the transported reductions. He suggests that better nutritional habits and a more stable economic and social situation were the major factors contributing to increased fertility rates among the Guarani neophytes.[10]

It is difficult to draw conclusions from the current inventory of mission Indian population histories. If we are all correct in our conclusions, no single trend exists. Yet with the exception of Paraguay, and Paraguay may always be an exceptional case, Indian numbers declined under missionary rule. This was clearly the case for Moxos. Even though a truly satisfactory population history would require the discovery of more precise information, the decline must be attributed in the long term to sex imbalances and sporadic epidemic disease outbreaks.

The decline began slowly. From 1745 to 1750, the censuses show a population loss of some 6.5 percent, and the 1752 count marks another 4 percent drop. These diminutions were directly attributable to the Portuguese occupation of the right bank of the Guaporé in the mid-1740s. Before this time, the Jesuits made regular trips across the river to seek new converts and even established the semipermanent Santa Rosa station north of the Guaporé. Portuguese arrival and Lusitanian insistence on making the river a dividing line between the Iberian empires deprived the Jesuits of their last fertile field for replenishing mission populations. With immigration largely suspended, long-term trends began to take a toll on Indian numbers.

In the last decade of the Jesuit century, mission populations decreased to levels characteristic of the first years of the eighteenth century, some 30 percent below their apex. In addition to the long-term factors already described, disastrous flooding in 1750–51 had a substantial impact. During this rainy season, many of the missions' crops and large numbers of their animals were lost. In the waters' wake came a series of epidemics that left no station unscathed. Then, in 1762, just as the missions began to recover from the effects of these events, a Spanish expeditionary force sent to counter Portuguese expansion into the Guaporé basin occupied the missions. This army, the largest European contingent seen in Moxos to that time, brought with it a demand for support from mission stores and from neophyte labor. The Spanish commanders were empowered to purchase on credit the supplies needed by their men, and, as missionary accounts taken at the time of the expulsion show, these demands were extensive and never paid in full. Mission stores, which had been rebuilt after the floods of 1750–51, were depleted in provisioning the soldiers. In addition, the presence of the Spanish army again triggered a series of epidemics, which struck hardest in the northern missions but affected the whole system.

The broad picture of Moxos mission demography shows that the rise and fall of the neophyte population was governed by external events — disease, absorption of new Indian immigrants, occupying armies. Although effective in laying out the major contours of the missions' population history, this systemwide portrayal masks a number of regional variants. Local trends are important for illuminating both the events of the mission regime and the post-1767 Jesuit legacy. Figure 2 compares the population changes of the eighteenth-century system using the geographic and cultural divisions devised by Jesuit directors of the missions: Mamoré, Pampas, and Baures.

The Mamoré region consisted principally of the Moxo Arawak, the Canisiana of San Pedro, and the Mobima of Exaltación. This was the original mission core and remained the center of Jesuit activity throughout the regime. The Mamoré trend line in figure 2 shows a relatively stable population for the eighteenth century: the total never varies more than 30 percent from a mean of 11,635 inhabitants. This numerical consistency is directly attributable to internal migration to the Mamoré stations as a result

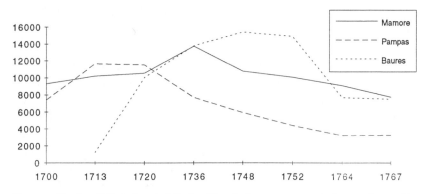

Figure 2. Regional Variations in Mission Populations, 1700–1767. *Source:* Appendix.

of their central administrative functions. Over the course of the Jesuit century, Loreto, Trinidad, and San Pedro all served as mission capitals, housing the superior and guarding food and materials reserved for the use of the system as a whole. The concentration of resources in these centers made them the logical points for supporting neophytes displaced from other areas. Refugees from the Portuguese conflict and from the periodic dissolution of missions — such as San Miguel, Santa Rosa, and San Luís — found their way to the Mamoré stations during the eighteenth century.

The Pampas stations suffered the most serious population losses during the Jesuit century. By 1767, the three remaining sites held populations of less than one-third their 1713 maximums. These missions were inhabited by many of the smaller ethnic groups of Moxos and occupied less promising settlement sites. Four of the Pampas stations — San Pablo, San José, San Luís, and Santa Rosa (1) — were abandoned between 1736 and 1758.

The Baures missions show the most rapid growth trajectory, increasing their numbers by over 50 percent between the time they were founded in the 1710s and 1736. Most of this growth came from the Baure peoples of the northern savanna and adjoining forest zones. But the Itonama Indians, settled at Magdalena, showed a remarkable demographic history under the Jesuits, increasing their numbers nearly four times between 1720 and 1767. This growth continued unabated even during the difficult years following 1750. One missionary attributed this phenomenon to the fertility of the Itonama women, an observation worthy of investigation by modern biologists.[11]

Previous paragraphs have called attention to the low levels of neophyte reproduction in the eighteenth century. However, during those periods when regional populations peaked — 1713 for the Pampas stations, 1736 for the Mamoré, and 1748 for the Baures — offspring exceeded replacement levels, led by the Pampas stations' 2.9 children per couple. And offspring in Magdalena exceeded two per union for the entire eighteenth century, reaching a high of 2.4 children in 1748. These statistics demonstrate that given favorable conditions, principally the absence of epidemic disease, mission populations were capable of sustaining and even increasing their numbers, suggesting a biological rather than a cultural explanation for Moxos missionary fertility patterns.

While extant data do not permit a thorough reconstruction of Moxos biological history, they do provide the basis for a number of observations. First, the mission period was punctuated by a series of disease outbreaks. Contemporary accounts mention a variety of diseases that afflicted the neophytes, including influenza, smallpox, dysentery, pleurisy, malaria, and undifferentiated fevers.[12] At least five major epidemics and four minor ones swept the missions during the Jesuit century, including the pandemics of 1700, 1727, and 1750 in which thousands died when disease swept the entire system.

While the qualitative evidence for frequent deaths is overwhelming, there is to date no documentary basis for establishing an overall mission mortality rate. Using sources that describe the first decade of Trinidad's history, Leandro Tormo Sanz has estimated a rate of 34.9 deaths per thousand for that station.[13] To see the wide range of estimates, compare this figure with the 70–85 deaths per thousand Sherburne Cook derived from California mission registers.[14] What Cook is able to document convincingly for California, and what I would like to suggest for Moxos, is that the mission period was critically important in the biological history of Indians outside the colonial core. Cook concludes that by 1830 the California mission population had reached stability. While Moxos' population curve continued its downward trend at the end of the Jesuit century, there were signs that Indian numbers were approaching an equilibrium. With the departure of most of the Spanish expeditionary force in 1763, the rate of population decline slowed. More important to long-term trends was the increase in the percentage of children in the Mamoré region between 1752 and 1764. Although the full evidence of biological accommodation cannot be demonstrated until the post-Jesuit period, the most important legacy of mission culture was a disease-resistant native population in Moxos.

As we saw in chapter 1, premission society was village based and only primitively segmented. Consolidation of the small village locus in the Jesuit century, while preserving traditional leadership, brought changes that supported the more complex societies characteristic of mission culture.

The contemporary Jesuit version of Moxos mission history emphasizes the important of a political restructuring of native society under their regime. The model cabildo introduced by Diego Francisco Altamirano's 1700 visita produced a set of offices for establishing and enforcing European patterns of religion and social change. Cabildo offices — two *alcaldes,* four *regidores,* and a *portero,* each elected annually — served as the missions' police forces and, with the guidance of the priest, as their judiciary.[15] The seventeenth-century Paraguayan mission cabildos, perhaps the models for their Moxos counterparts, were more complex, including a *corregidor,* two *alcaldes ordinarios,* two *alcaldes de la Hermandad,* an *alferez real,* four regidores, an *alguacil mayor,* and a *mayordomo.*[16] Modern works on the Jesuit missions invariably mention the cabildo officers but insist that these positions were largely ceremonial. The Moxos experience offers strong evidence for another view of mission politics, one stressing real native influence in the system.

In most cases caciques merged with the cabildo: past leaders continued to hold political power, uninterrupted by the onset of mission rule. Manoel Felix noted that, in Magdalena, those who held the principal mission offices were all former caciques, and a report written in 1764 notes the presence of traditional leaders in the Baures missions, still called aramas sixty years after their entry into the system.[17] The fate of the shamans under mission rule is less clear, but surviving evidence suggests that they entered the stations and perhaps even joined the new spiritual elite, as in one case where a former hechicero was described as always "the first to mass and conversion."[18] Such persistence of aboriginal leadership illustrates a process of accommodation typical of mission culture. Accommodation also penetrated the ranks of those who had been ordinary villagers outside the missions.

In tropical forest culture, the vast majority of the population performed their work differentiated only by age and sex. The missions brought with them a sophisticated division of labor and created roles that had been unimaginable in aboriginal society. Jesuit censuses taken in the mid-eighteenth century show that part of this social complexity was based on the breakdown of the adult population into marital statuses. As had been true in premission native society, most adults were married, 76 percent of those enumerated in the censuses. However, these data also show that a significant percentage of the mission populations were single (17 percent) and widowed (7 percent), categories stigmatized by custom and necessity in the native world. These segments of the population, no doubt created by missionary-enforced strictures against infant betrothal and polygamy, performed special functions in the Jesuit system. For instance, Guarani widows became handicraft specialists and cared for orphans.[19]

Jesuit correspondence from the Moxos missions also cited the growth of a group of functional specialists in the population. As early as 1697, San Javier counted fifty "masters of carpentry and other offices" among its inhabitants, and mature missions saw their craftsmen organized into a guild, governed by its own officers.[20] The extent to which this division of labor affected mission social structure emerges with the examination of the single surviving manuscript census of the era, a document prepared at Reyes six years after Jesuit exile.[21]

The 648 individuals enumerated in this census show occupational and kinship groupings that both segregated the neophytes into a series of hierarchies and bridged the traditional linguistic boundaries of the native peoples. The document divides the mission Indians into two functional categories, each with its own leadership. The first, called *Familia,* subsumed the native political leadership and those neophytes trained in European arts and offices. These specialists — fourteen singers and religious assistants, an equal number of blacksmiths, seventeen carpenters, ten weavers, seven tallow makers, and two caciques — were likened by one contemporary observer to a nobility that partook of the food surplus produced by other members of the mission in exchange for performing their vocations.[22] Further evidence of the Familia's elite status comes from records of office holding in the mission. Although they comprised only 28 percent of the population of Reyes, members of the Familia held 75 percent of the missionwide offices.

The common folk, denoted *Pueblo* in the census, were divided into three groups (*parcialidades*) — Macarani, Majieno, and Romano — corresponding to the major linguistic elements resident in the mission. Leadership of each of these subdivisions fell to a captain aided by one or two lieutenants. In Reyes, the Pueblo furnished labor to the mission agricultural and herding enterprises, occupations requiring a division of residence between the central settlement and outlying farms and ranches.

In addition to the hierarchical divisions in Reyes, the census illuminates, through its enumeration of individuals and their family connections, the presence of well-developed kinship networks operating within the mission. Of the 270 surnames mentioned in the document, 114 (42 percent) appear in more than one family unit. In the Pueblo, surname repetition occurs most often (78 percent) within the same parcialidad or linguistic group. In cases where surname repetition crossed linguistic barriers, 82 percent occurred on the distaff side. Since the parcialidades represented the major native groups in the mission, these patterns of surname sharing indicate both the continued maintenance of strong ethnic identification within the mission and the continuation of the premission practice of exchanges of females across lineages.

In the Familia, shared surnames appear almost twice as frequently as among the Pueblo. Surnames held by Familia members recur in all three parcialidades, tracing patterns of kinship and communication between the governors and the governed. These links showed themselves as large, extended families. Consider these two examples. The lieutenant of parcialidad Macarani, Ygnacio Chupi, was married to Martina Chanita. The same parcialidad held Ygnacio's sister Martina Luisa, her husband Agustín Subi, and his brother Juan. Martina Chanita's relative, Pascuala, also appears in the census, living in parcialidad Romano with her husband Mateo Yuire, the mission alcalde. In this case, the census shows a set of links between the Chanita and Subi families, members of different ethnic groups.

The marriage of Manuel Yuire, *fiscal* of parcialidad Romano, to Manuela Mabeia provides evidence of an even more extensive kinship network. The Yuire family included Pablo, the second fiscal of Romano, and Luís, cacique of the mission. A third relative, Lorenzo Yuire, was married to Manuela Chito, whose kin included three married brothers from parcialidad Romano. The census also records that Manuela Mabeia's married sisters, María and Rosa, were both members of the Familia. This familial constellation, charted below, held ten families and twenty-eight individuals (twenty adults and eight children), over 4 percent of the total population of Reyes. That the cacique of the mission belonged to this group seems more than coincidental.

The social arrangements shown in the Reyes census — particularly the extended families and lineage linking through marriage — document overlapping influences of aboriginal and European kinship systems, each reinforcing the other. And while these data may be unique in their detail, the structures they describe were clearly present in other missions.[23] The Reyes

Manuel Yuire (Romano, fiscal) — Manuela Mabeia

Pablo Yuire (Romano, fiscal) — Gaspara Curiyania   Maria Mabeia — Mariano
                                                  Cuanea (Familia, cantor)

Martín Yuire (Romano) — Tomasa Yuari   Rosa Mabeia — Francisco
                                                  Biquina (Familia, cantor)

Luís Yuire (Familia, cantor, cacique) — Estefa Puama

Lorento Yuire (Familia, cantor) — Manuela Chito
                                  Manuel Chito (Romano) — Rosa Sirene
                                  Miguel Chito (Romano) — Petrona Chiano
                                  Ylario Chito (Romano) — Bacilia Mueia

Figure 3. Family Ties in Reyes, 1773.

example also shows the degree to which the mission community no longer followed its aboriginal ways. A quarter of the population now functioned as economic specialists and were no longer engaged in subsistence activities. The fact that these same specialists occupied the mission offices, to a degree disproportionate to their numbers, demonstrates that they combined political leadership with economic specialization. This elite was supported by a large group of farmers and herders who preserved their aboriginal ethnic identification.

Yet as power and privilege divided mission society, intrafamily networks crosscut the Familia and Pueblo and gave them cohesion. These networks bridged the traditional cultural barriers within the missions and provided people outside the elite sector with access to those who held power. The development of such systems strikes a familiar chord with one accustomed to viewing Iberian patterns of family alliance, an observation further strengthening the image of mission culture as a vehicle for accommodation between the native and Spanish worlds.

DAILY LIFE OF THE MISSION INDIANS

The Indians saw European-oriented changes in their daily lives as they did in their social relations during the Jesuit period. Mission culture established a set of practices and regimens that governed both the trivial and the extraordinary. From dress to politics, from subsistence to worship, mission life brought new modes to the savanna. However, in daily life as in all else,

Mission Indians: Gentiles and Neophytes   89

European introductions combined with native tradition to produce a distinctive amalgam.

Mission clothing bore the stamp of European style and morality. In pre-Jesuit times the Indians wore little clothing. In fact, nudity was so much a part of Moxo culture that the first missionaries were called "the dressed ones" in the local language.[24] Written accounts and the drawings shown in plates 4 and 5 illustrate typical mission-age clothing. The neophytes adapted the short skirt or *tipoy,* which females had worn in premission days, into a basic chemise for both sexes. The drawings depict garments worn at the end of the Jesuit century; they suggest that the female style may have been more decorative than the male version.

The same accounts describe a native fondness for personal ornamentation. At the time of their initial missionary contact, the Arawak speakers of the Mamoré maintained their coiffures fastidiously, a practice continued in the missions. Father Eder described a ritual of shampooing, combing, and braiding with ribbons and feathers as typical of the northern missions in the 1750s.[25] Additional ornamentation came from body paints applied to exposed arms and legs, necklaces, earrings, bracelets, and anklets of animal, vegetable, and glass components, and from a variety of rattles attached to various body parts. All of these customs continued under the Jesuits' eyes despite their heathen connotations.[26]

The missions changed the tempo of Indian life, too. Contemporary accounts of mission activities as well as modern reconstructions of the mission experience emphasize the central role of Catholic ritual in orienting the neophytes' existence. "There were definite times for rising, going to bed, attending church, laboring in the fields, and working in the town. In going to work in the fields, groups of converts marched from the village square carrying a statuette and accompanied by musicians who made the morning air tingle with their music."[27] This description, penned in the 1930s, now seems more rhetorical than factual. Nevertheless, religious observance did serve as the mission clock and calendar. Catholic ritual ordered the neophytes' daily activities. In the stations the workday began and ended with a tolling of church bells and brief worship services directed by the priest and his Indian spiritual assistants and musicians. But the introduction of the concept of "daily" routine should not be confused with the institution of a factory system. The Indians retained a rather casual approach to their work, observing a regimen that Tormo Sanz has calculated at five hours per day.[28]

Plate 4. Typical Male Mission Indian Attire, ca. 1750. *Source:* Eder, *Breve descripción de las reducciones de Mojos,* Illustraciones. Reprinted with permission.

Plate 5. Typical Female Mission Indian Attire, ca. 1750. *Source:* Eder, *Breve descripción de las reducciones de Mojos,* Illustraciones. Reprinted with permission.

The Catholic calendar superimposed a second cycle onto mission life, which allowed for breaks in the work routines. The preface to Father Marbán's grammar notes that eleven holidays were observed in the seventeenth-century missions. Days such as Easter, All Saints' Day, Epiphany, Corpus Christi, and Christmas occasioned systemwide pageants, parades, and contests. The missionaries' accounts of religious ceremonies are too copious and repetitive to merit extensive citation. Two examples of mission Holy Week observances will give the reader a feel for their flavor. An anonymous account written in 1713 describes a period of total absorption and great spiritual outpouring. As Holy Week drew near, Indian cowboys drove herds of cattle into the mission corrals to furnish food for the celebrants. Palm Sunday signaled the beginning of a cavalcade of confessions, masses, and processions. The writer was particularly impressed by the neophytes' spiritual fervor. He describes observants marching through the streets striking their breasts with their fists and flagellating their backs with whips. At times the collective passion for penance became so intense that children joined their parents in these acts.[29]

A second account of Holy Week in the missions, written in exile by Father Eder, describes the celebrations as they occurred in San Martín at the end of the Jesuit century. Eder relates that on Holy Saturday, the neophytes erected two effigies in the center of the mission plaza: the first was made of rags and represented Judas Iscariot; the second, in the form of a black boy hung upside down, the devil incarnate. After filing into the plaza, the men solemnly drew their bows and filled both effigies with arrows, after which they dragged the figures through the streets and burned them. Eder remembered these ceremonies with amusement, concluding his vignette with the observation that one year, because of a dyer's error, the Judas effigy emerged with dark rather than light skin. Perhaps conscious of the irony in his words, the priest-chronicler reports that this year the pageant stopped until the dyer retouched the dummy to make its skin more the color of a *caraiono,* a Spaniard.[30] The celebrants knew their Scripture—and their adversaries.

The fiesta cycle served a social as well as a religious function. Mission celebrations, like their counterparts in the secular world, intertwined sport and feasting with Christian ritual. Horse racing and traditional games, such as that played by sides kicking a heavy rubber ball, entertained neophytes celebrating Epiphany. Eating and drinking enhanced the merriment. At one three-day fiesta held at San Javier, the neophytes consumed 500 fish,

2,000 manioc and corn loaves, and a "considerable quantity of chicha [maize beer]."[31] In addition to the communal feasts, holy days marked the occasions when common resources were distributed. The 1713 account of Holy Week cited above notes that the celebration of St. Joseph's Day was especially generous in Moxos, but that all celebrations signaled a time when gifts of food and clothing were given to the old, widowed, and orphaned. Other witnesses reported that presents of trade goods, food, and cloth were given at regular intervals and on special occasions, such as nuptials, not a part of the established spiritual calendar.[32]

Familia

The neophytes' daily activities reflected the elite-commoner distinction of Familia and Pueblo. Members of the Familia held positions described in European terms. Political specialists, shown in the Reyes census as a cacique and eleven officers of the cabildo, provided leadership and enforced the laws of the mission regime. These functionaries, apparently all men, assigned tasks and set work quotas for their people. They arranged for crops to be planted and harvested, for the management of mission herds, for the production of cloth and handicrafts in mission workrooms, and for the maintenance of mission streets and buildings. While some of these tasks were accommodated easily to traditional savanna rhythms, others did not and required inducements to establish and maintain them. The caciques and alcaldes (cabildo officers) reinforced their positions by the use of European symbols, trading on tangible signs of their offices — titles, clothing, and the Spanish language.[33] However, the political leaders were reinforced in their positions principally by their access to mission herds and stores. They joined the priests, often by literally passing goods from hand to hand, in distributing regular food and periodic gifts of clothes and European trade articles to their people.

The political specialists' law enforcement responsibilities subsumed police and judicial powers. The cabildo officers were charged with apprehending those who fled the missions, failed to follow prescribed activities such as church attendance, or reverted to "gentile customs" such as adultery or drunkenness. One source claims that the cabildo attempted to enforce discipline through an intelligence network that encouraged neophytes to denounce offenders.[34] If this strategy was ever hatched, however, it never spread widely. The Reyes census shows that cabildo officers held full-time jobs in the mission economies; their work as musicians, carvers, or cowboys would have given them little time to exercise intelligence functions. Punishment was carried out by the political officers. It ranged from reductions of rations or public penance for minor offenses to haircutting for those guilty of more serious crimes, such as repeated failure to perform assigned tasks. Those deemed incorrigible or guilty of particularly serious crimes (arson was adjudged harshly in the thatched-roofed missions) could be banished from their homes or, in the gravest cases, turned over to civil authorities in Santa Cruz.

If the political specialists were the most prominent members of the Familia, the artisans were the most numerous. Carpenters, carvers, weavers, cooks, and smiths predominate in mission records, but painters, copyists, and even a watchmaker appear as well. Native weaving skills were transferred wholesale into the mission enterprise. Early vocabularies provide evidence for the importance of weaving among the savanna people. Marbán's *Arte y vocabulario de la lengua Moxa,* for example, contains over fifty words describing the tools and techniques of cloth making, including separate expressions for fine thread, thick thread, hammock thread, broken thread, spun thread, and wrapped thread. Father Eder was impressed, no mean trick as we have seen, with Indian weavers who worked skillfully in cotton and feather fibers.[35] Featherwork, drawing directly from native tradition, became a luxury export and received particular attention for its soft texture and imaginative design. Cotton cloth was sewn into chemises for the neophytes' use or was sent to Spanish markets in Santa Cruz and Cochabamba.

Starting at the end of the seventeenth century, mission construction encouraged the development of skilled woodworkers. Carpenters shaped the wooden superstructures characteristic of mission architecture. Each mission trained a staff of carpenters to build and maintain local structures. However, undertaking a large project, such as the erection of the new church at San Pedro in 1740, required the services of carpenters from the entire system. Perhaps the most eloquent testimonial to these men's skills is the durability of their work. Many of the Jesuit churches survived well into the nineteenth century, and at least three stood on their mission foundations as late as the 1940s.

Although the carpenters' works are no longer available for viewing, the carvers' works appear in museums and private collections throughout the world. Jesuit sources stress the neophytes' skills in crafting church decoration and Christian iconography. One Jesuit wrote that his carvers copied an

Italian sculpture of Christ's scourging so skillfully that viewers could not tell which statue was the original.[36] Mission artisans produced tables, chairs, and ornamental supports for the mission churches, all crafted in Amazonian hardwoods. These same men also built furniture, especially chests and carved cabinets or *bargueños,* which entered the secular markets of Peru. One surviving example of the carvers' skills, now part of a private collection in Sucre, is a huge upright chest (1.85 meters × 1.1 meters × .78 meters) built of mahogany and inlaid with Amazonian rosewood and shell. It is inscribed anthropomorphically:

J— + —M

FLH Fray Fernando

Arroyo, hizo y me asió

en el año 1715

La Concepción

J— + —M

FLH Friar Fernando

Arroyo, made and held me

in the year 1715

La Concepción

Recent works by the Bolivian scholar Rogers Becerra Casanovas include illustrations of the remarkable output of mission craft specialists.[37]

Indian smiths produced a variety of utilitarian articles, including agricultural implements, bronze sugarcane grinders, and construction hardware. A reading of the inventories of mission property produced at the time of the expulsion in 1767 adds balconies, carpenters' tools, locks, bells, and caldrons to the list of the smiths' works. By the end of the Jesuit century, Indian ironworkers had become so skilled at their craft that the first Spanish expeditionary force carried mission-made cannons into battle against the Portuguese.

The last major segment of the Familia consisted of those who aided the priests in their celebrations of worship. Sacristans, literate in Spanish and perhaps in Latin, helped to perform the liturgy. Musicians, both singers and instrumentalists, achieved remarkable proficiency. Native orchestras included both European instruments — violins, harps, organs, woodwinds, and brasses — and the native flute pictured in plate 6. This aboriginal instru-

Plate 6. Mission Indian Flutist, ca. 1750. *Source:* Archivo General de Indias, Seville, Estampas 201. Reprinted with permission.

Mission Indians: Gentiles and Neophytes   97

ment, fashioned from palm leaves to lengths as great as two meters, produced rich, deep tones to balance the higher-pitched violins and woodwinds. A study examining surviving musical scores discovered at Mission San Ignacio testifies to the proficiency of mission musicians. Indians made copies of scores by famous composers of the colonial period, such as the Chuquisaca native Juan de Araujo (1646–1714) and the Italian Jesuit Dominico Zipoli (1688–1726).[38]

Pueblo

Daily life for members of the Pueblo more closely resembled that of pre-Jesuit days. Under the Jesuits, the Pueblo became the manual labor force, concerning itself primarily with subsistence, construction, and transport.

Agriculture and herding were the primary subsistence activities in the Jesuit century. Agriculture became more seasonal than it was in aboriginal times. The introduction of annual crops set a regular cadence to planting, weeding, and harvesting, new to manioc cultivators, but the basic agricultural techniques continued unchanged. Farming in the Jesuit century emphasized native cultivars, keeping maize and manioc on the riverfronts near the missions. In the eighteenth century, sugarcane, produced both for local consumption and for export, shared these choice locations. Cacao and rice, crops introduced to Moxos by the Jesuits, were planted in fields removed from the central stations. Because these crops were raised as perennials, they did not require permanent satellite settlements. This pattern of land tenure concentrated the agricultural labor force on the mission grounds and made it available for other kinds of work as well.[39]

One important change in native agricultural techniques occurred during the Jesuit century. The missionaries introduced a dual system of production that separated traditional family-based agriculture from community-oriented enterprise. In the Guarani missions, this communal-work model—in the form of the *tupambaé* or community plantation—was part of the native practice. However, in Moxos there is no premission evidence of the mixed private and community economic enterprise described by an eighteenth-century missionary:

> Each family is allotted the amount of land necessary for its subsistence, and [it is allotted] to the person for his living; the working of these lands is ordered to banish idleness and poverty. The advantage is that the families are almost equally rich, that is to say, that each household has enough goods so as not to fall into misery; but no one of them has such a

great abundance that it can live in softness and luxury. Besides the goods given to each family for its use — be it land or animals — each village has goods in common and from which they apply the incomes to the maintenance of the Church and to the old beyond a state of working.[40]

The community activities became the basis for an economic system in which agricultural surplus, herds, and handicraft production entered a common storehouse as a hedge against hard times or for sale in the secular economy. These storehouses and the communal traditions that filled them, a mission parallel to the highland *caja de comunidad* (community chest), formed a palpable source of mission wealth.

Herding involved a more extensive pattern of Indian labor. Although mission herds were allowed to roam freely on the grasslands, they had to be driven to high ground in the rainy season and into the mission centers for slaughter. Indian cowboys moved with the cattle, living off the land and from supplies cached at strategic points on the range. The Reyes census shows that the cowboys had dependents in the central mission, but the exact nature of their family lives remains unclear. Father Eder's observations of the cowboys are reminiscent of European descriptions of the gauchos of the Río de la Plata region. He was impressed with their skills as horsemen and with their prowess as hunters. The Moxos cowboys rode with a saddle and bitless bridle; they used braided rawhide ropes to herd cattle and to lasso their quarries, which even included fierce jungle cats.[41]

Members of the Pueblo were involved secondarily in construction activities. In agricultural slack times, they aided the carpenters in building, supplementing Familia expertise with their brawn. Pueblo activities included making adobes, gathering roof thatch, hauling timbers across the savanna, and putting them in place. This last activity exposed the laborers to danger as the lowering of massive tree trunks into foundation holes risked digits and even limbs to amputation. The major source on Indian activities during the late mission period reported that Indians of the northern savanna still practiced the earth-moving techniques of the prehistorical period. Father Eder describes the construction of raised roads that connected settlement sites and also provided water, collected in the troughs the earth-moving produced, for use in the dry season.[42]

Pueblo members also composed the mission defense forces. Militias were formed to meet the threat of Portuguese invasion of Moxos in the 1740s. For example, although the Magdalena militia never entered combat as a unit, it demonstrated its might to the Portuguese interloper Manoel Felix de Lima. This military force consisted of a cavalry unit and an infantry of bowmen, who paraded before Manoel Felix naked, "their bodies stained red as if for battle, stamping their feet and setting up a warwhoop."[43] Then, to the visitor's surprise, the archers pulled into tight formation and released a barrage of arrows toward the great cross in the center of the mission plaza. These exercises served a more serious purpose, for mission Indians formed an integral part of the Spanish strategy for their defense of the Guaporé frontier against the Portuguese.

When war came in 1762, the neophytes supported the Spanish cause with labor and combatants. As auxiliaries, they dug battlements along the left bank of the Guaporé and built bridges across the marshes of the Machupo River for the transport of artillery and supplies to the Spanish positions. As combatants, neophytes fought alongside their European allies. One of the Spanish commanders, Colonel Antonio Aymerich y Villa-juana, listed eighty Canisiana among his levies. Mission Indians also fought with Alonso de Verdugo's force when the Portuguese attacked the Spanish fort of Santa Rosa in 1762.[44]

The mission transportation service operated with Pueblo labor. Because of the incessant need for supplies and communication, the Jesuits were concerned with maintaining reliable routes connecting the missions with the core of the viceroyalty. By the end of the seventeenth century, the missionaries had established a land and water route up the Beni drainage, which connected the stations with the highlands without circling south through Santa Cruz. Fifty years later all the stations were part of a smoothly running transport network. Indian rowers and captains formed the backbone of the system, plying the Mamoré and Beni in huge canoes similar to the one pictured in plate 7. These crews made regular voyages between the missions and the ports of Santa Cruz, and even entered the city to trade on their own accounts. On his visit to the missions in 1747, the bishop of Santa Cruz found that the boatmen had covered the river route between Loreto and Exaltación (some 300 kilometers), with stops in each mission port, in less than two weeks.[45] The Indians also maintained a mule train tethered at San Ignacio for making the trek between the Mamoré stations and those located on the western savanna.

An Indian version of Jesuit-century history stresses the importance of aboriginal participation in the formation and functioning of mission culture. Far from unwitting, the savanna peoples made a series of conscious

Plate 7. Indian Canoe from Late Mission Period. These great canoes plied Moxos' river networks into the twentieth century. Note the passenger compartment aft and the galley forward. *Source:* Eder, *Breve descripción de las reducciones de Mojos,* Illustraciones. Reprinted with permission.

decisions based on their own self-interest: to receive the missionaries' gifts and then the missionaries themselves; to abandon their villages and enter the reductions; and, finally, to accept new regimes of subsistence, social organization, and spirituality. As the order of this sentence suggests, Indian actions composed a process, each step building on the previous one. But what forces, what attractions guided the Indians in their decisions? Given the European history of Moxos traced in chapter 2, coercion, a common explanation in mission studies, cannot be cited as an important motivation. Yet there was a powerful force that attracted the native people to the missions and kept them there.

In his eighteenth-century treatise on American Indian languages, Lorenzo Hervás y Panduro relates how the Canisiana Indians entered the mission system. A Jesuit missionary, learning that some of his neophytes' kinsmen had been captured by their enemies, visited the Canisiana chiefs and offered axes as ransom for their prisoners. The chiefs, delighted at the prospect of such an unequal exchange, immediately turned over their captives and asked if there were more axes where those came from. After a brief visit to the nearby mission, the chiefs returned with their people and belongings in tow. The Canisiana eventually settled in a station of their own, christened San Pedro. Hervás attributes this chain of events to the "profound effect that true faith can have, even on the most bestial of men."[46]

But I would argue that Hervás misinterprets his source. Axes rather than faith served as the impetus for Canisiana conversion.

The distribution of manufactured goods became an indispensable part of relations with native people along the frontier. Europeans saw this activity as a way of influencing Indian behavior, of gaining loyalty and support. However, as Amy Bushnell has shown for Spanish Florida, the native people viewed the goods as their due and reacted unfavorably when supplies were cut off or delayed.[47] Alfred Métraux has called the introduction of metal tools in the Amazon basin a "revolution of the ax," pointing to the tremendous labor savings resulting from the replacement of stone with metal implements.[48] So it was in Moxos. According to the missionaries' own testimony, although not according to their emphasis, the Indians began to associate material rewards with their participation in the missions. Once the area's tropical forest gardeners fell heir to iron tools adapted to their traditional tasks, they readily laid aside their locally made stone and wooden prototypes to embrace an iron age and its Jesuit apostles with open arms.

An Indian version of history, despite its articulation among the peoples of nuclear America, remains largely unexplored in studies of the Spanish mission experience. For even though the missions are among the earliest subjects of Latin American history, the accepted image of the Indians within them is one of passive participants, a dark background for white action. A well-received recent textbook underscores this active-passive dichotomy, characterizing the role of Paraguayan missionaries as an "authoritarian paternalism" and depicting Guarani neophytes as absorbing only a "thin veneer of European culture imposed upon them by the missionaries."[49] This reading of mission history denies the mission Indians their due; it hinders an understanding of both the past and the present. An Indian version, as shown here and in recently completed studies of other mission areas,[50] stresses the active roles the neophytes played in determining their destinies, an especially important point to raise in reconstructing the history of Moxos, a region in which native people continue to struggle against discrimination and negative stereotypes.

V THE MISSIONARIES: FATHERS AND BROTHERS

Missionaries, priests and lay brothers, comprised a hundred-year Jesuit presence in Moxos. While this study has stressed the importance of native people in mission culture, it does not intend to diminish the contributions made by the Jesuits. These men brought with them a material culture radically different from that of the savanna peoples and a spiritual vision shaped by their training in post-Tridentine Christianity. An examination of the Jesuit missionaries as a group illustrates their importance in the formation and function of mission culture in Moxos.

DEMOGRAPHY

The size of the Jesuit staffing in the Province of Peru grew rapidly through the sixteenth century. From an initial contingent of five priests, the Society expanded to 105 priests and brothers by 1578 and 133 eight years later.[1] From the end of the sixteenth century until the suppression, the Society in Peru maintained a staff of between 450 and 520 men.

As figure 4 shows, the foundation and growth of the Moxos missionary population took place after the stabilization of the Province's staff as a whole. The Moxos Jesuit population expanded rapidly as the missionary system spread across the savanna. The three priests resident in the 1660s and early 1670s were reinforced to eleven in 1690, to twenty-eight by the end of the seventeenth century, and to thirty-six by 1706. By the second decade of the eighteenth century, the missionary population had reached a level within 10 percent of its maximum, the fifty-three priests and brothers recorded in 1741. Figure 4 also illustrates a drastic diminution of missionary strength in the decade between 1754 and 1764, a trend that had not

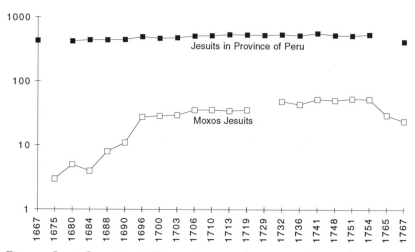

Figure 4. Jesuit Operatives in Peru, 1667–1767. *Source:* ARSI, Peru 6–Peru 11.

completely reversed itself by the year of exile. Again the reasons for the decline follow the events of the Jesuit century. A decreasing Indian population in the missions, the stress brought on by the years of Portuguese hostilities along the northern border, and a breakdown in the mechanisms for supplying new operatives from Europe resulted in a dwindling of the missionary population. By the end of the Jesuit century, only twenty-four priests staffed the stations. These aggregates of growth and decline establish a base for understanding the missionary achievement.

In addition to listing their numbers, the historical record preserves a rudimentary composite biography of the Jesuit operatives. Personnel documents record information on the missionaries' careers in their order and on the savanna. These sources identify 299 men as having served in Moxos and separate them into two broad categories, fathers and lay brothers, based on their religious training. Priests received rigorous academic preparation, often lasting a decade or more, concentrating on theology and sacred philosophy. After a short probationary period, they took final vows and entered their vocations. Lay brothers normally lacked formal academic backgrounds but went directly into their probations and vows.

A comprehensive study of missionary departures from Europe shows that brothers were never a large component of the missionary experience in the Indies. Spanish port records show 360 brothers among 1,221 Jesuits leaving the metropolis.[2] The Moxos data extended this trend; priests out-

The Missionaries: Fathers and Brothers

numbered lay brothers more than seven to one. The brothers never reached 20 percent of the mission staff, and in the years of the largest Jesuit presence, 1715–50, they averaged some 12 percent.

Although few in number, these men possessed technical skills important to the missionary enterprise. Brother José del Castillo opened the Jesuit age when he entered Moxo territory as the surgeon to a Spanish expeditionary force. Lay brothers also performed important works as architects, musicians, woodworkers, and agronomists. The scarcity of lay brothers forced the Moxos priests to learn practical arts and to rely on the skills of their neophytes. It was the priests and Indians who largely built and maintained the mission complexes, making them all the more remarkable.

Age statistics, preserved in the personnel records, show that while the missionaries entered the Society at an early age, they were hardly smooth-cheeked youths when they arrived in Moxos. A random sample of eighty-nine priests and eight brothers taken from the period 1668–1764 shows a mean age of 30.4 years at the beginning of the priests' missionary service. Although their sample size is small, the mean age of the brothers was significantly higher, 34.6 years. Many of these men took holy vows after practicing secular vocations, which explains both their greater age at entry and their well-developed practical skills.

The missionaries also had considerable experience in religious life. The ninety-seven Jesuits in the sample average 18.3 years at the time of their admission to the Society, making 12.1 years the mean length of service for those entering the missions. Again the lay brothers had a higher average entry age, 23.5 years, and despite their shorter periods of religious instruction, the brothers' mean length of service in the Society when entering the missions, 10.9 years, was considerable. These statistics show the Moxos Jesuits arriving on the savanna unaccustomed to missionary work in the tropical world but well tested by the rigors of their order.

The Moxos missionaries represented a variety of national origins. Among the 299 priests and brothers identified, Spaniards comprised the largest single contingent, 116 or 39 percent. Next in number were the Creoles (American-born) at 103, 35 percent, followed by 70 non-Spanish Europeans (23 percent). These figures appear in table 9, which compares the Moxos data with those of other Jesuit provinces.

Columns 1–3 break down the Hispanic missionaries into Spanish and Creole components. In Moxos, the proportions of Spaniards and Creoles were nearly equal for the duration of the Jesuit century, with Iberians

Table 9: National Origins of Jesuit Operatives in the Americas

Area	Local Creole	Other Creole	Spanish	European	Total
Moxos	14 (5%)	89 (31%)	116 (40%)	70 (24%)	289
Paraguay	76 (4%)	440 (22%)	995 (51%)	452 (23%)	1963
Chile	172 (50%)	37 (11%)	80 (23%)	53 (16%)	342
Peru (1767)	234 (55%)	34 (8%)	112 (27%)	42 (10%)	422
Mexico (1767)	387 (57%)	35 (5%)	169 (25%)	87 (13%)	678
California (1767)	2 (4%)	12 (23%)	14 (27%)	24 (46%)	52

Sources: ARSI, Peru 5–7; Hugo Storni, *Catálogo de los Jesuitas de la provincia del Paraguay (Cuenca de la Plata) 1585–1768* (Rome: Institutum Historicum, S.I., 1980), passim; Walter Hanisch Espíndola, *Historia de la Compañía de Jesús en Chile, 1593–1955* (Buenos Aires: Editorial Francisco de Aguirre, 1974); Rubén Vargas Ugarte, *Jesuitas peruanos desterrados a Italia* (Lima: n.p., 1934), 201–56; Rafael de Zelis, *Catálogo de los sugetos de la Compañía de Jesús que formaban la Provincia de Mexico en el día del arresto, 25 de junio de 1767* (México: Imprenta de I. Escalante y Cía, 1871), 4–49; and Gerard Decorme, *La obra de los Jesuitas mexicanos durante la época colonial*, 2 vols. (México: Antigua Librería Robredo de José Porrua, 1941), 2:543–44.

dominating the early years, Creoles the middle period, and a rough parity obtaining after 1750. But hidden in these figures is an important difference in the origins of the two major components. While the birthplaces of the European-born spread themselves across Spain and the continent, American-born Jesuits were overwhelmingly Peruvian. Charcas, the administrative district closest to the missions (designated as local Creole in the table), contributed only 5 percent of the total missionary population. Peru, that is, the Audiencia of Lima, claimed 87 of the Creole missionaries; of these, 46 (52 percent) hailed from Lima and its port, Callao.

Such a disparity may be attributed to several factors. The total population and its distribution within the viceroyalty was skewed toward the region adjudicated from Lima, a region roughly corresponding to modern Peru. Three surveys of Spanish America written in the seventeenth and eighteenth centuries suggest that this area held roughly twice the number of inhabitants as Charcas (modern Bolivia).[3] Another reason for the Peruvian dominance of Moxos' Creole missionary force lies in the locus of the Jesuit system. The Province of Peru, to which the missions belonged, maintained its administrative center and most important educational facilities in Lima. Thus the province made its strongest recruiting efforts in the capital and its environs. It is also illuminating to compare Moxos with Paraguay and California, the other areas with small local Creole populations (see table 9).

In Paraguay, the small European population waged continuous battles with the Jesuits over Indian labor and political influence, making local Creoles unlikely recruits. The California Jesuits offer a more comparable population. Here, as in Moxos, the systems existed on the frontier of well-established parts of the empire. The low levels of local Creole participation in these areas, despite the existence of long-lived Jesuit colleges in Durango and La Plata, the nearest administrative centers, suggest a lack of enthusiasm for service on the frontier by those born closest to it.

The tension between Creoles and Spaniards in colonial Latin America is well known. Investigations of the internal workings of the Franciscan order in colonial Peru have uncovered Creole-Spanish rivalries, which tended to produce a peninsular domination of mission fields.[4] The figures in table 9 also show a majority presence in Paraguay. These statistics and complementary documents have led some historians to describe Europeans as more dedicated to missionary work than their American-born counterparts.[5]

The Moxos experience presents a pattern at odds with the image of a Spanish or European domination of the mission enterprise. While the Spanish-born was the largest single element in Moxos' personnel rosters, it never reached a majority, except in the very early years when the missionary corps numbered less than ten. Over the course of the Jesuit century, the Creole contingent effectively balanced the numbers of their Spanish coreligionists. Creoles also matched their Spanish colleagues in office holding. During the century of Jesuit presence in Moxos, fourteen men held the post of superior, the local director of the missions. Nine Creoles, all Peruvians, held the office for a total of fifty-six years. And, of the seven named vice-superior, a position created circa 1720, four were American-born.

The non-Spanish component, also shown in comparative perspective in table 9, set the Jesuit experience apart from that of the other missionary orders in the Indies. By a series of decrees, the Crown conceded to the Society the right to recruit outside Spain itself. In 1715 those recruited might include men from "the Kingdoms of France and Poland, from Bavaria and Flanders, from the Republics of Venice and Genoa, from Rome and all other nations which compose Italy, excluding only the Kingdom of Naples."[6] And for once a royal decree was observed to its letter. In the eighteenth century a quarter of the Moxos operatives came from non-Spanish Europe; Italians and Germans comprised the largest groups of recruits, but missionary rosters show Hungarians, Frenchmen, Flemings, Belgians, and even an Irishman, John Brand.

The Missionaries: Fathers and Brothers 107

Once they began to arrive, these "foreigners" had an immediate and lasting effect on the missions. The first non-Spanish Europeans reached Moxos in 1696; by 1723 non-Spaniards numbered some 30 percent of the missionary population. While their numbers fluctuated over the course of the century, the impact of this international brigade proved profound. At a time when demands for new recruits was intense, foreign recruitment enabled the Society to spread their staffing burden over a wider population base.[7] However, the foreigners also made the Jesuits vulnerable to charges of disloyalty to the Crown. When the Gallicanist advisors to Charles III attacked the order in the 1760s, they pointed to its cosmopolitan makeup as evidence of its questionable allegiance.

RECRUITMENT AND TRAVEL

The missionary force consisted solely of volunteers. All entered Moxos of their own volition, some after many years of waiting. However, the procurement of priests and brothers suitable for service in Moxos and their placement in the centers themselves involved considerable feats of persuasion and logistics. This effort combined the resources of the Jesuit Province of Peru, Jesuits colleges in Europe, and the Spanish Crown.

Under the terms of the Patronato Real, the Spanish monarchs exercised control over all missionaries bound for the Indies. However, as a practical matter, the Crown seldom asserted its rights at the individual level, confining its efforts to regulating the acceptable nationalities and numbers of missionaries who departed from Europe. Beginning in the second half of the sixteenth century, a mechanism for recruitment of European Jesuits for American missionary service developed. Law and custom prescribed a four-step process in which: (1) the religious hierarchy made a request for the desire number of operatives; (2) the Council of the Indies forwarded these requests to the Jesuit provincials in Spain, who moved to seek volunteers; (3) the volunteers selected by the provincials presented themselves and their credentials to the council; (4) the council gave its permission for departure and disbursed funds to cover travel expenses.[8] In reality, recruiting was never so simple.

Faced with increasing demands for manpower, the Jesuits developed a variety of recruiting strategies. The Province of Peru, like its counterparts in other regions of the Indies, began to rely on a delegate sent to Europe once every three years to represent the province in general meetings at Rome.

The procuradores took advantage of their stays to present Peru's requests for new missionaries and often made extended trips through Europe in search of priests and brothers. Pedro Marbán, Moxos' first superior, came to Peru as the result of a visit by the procurador Juan de Ribadeneira, and several of the German priests who arrived in the 1710s were similarly attracted to mission work.[9]

The Jesuits also made effective use of missionary marketing. The "Jesuit Relations," first published in French at the beginning of the eighteenth century and translated into German, English, Italian, and Spanish by 1753, are the best-known examples of this genre.[10] These letters and short essays portray the lives of Jesuits working in the Americas as well as in Africa and Asia. Best-sellers in their day, the relations were written without overt propagandistic overtones but expressed the heroism and purpose of the missionary experience.

The relations that treat Moxos missionaries offer typical portrayals. Take the short biography of Cipriano Barace recorded in the French edition of the work. Although this priest was the first Jesuit martyr in Moxos, the letter presents his death as a mere denouement. Instead it concentrates on the strange customs of the aboriginal people, and on Barace's role in congregating them into settlements and introducing them to Christianity. When the Baures ended Father Barace's life at the ripe old age of sixty-one, they could not dim his achievements in having created a thriving mission system.[11] These relations apparently had their desired effect. A study of German Jesuits relates that these accounts captured young seminarians' imaginations. They rushed to volunteer for service in the Indies, prompting complaints from German superiors who resented the potential loss of the students.[12]

The Jesuits employed other types of formal recruiting strategies, too. In some circumstances provincials would make direct appeals for missionaries. This device was employed in Peru during the initial period of the Moxos missions.[13] Recruiting manuals, such as the surviving *Instruction pro candidatis ad indios,* were circulated to European and American colleges to give potential missionaries inspiration from the Scripture and the writings of Ignatius Loyola. A manuscript entitled "Mission a las Indias con advertencias para los religiosos de Europa que la huvieren de emprender" is a veritable step-by-step manual for entering the missions, from how to ask permission from the local superior to saying good-byes to parents and how to conduct oneself aboard ship.[14] The production of such works shows the extent to which the Jesuits were willing to offer aid and encouragement to potential recruits.

When all else failed, the Jesuits apparently resorted to effectively lowering their standards, recruiting increasing numbers of students for missionary work. A careful analysis of sailing records in the seventeenth and eighteenth centuries shows that 27 percent of European Jesuits (compared to 4 percent of Franciscans) bound for the Indies had yet to finish their spiritual formation.[15] The Moxos data conform to this conclusion, including the marked upswing of students arriving at the end of the Jesuit century. Moxos Jesuits denoted students reached a high of 32 percent in 1750 with the arrival of fifteen new European operatives in 1748, twelve of whom were students.

Yet the weight of evidence argues that even these means were insufficient to meet the need for missionaries. By the onset of the Moxos enterprise in the 1680s, Spanish colleges proved unable to provide the manpower necessary to staff a worldwide Jesuit network. By the beginning of the eighteenth century, the quotas authorized by the Council of the Indies were consistently unfilled. Even opening the missions to "foreign" recruits failed to reach the limits authorized by the Crown. Between 1723 and 1747, requests for ninety Moxos missionaries were approved by the Council of the Indies, yet only sixty-five men sailed for Peru.[16] Given chronic underenrollment, a relatively minor incident such as the wreck of the schooner *Venezia* — which foundered in 1758, drowning twenty-one Jesuits destined for Moxos — contributed to the downward trend in missionary manpower illustrated in figure 4.

Once approved for service, the missionaries-to-be began a long trip to the missions. From Lima, the recruits had to traverse a coastal desert, the western Andean slope, and the intermontane high plain before descending through the tropical forests east of Cochabamba to the savanna. Europeans endured an even more involved itinerary. Italians and German Jesuits traveled to Genoa, which served as a point of embarkation for a voyage to the Andalusian ports of Spain. Here the missionaries-to-be began what was normally a long wait for a berth to America. During this period, the European Jesuits entered a program of orientation and practical training. The Spanish residences held retired missionaries who passed on their experiences to their young colleagues. The hiatus also gave non-Spanish Jesuits a chance to learn Castilian and to practice practical skills. A missionary bound for Mexico in the eighteenth century wrote of his two-year stay in Sevilla:

We studied not only astronomy, mathematics and other interesting knowledge, but we ourselves made all sorts of trinkets and worked at things. Some of us made compasses or sun-dials and others cases for them; this one sewed cloths and furs, that one learned how to make bottles, another how to solder tin; one busied himself with distilling, a second with the lathe, a third with sculpturing, so that we might gain the good nature of the wild heathen and more easily give them the truths of Christian belief.[17]

Once disembarked from Spain, European Jesuits endured a two-month sea voyage and, depending on their port of entry, a northbound or southbound trek of one thousand to fifteen hundred kilometers. The early European arrivals took the annual fleet from Spain to the Caribbean, disembarked in Puerto Bello, crossed the isthmus of Panama, and proceeded down the Pacific coast to Lima. Once Buenos Aires was opened to regular navigation from the metropolis in the second decade of the eighteenth century, European Jesuits followed a more direct route to Moxos. A party of six Germans and one Spaniard followed the route from Buenos Aires to the Argentine cities of Santa Fé, Santiago del Estero, Córdoba, and Jujuy to Potosí, Oruro, Cochabamba, and Santa Cruz in present-day Bolivia on their way to the missions. The overland segment of the trip took fourteen months in 1717 and 1718.[18]

Expenses for the journey were shared by the recruit's home province and the Spanish Crown. The province bore the cost of maintenance from the onset of the Jesuit's trip to the time he boarded a ship bound for the Indies. The burden to the province often mounted as the protomissionary waited for his vessel to sail. As a remedy to expensive delays, the Jesuits constructed their own one hundred-bed residence in Santa María near Cádiz. At the point of departure, responsibilities shifted to the Crown, which provided passage and maintenance on board as well as a per diem, which was to carry the missionary to his site. In addition, Spanish authorities provided each missionary with the basic supplies for his passage and overland trip to the missions. Pedro Borges Morán has published the contents of these supply packages, detailing twenty items of food, clothing, and equipment.[19]

MISSIONARY SERVICE

Upon reaching Moxos, the novice missionary began to learn a whole new way of life. The transition was cushioned by a period of greeting and in-

Table 10: Missionary Service in Moxos, 1668–1767

Time Period	Number of Missionaries	Mean Serivce in Years
1668–1700	38	16.28
1701–40	34	18.60
1741–67	36	20.83
		Mean for the Century 18.57

Source: ARSI, Peru 6–Peru 10.

country training. The arrival of fresh men signaled a period of celebration in the missions. For example, one German Jesuit was welcomed to Loreto by a company of neophytes playing trumpets, clarinets, and flutes. The celebration continued with a procession through the streets and ended with a Te Deum mass in the church.[20] After his welcome, the new operative spent a period of orientation learning basic skills at the side of a veteran missionary before receiving his first assignment.

Once in the missions, the men tended to stay. A breakdown of personnel records shows missionary careers characterized by long service. Table 10 displays the priests' and brothers' terms of service broken into the three major chronological periods of the Jesuit century.

The differences in mean service shown in the table are not statistically significant, but the lengths of service in all periods are nothing short of remarkable. Biographies of Franciscans working in California in the eighteenth and nineteenth centuries show that long service characterized this enterprise as well.[21] But the California experience took place in a climate the Europeans found much healthier than that of Moxos. Life in the tropics before the advent of inoculations against diseases such as malaria and yellow fever was almost certainly shorter and unhealthier than life in temperate zones. Perhaps more meaningful as a comparison than the Franciscan experience in California is a study of the order's efforts in a tropical forest zone. While he was unable to quantify their stays exactly, Jay Lehnertz's work on the Peruvian central montaña suggests a mean service shorter than ten years.[22] But however one reads the context of Moxos missionary service, such long periods on the savanna testify to the physical and psychological strength of the Jesuit fathers and brothers.

In Moxos long service was buttressed by a pronounced tendency to stay in the same station for many years. Analysis of the records of 110 missionaries who served on the savanna between 1713 and 1767 shows that ninety-two men served in one station for their entire careers, and that of those who did relocate, more than half did so when their former stations disappeared. Such continuity worked to the Jesuits' advantage, allowing the missionaries to develop familiarity with local conditions and fluency in an Indian language. These statistics contrast with the Franciscan data cited above. The California missionaries averaged nearly three changes of mission over their careers, and Lehnertz concludes that constant staff turnover and frequent changes of residence seriously hampered the Franciscans' efforts to establish viable missions among the Campa peoples of the montaña.[23]

The missionaries' long residences took place under very difficult conditions. Even the most dedicated of the fathers and brothers suffered from the rigors of Moxos' tropical climate and from the isolation concomitant with the missionary experience. Pedro Marbán commented on the discomfort of living beneath a sun intense enough "to convert a person to ashes." Describing the humidity, he wrote that in Moxos one sweated so much as to "irrigate the ground or make a water soup for nourishment."[24] Ubiquitous swarms of insects added to the Jesuits' misery. One brother mused that in order to suffer in silence both the heat and the mosquitoes one had to be a saint.[25] The mosquitoes were a greater health hazard than these men knew, for they constitute the primary vector for malaria and yellow fever, diseases still endemic on the savanna today.

Another recurring theme in the missionary record is solitude. The lack of fellowship produced complaints among even veteran missionaries. Antonio de Orellana openly bemoaned the lack of sure correspondence through Santa Cruz; he accused the mission boatmen of using his letters to roll cigarettes.[26] Isolation proved especially hard for members of the international brigade. One German Jesuit lamented to his family in Augsburg that his experience in an Indian-speaking region of the Spanish Empire had deprived him of all use of his mother tongue.[27] Under the terms dictated by the time and place, the Moxos stations became worlds of their own — small, enclosed, and absorbing.

Not all the Jesuits stood up to these conditions. Some men did not prove equal to the physical demands of mission life. One German priest, Joseph Schwendtner, left the missions after eleven years and served the rest of his life in the Santa Cruz residence. In describing his own transformation from scholar to laborer in Moxos — "I now manage the plow with the same frequency and dexterity that I once did the pen" — a fellow priest observed that Schwendtner never mastered the rigors of physical labor.[28]

Poor health proved a greater obstacle to service. Accounts of sickness and death punctuate missionary correspondence for the entire Jesuit century. Cipriano Barace and his highland Indian companion were stricken with fevers in 1682, and, within a year of 1750, five priests died of disease exacerbated by the Portuguese conflict. Perhaps the most revealing account comes from the 1730s, when Father Miguel Sánchez reported that disease had diminished the mission staff to the point that in six stations there was only one priest, and in another seven, one of the fathers was habitually ill. While surviving records do not support the compilation of a life table, they make clear the heavy toll that the tropical climate and diseases exacted on the missionary force.[29]

Others departed the missions tapped for special work or for advancement in the provincial hierarchy. Juan Rehr, a Hungarian priest who served in San Borja, left the savanna to apply his architectural skills in Lima, repairing the damage of the 1746 earthquake. Several of the Moxos Jesuits served as leaders at the provincial level. Antonio de Garriga, Miguel Sánchez, and Pascual Ponce all succeeded to the Peruvian provincialship in the eighteenth century, and Antonio de Orellana became rector of the San Pablo college in Lima in 1712. Garriga had perhaps the widest experience of any of these ex-missionaries. Born and educated in elite circles in Spain, he entered the Society of Jesus in 1684 at the age of twenty-two. After his training, he volunteered for service in Peru and passed almost immediately into the missions. Four years later, in 1701, he was ordered to Lima under the sponsorship of the visitor Diego Francisco Altamirano, where he worked at the college of San Pablo. Returning to Moxos in 1706, he aided the conversion of the Kayubaba in the mission of San Pedro. Garriga's election as visitor and vice-provincial of Paraguay took him across the continent and then back to Peru between 1708 and his death in 1733.[30]

But these administrators stand out as exceptional cases. A modal career was probably quite similar to that of Francisco Xavier Eder, whose chronicle tells us much of what we know about Moxos in the mid-eighteenth century. Eder was born in Hungary in 1727 and entered the Society of Jesus at the age of fifteen. He came to Peru while still a student and finished his theological training in Lima in 1751. Then, from 1753 to 1767, Eder served in the mission of San Martín on the northeastern savanna. He is known today primarily for his history, written and published in exile, rather than for his missionary service.[31] But men such as Eder, through their numbers and their years of immersion in the missions, made the greatest contributions to the introduction and growth of mission culture in Moxos.

From the priests' and brothers' perspectives, missionary service centered on their attempts to create and administer Indian communities based on Iberian models of religion, politics, and economics. Their work in Moxos was guided by abstract and practical instructions from their corporation and by a store of mission experience accumulated by members of the Society in the Peruvian highlands and on the savanna.

The Jesuit theological vision of the missions reflected two distinct philosophical currents. Half of the vision, very much in keeping with an Enlightenment view of natural man, is what Josep Barnadas has called the "Jesuit utopian impulse," an emphasis on the unspoiled nature of the Indian and his environment.[32] The eighteenth-century Moxos missionary Alonso Messia clearly voices this utopian impulse in describing Indian worship in the stations. To his mind, the more pristine conditions provided on the savanna had cleansed Catholic worship of many of its secular additions. He cites the missions' celebration of the Jubilee of the Forty Hours, which eschewed the European observance of sporting events.[33]

The second current, equally strong in theory and practice, appears unalloyed in the writings of the great Jesuit intellectual José de Acosta. His magnum opus, *De procuranda indorum salute* (1576), divides the infidels of the world into three types, ranging from the Chinese, who manifested all facets of culture, to people whom Acosta describes as "scarcely human."[34] This last type, into which the savanna tribes clearly fall, were to be treated as children, their conversion accomplished by equal measures of cajolery and force. Eder's chronicle of the Baure stations at the end of the Jesuit century reflects Acosta's view, characterizing the native people as capricious, vindictive, and only superficially converted to Christianity a century after the onset of the missions. He concludes by answering those who criticized the Jesuit regime as paternal by asking rhetorically, "who in the world could be more infantile than these [Indians]?"[35]

The First Provincial Congregation of the Society in Peru, held in 1576, also contributed to the theoretical underpinnings of the Moxos effort. First, it affirmed the importance of native languages as the basis for conversion and established a catechism that would serve as the basis for translations. Second, after discussing the possibility of taking over existing parishes, making transitory missions, and concentrating efforts on colleges for the education of Indian nobles, the delegates chose the establishment of permanent mission centers as the preferred strategy for converting the Indians of Peru.[36]

Formal instructions added a second layer of structure for the Moxos missions. Peru's first Jesuit priests carried with their baggage a set of instructions from General Francisco de Borgia. Relying on the Jesuit experience in the Far East, the general ordered his men to follow a cautious course, which was to characterize their approach in Moxos a century later. He insisted on a concentration of resources, careful evaluation of the native people as subjects for conversion, an avoidance of martyrdom, and regular correspondence between priests in the field and their superiors in the administrative centers.[37]

The provincial of Peru issued his own set of instructions to the missionaries. With his approval of the Moxos missions in 1676, Hernando Cabrero established the formal outlines of the Jesuit enterprise in fifteen instructions and nine orders. These documents speak to the temporal and spiritual conduct of the missionaries. Their provisions include the naming of a superior of missions, an authorization for use of material inducements in establishing the centers, an order for careful observance of spiritual exercises among the priests and brothers, and the institution of a consultative model for mission governance.[38]

By the time the Jesuits entered the savanna, their order had accumulated a considerable store of missionary experience in the Peruvian highlands. Abortive efforts at Huarochirí and Santiago del Cercado prefigured the establishment of a huge missionary complex among the Lupaqa at Juli near Lake Titicaca in 1576. Here the Jesuits enjoyed considerable success in winning over the Indian population with their fluency in Aymara, their strict observance of sacred vows, and their redistribution of ecclesiastical fees among the populace.[39] The Juli station also established the viability of Spanish models of government and the teaching of European arts and offices to Indian neophytes. Perhaps most important, Juli marked the use of a mission strategy in which the Indians were segregated from the secular world. Spaniards were prohibited from entering the missions except for specific tasks, and the Lupaqa were encouraged to maintain a separate existence as well.

While the Moxos missionaries were influenced by this reservoir of corporate theory and practice, their work soon produced another body of knowledge based on local conditions. Father Eder left a terse summary of his view of the missionary experience. For him, the fathers and brothers served as "head of the mission, its judge, master, spiritual leader, physician, economist, and finally its slave."[40] While Eder's vision underestimates the role played by the neophytes, its emphasis on the missionary as jack-of-all-trades and the experience as a mixture of the sacred and the profane provides an accurate summary of the Jesuit *vie quotidienne* in Moxos.

The missions began with a congregation of Indians at a central location. This gathering of the flock, a reduction in the language of the time, was an ongoing activity in the Jesuit century, as new stations were founded and infidels were added to established ones. The tactics the Moxos Jesuits developed and perfected for attracting native people to their missions bear remarkable resemblance to those still used in the Amazon. The missionary, usually accompanied by neophyte assistants, entered the savanna at the end of the rainy season. He traveled on foot and carried little: a drinking cup, short rations of manioc flour and parched maize, a bow and arrows, a machete to clear his trail, trade goods and the tools of his trade—a Bible and missal. Once he made contact with a native village, the missionary proceeded with caution. He attempted to gain the Indians' confidence by leaving trade goods at strategic locations near the village. Then he waited for a response. If the Indians were amenable to his presence, they approached him. As a token of good faith, the headman might allow a few boys to accompany the missionary back to his station. Here they learned the primary mission language and prepared themselves to serve as intermediaries between their people and the priests when the time came for the village to join the mission.

If the Indians did not approach the missionary directly, he followed a series of alternative strategies. A favorite tactic was to capture a stray member of a village and take him back to the nearest station. The Jesuits made contact with the Mobima in this way, taking prisoners and then returning them to their villages with tales of the good life in the missions. The missionaries also became adept at manipulating the intergroup rivalries of the savanna peoples to convince the reluctant to enter a mission. The Mopecianas entered San Javier to gain the missionaries' protection against the Canisianas, who had taken some of their number captive.[41] And the governor of Santa Cruz reported that the Bauranos of San Ignacio refused initial Jesuit blandishments. Only when the priests succeeded in reducing their traditional enemies did these people consent to enter the station.[42] When all else failed, the Jesuits were not above calling in Spanish troops to aid their cause. On at least four occasions — in 1678, 1697, 1702, and 1709 — expeditions from Santa Cruz entered the savanna, with Jesuit blessing, to put down Indian resistance to the missionaries.

With the congregation of the last major savanna peoples in the 1710s, missionary activities took on a distinct parish-work flavor. Diane Langmore, a historian of the Pacific Islands who has noted a similar transition in the nineteenth-century missionization of New Guinea, introduces Weberian terminology to describe the changes in missionary life-styles.[43] After the passage of a thirty-year charismatic age, the Moxos priests and brothers entered a more rational-legal stage, spending less time in the search for natives in the bush and more time in ministering to the material and spiritual needs of the resident neophytes.

As the missions reached a mature stage, the priests turned their attention to education. As their counterparts in the secular world did, mission schools mixed conversion with instruction in reading, writing, and figures. The Jesuits' concern for teaching in the native vernacular produced a number of grammars and religious tracts written in Moxo, Baure, Mobima, Kayubaba, Itonama, Sapibocona, and other savanna languages. The principal survivors of this effort are Antonio Maggio's *Arte de la lengua de los indios Baures de la provincia de los Moxos* (1749) and Pedro Marbán's *Arte y vocabulario de la lengua Moxa* (1703). These works are useful not only to the historical linguist trying to assess the impact of European contact on the grammar and syntax of savanna Arawak but also to the student of Jesuit systems of conversion and instruction. One text used in Moxos is the short catechism translated below from Marbán's work. Originally printed in Spanish and Moxa, and based on the compiler's experience as a pioneer missionary, it illustrates the concepts the Jesuits tried to impart to their charges.

Question: Tell me children, is there a God?
Answer: Yes, there is.
Q: How many gods are there?
A: One and no more.
Q: Where is God?
A: He is in the heavens, in the earth, and everywhere.
Q: Who is God?
A: He is the Father, the Son, and the Holy Spirit, three persons in one God.
Q: Is God the Father?
A: Yes, He is.
Q: Is God the Son?
A: Yes, He is.

Q: Is the Holy Spirit God?
A: Yes, He is.
Q: Are there three Gods?
A: No, only One and no more.
Q: Well, how is it that there are three persons and only one God?
A: Because this is the true being of God.

Apparent from this brief dialogue is the rigid nature of the eighteenth-century missionary approach to conversion. Marbán's text is a literal translation of the brief catechism the First Provincial Congregation had established a century and a half before. It makes no allowance for aboriginal tradition or nuances in language. Despite his thirty years in the area, Marbán found no way to express central Christian concepts in the Moxa language. For instance, his translation of the catechism includes the words *Espiritu Santopoze* (Holy Spirit), and *Dios* (God), both direct loans from the Spanish. With such texts serving as the basis for Indian instruction, it is little wonder that the neophytes would be accused of acquiring only a superficial knowledge of Christianity.[44]

The children took to their lessons with enthusiasm. Visitors to the missions marveled at the students' ability to read and recite sacred passages; resident priests made similar comments, even though some expressed reservations about the students' level of comprehension.[45] But even if the dogma were imperfectly received, the lessons had their effect. A number of the neophytes, largely members of the Familia, learned to speak and write Spanish. This facility would serve them well, especially in the post-Jesuit period when contact with the Spanish world increased.

Adult instruction followed more imaginative approaches. An important part of adult conversion centered on the use of visual illustrations of the abstract tenets of the new faith. Paintings showing holy figures and extraterrestrial images, especially heavenly bliss and hellish torment, became an essential part of adult conversion activities. These canvases were often produced and maintained by highland artists and transported to the missions for use there. The Jesuits also employed native traditions in music and dance to reach their adult charges. As early as the 1690s, the Mamoré missions boasted native musicians who performed during the mass and supported conversion activities set to music. Dance became a medium of religious celebration, with the missionaries encouraging the native peoples to weave their own patterns of choreography into Christian services.[46]

The impact of Indian schooling is a topic of considerable interest among scholars of the North American experience. Historians of the British colonies and early American Republic have pronounced Indian schooling a failure, citing scanty resources, Indian resistance, and a lack of available teachers.[47] But as these scholars demonstrate, the British experience was different than its South American counterpart. After very brief experiments with instruction in native languages, English-language teaching became a universal practice in North America. North American Indian schools, most operated as boarding facilities, forced pupils to abandon their families and live in the European world, a policy that produced few candidates for instruction and even fewer graduates. Finally, the North American Indian schools attempted nothing less than the total integration of the native population into white society.[48] Mission culture offered a more realistic approach to Indian education. In Moxos, instruction took place in the neighborhood and was conducted in native languages. Under European tutelage, Indian neophytes gained a real capacity to deal with the world outside the missions while they continued to live within them.

The missionaries also introduced the basic elements of European technology to Moxos. As I described in chapter 3, the Jesuits were heavily involved in construction, in agriculture and ranching, and in cottage industry. Much of the responsibility for introducing European modes of production fell to the lay brotherhood. Brothers such as Diego Urbe, Jorge Ligardo, and Alberto Marterer brought a variety of skills to the missions, among them woodworking, foundry, weaving, and agronomy. Following European tradition, they trained native apprentices, who in turn practiced and taught in other mission centers.[49]

One area where European technology produced mixed results was in the practice of medicine. The priests and brothers spent part of each day ministering to the sick. In healthy times these visits were interspersed with a regular regimen of counseling and religious instruction. In times of disease outbreak, such as during the major epidemics of 1730 and 1751, mission medical practice reverted to triage. The missionaries were largely helpless in the face of European diseases introduced among the savanna people. Their medical practice mixed scientific and folk cures. Quinine was widely prescribed in the Moxos missions for the treatment of tropical fevers. Made from the bark of the cinchona tree, this medicine, initially harvested in the sub-Andean forests of what is today southern Ecuador, became the staple of mission pharmacies and entered Europe under the name Jesuit Bark. Other remedies applied to the sick included a variety of tropical herbs and the application of bleeding.[50]

While the priests were less skilled than their brothers in arts and offices, they exercised control over the spiritual life and management of the missions. Through their investiture by the church and their control of the distribution of European goods shipped from Peru, the priests directed the formal institutions of religion and government in the stations. Their role as guardians of the rites and traditions of the Church gave them extensive influence in religious affairs. They interpreted the mysteries of their faith and preached a Christian interpretation of morality from the pulpit and the street. As spiritual leaders, the priests also presided over the events that marked the passage of time in the missions. Each day they celebrated the masses with which mission activities began and ended. They also presided over an elaborate fiesta cycle. On three occasions — Christmas, Easter, and the local saint's day — the priests generously distributed food, clothing, and trade goods from mission storehouses. One Jesuit used the symbolism of Christ's dividing his clothing among the twelve disciples as he distributed raiment among the widowed and orphaned of the mission Concepción.[51]

In addition to their spiritual leadership, the priests exercised titular control over mission politics. Histories of the Jesuit missions often depict the priests as exercising unchecked power in naming officials and dispensing justice. One general study of the missionary enterprise offers the following analysis: "Indians were appointed as overseers and headmen, but they had little authority. In reality the Jesuit was master of all he surveyed."[52] But, as the preceding chapter stressed, the political structure of the Moxos missions confirmed traditional aboriginal leadership and gave them Spanish titles. The missionaries confirmed and legitimated the neophytes' choices but seldom overruled them. This policy of recognizing native modes of government made for firm bonds between the Jesuits and traditional Indian leaders. By holding themselves above partisanship, the missionaries were able to function as arbiters among conflicting interests. Antonio de Garriga's published orders regulating each mission's rights to harvest forest products offers one example of this arbitrating role. In the Moxos system, priests functioned in harmony with the traditions of mission culture.

In describing the missionary experience, this chapter addresses several topics at issue in the general historiography of Latin America. Perhaps most poignantly, it speaks to the mind-set of the missionaries. Historians have

R.P. Dominicus Mayr, Waldensis Suevus S.I.
10.Augusti 1680. propè celeberrimum ad Sylvam
Ordinis S.Bernardi Monasterium natus est: diem
verò supremum obiit 1741. in Apostolicis Moxorum
Missionibus labore plurimo confectus. Ejus Cada,,
ver, quamvis, cum tumulo inferretur, viva calce
fuisset obrutum, reserato tamen elapsis post fa,,
ta duobus annis Sepulchro, integrum, flexile, et re,,
centi Sanguine manans, Sacerdotalibus Vestibus
etiam illæsis, in clarum Angelicæ vitæ testimonium
repertum est.

long faulted Hispanic missionaries in general and the Jesuits in particular for a paternalistic attitude that stifled their avowed raison d'être of integrating the Indians into the mainstream of the colony. Relations between missionaries and neophytes have been characterized by such expressions as "theocratic dictatorship" and "perpetual childhood." Writing on the Paraguayan missions, J. H. Parry concludes that "they had little power of internal growth, however; the Indians in them were treated, kindly but firmly, as perpetual minors." The logical outcome of such a system was that "when the Jesuits were expelled from the domains of the Spanish Crown the cloistered jungle Utopias collapsed."[53] As this book will subsequently show, the Jesuits' departure from Moxos did not signify the end of mission culture. The missions did not collapse, and, more important for the history of the region, the new cultural amalgam that developed during the Jesuit age gave the Indians a basis for resisting new demands of the Jesuits' secular successors. Paternalism, as a state of mind, was a natural outgrowth of the colonial relationship, especially in this age of monarchy. After all, the missionaries were fathers and shepherds with their children and flocks to care for. Illustrations of this *mentalité* appear repeatedly in the surviving iconography of the period and in the correspondence of the fathers and brothers. But, in reconstructing the missionary age, we must pay attention to what these men did as well as to what they said. The Moxos experience is filled with examples of priests accepting native modes of government, technology, and intergroup relations. The missionaries may have wished for a paternalistic society in the reductions, but the reality was quite different.

The Jesuit century in Moxos adds to our understanding of missiology. The use of a congregation strategy for organizing the mission populations, the missionaries' training in native languages, and Jesuit insistence on regular communication between the field staff and their superiors were consistent features of the Moxos enterprise. However, two factors stand out as critical in the Jesuit establishment and maintenance of their Moxos missions.

Plate 8. Dominikus Mayr, S.J., Moxos Missionary, 1718–41. This illustration accompanies a compilation of Mayr's letters to his family published by his father as *Neu-aufgerichteter amerikanisher Maherhof* (Augsburg, 1747). The missionary's erect posture and beatific expression, and the subordinate, grateful pose struck by the accompanying Indian neophyte, typify both contemporary European representation of the missionary experience and the mind-set that underlay it. Courtesy of New York Public Library.

The importance of the dedication of the fathers and brothers cannot be overstated. Their long service records provide statistical evidence of a diligence that can only be described as remarkable. The field correspondence cited throughout this chapter testifies definitively to the Jesuit esprit de corps. Despite their occasional discouragement and incessant physical discomfort, the missionaries kept alive a fierce determination to create Christian communities on the savanna, "to harvest souls or receive martyrdom as an acceptable obligation to God."[54] And martyrdom proved more than a figure of speech. Cipriano Barace and Balthasar de Espinosa both met death at the hands of the Indians they sought to convert.

A second key to understanding the Jesuit approach in Moxos was the emphasis they placed on European material culture as an integral part of the conversion process. The traditional view of missionary activities emphasizes their religious nature, a spiritual conquest in both the contemporary and modern usage. But, as Urs Bitterli has pointed out in a general context, in many ways the missionaries behaved like European traders.[55] The Moxos Jesuits introduced numerous utilitarian and ceremonial goods to the savanna. Musical instruments, medals, axes, knives, machetes, and the profusion of sacred objects described in the mission inventories swiftly secured the Jesuits a position as reliable sources for objects never before seen on the savanna but greatly desired by its inhabitants. Seen in this light, the activities of the fathers and brothers were as much a material as a spiritual conquest.

VI MISSION CULTURE UNDER SPANISH RULE

When the Jesuits departed the savanna in 1767, they left behind a resilient mission culture based on firm foundations. The population was resistant to European diseases and cohesively organized into small urban communities. A native political elite, enjoying popular support, had gained valuable experience during the Jesuit years. By 1767 members of the communities had become fluent in Spanish and showed remarkable skill in European arts and industries. The missions also retained a considerable material base. Although deprived of their access to Jesuit coffers, the Indians inherited the sumptuously appointed churches, well-equipped workrooms, and, most important, the riverfront lands and cattle herds amassed during the Jesuit century. But as the Jesuits left their posts, they were replaced by men of a different stripe.

The year 1767 marked the onset of secular Spanish rule in Moxos and the establishment of a new set of economic and administrative institutions on the savanna. From an imperial perspective, Spanish rule in Moxos coincided with the apex of a movement designed to restructure the Indies, to secularize and commercialize Spain's overseas domains, and to bind them more closely to the mother country. A series of reforms, fostering industry and trade and altering Moxos' relationship with the rest of the colony, occurred after Jesuit exile. Locally, a significant alteration in the European component of mission culture began in 1767. In place of the fathers and brothers came functionaries more closely tied to secular Spanish society. These men saw Moxos as a source of wealth to be siphoned off for uses outside the savanna. The combined impact of local and imperial events posed a serious challenge to the survival of mission culture in Moxos. Faced with a new economic orientation and with a new cast of European characters, the mission Indians searched for new strategies, which they applied with varying intensity and effect, for maintaining mission culture in the last half-century of the colonial period.

ADMINISTRATIVE CHANGES, 1767–1825

The royal orders banishing the Jesuits contained a provision for establishing new administrative regimes in the mission areas. In addition to the twenty-nine general points of the exile decree, the document included an appendix for use in the colonies. The appendix included a special instruction that "in all the missions formerly administered by the Jesuits in America and the Philippines, an interim governor of good character will sit in the name of the sovereigns and attend to the missions according to the Laws of the Indies, and it will be advisable to establish there Spaniards, to open and facilitate commerce."[1] This interim governor was to be replaced by a permanent functionary appointed by the viceroy.

The Council of the Indies was first inclined to apply the administrative organization developed for the Paraguayan missions to Moxos. There a governor, resident in the former mission capital and reporting directly to the viceroy, oversaw subordinates in each station and established a new regime that recognized the neophytes as full citizens of the empire. However, the realities of the Moxos situation — chiefly its isolation from other Spanish centers in Charcas — forced modification of the initial plan, and, in 1772, the Council established a new administrative mode: a governor would live in the missions but would be subject to the authority of the governor of Santa Cruz.[2] As commander of the Spanish force protecting the Guaporé frontier, Colonel Antonio Aymerich y Villajuana inherited the interim position spelled out in the exile decree. Aymerich's tenure, which included four years of interim service and a year as confirmed by the Council of the Indies (the last five years of his life), began an institution that would last for the duration of the colony, until 1825.

The second durable European fixture of the post-Jesuit age was the position of *cura doctrinero*, literally priest doctrinary but in reality a lay functionary. In Moxos the position was created ad hoc, with replacement of the Jesuits in mind, to administer both the temporal and spiritual welfare of the neophytes under the governor's direction. It was codified in a rule (*reglamento*) issued by the bishop of Santa Cruz, Francisco Ramón de Herboso, in 1772. The reglamento called for two *curas* (used hereafter to

126 *Mission Culture under Spanish Rule*

describe the position) to occupy each station, a *cura primero* with a salary of six hundred pesos per annum, and an assistant (*cura segundo*) with a four hundred-peso salary.[3] The curas were named by the bishops of Santa Cruz, and while their powers would vary over time, they lived and worked in the mission centers until the end of the colony.

Colonel Aymerich and the curas began their tenures as soon as the last Jesuits left Moxos. While the Crown had intended to send curas to all the Jesuit centers, the necessity of finding replacements to staff both the Moxos and Chiquitos missions, some thirty-five sites in all, exceeded the pool of candidates available to Bishop Herboso. Nevertheless the bishop found six curas to accompany the Spanish troops who delivered the order of exile. Aymerich assigned these men to the principal stations of the Mamoré — Loreto, Trinidad, San Javier, San Pedro, Santa Ana, and Exaltación — and consolidated the remaining missions by ordering the abandonment of San Martín, San Simón, and San Borja at the same time. A year later, reinforcements from Santa Cruz increased the number of curas to fourteen and placed at least one cura in all of the remaining savanna centers.[4]

The creation of overlapping jurisdictions and competing responsibilities immediately led to friction between the new Spanish functionaries. Only four months after assuming the governorship, Aymerich wrote to the judges at La Plata that some of the curas were "conspicuous only in the poor examples and inadequate instruction they give to their charges."[5] A succession of governors accused individual curas of abusing Indians in their missions and squandering the economic resources they had inherited from the Jesuit century. The curas countered that their effectiveness was being compromised by outside interference.[6] This rift within the European population of Moxos created an administrative climate very different from that of the Jesuit years. The unified administration of the priests and brothers gave way to fifteen years of unresolved struggle between two Spanish factions, one occupying Trinidad, the other spread across the remaining missions.

The impasse between governors and curas entered another phase with Lázaro de Ribera's arrival as governor in 1791. Ribera, a Spanish-born bureaucrat with American experience in Lima, Chile, and Buenos Aires, arrived at his post imbued with the spirit of reform.[7] His tenure in Moxos was characterized by decisions that developed the area's export products and asserted the interests of the Spanish Crown over those of local Creoles. Although Ribera's governorship took place on the distant frontier of Spanish

America, to be understood it must be placed in the context of the empire-wide revamping of the Spanish bureaucracy in the eighteenth century.

When the Bourbons ascended the Spanish throne in 1700, a period of administrative and economic readjustment and a reassessment of the relationships between the Iberian metropolis and its colonies began. The Bourbon period saw the triumph of mercantilism, with its emphasis on commerce and industry, as an economic philosophy and believed an activist state was the best means of fostering it. The Bourbon period also marked an attempt by a succession of ministries to gain greater revenues from the colonies and to strengthen imperial defense capabilities. These reforms reached their apex in the reign of Charles III (1759–88). The Jesuit expulsion, the creation of the Viceroyalty of Río de la Plata (1776), and the establishment of the intendant system within the new viceroyalty (1782) all occurred during this period.[8]

These events were of direct significance to Moxos. The first removed an important component of mission culture; the second reoriented the area's administrative locus away from Lima and toward Buenos Aires; the third marked a general economic transformation of the mission economies, for even though Moxos never actually became part of an intendancy, its orientation mirrored the movement toward commercialization that characterized the system in general. Moxos became a military governorship in 1777, and similar arrangements were made in Chiquitos, the Guarani missions, and Montevideo. This new form of government recognized Moxos' continuing role in imperial defense against the Portuguese and brought a series of military men to the savanna.

Ribera was remarkably different from his predecessors. Neither a soldier nor an absentee, Ribera's eight-year administration would show him to be one of a new breed of bureaucrats then in ascendancy in the Andes, men who favored energetic planning and active execution of initiatives.[9] Soon after he arrived, the governor began an extended visit to the mission stations. This trip produced a series of statistics, the empirical basis for Ribera's administrative reforms, and a set of orders issued immediately after the governor's return. Ribera discovered that, during the period when their activities were unsupervised, the curas had initiated trade with Santa Cruz merchants, seriously diminishing receipts of the authorized system in which savanna products were exported through a Crown-sponsored marketing system centered in La Plata. One of the governor's first acts was to prohibit this illicit commerce, which he termed "free trade."[10]

Ribera's experience in Moxos, and in all probability his predilections on assuming the governorship, convinced him that significant changes in mission administration were in order. These changes, described in a fifty-seven-point "New Plan," established Ribera's and his successors' authority over the curas through the creation of new administrative positions. Business managers would be responsible to the governors and would live in the mission centers.[11] The New Plan confined the curas' duties to spiritual matters, chiefly maintaining regular worship services. The administrators became the instruments for the wide-ranging economic reforms to be discussed later in this chapter and for making sure that mission production entered royal coffers rather than those of the curas and their relatives.

The New Plan also stressed the importance of the monarchy as a focus in mission life. Portraits of the king and queen were to be displayed in each station and the sovereigns' birthdays observed as major holidays, replete with celebrations and double rations of meat. The governor even composed a secular catechism that unctuously extolled the power and majesty of the sovereigns with dialogue reminiscent of the Jesuits' catechism reproduced in chapter 5:

Question: Who are you?
Answer: I am a loyal vassal of the King of Spain.
Q: Who is the King of Spain?
A: He is a Lord so absolute that he recognizes no greater temporal authority.
Q: And where does the King derive his royal power?
A: From God himself.
Q: Was the King anointed by Christ?
A: Yes, father, as is seen in the Holy Scriptures.[12]

Like many a modern bureaucrat on the fast track, Ribera left much of the implementation of his plans to others. In 1792, only a year after the promulgation of the New Plan, he departed the missions for a position as intendant of Paraguay.[13] It became the work of Ribera's successors to enforce the plan's far-reaching implications for the lives of mission Indians and to establish a new modus vivendi with the curas. Succeeding governors found this anything but easy.

Miguel Zamora y Treviño arrived in the mission capital in 1792 to receive both the standards of office and the blueprint for the New Plan from Ribera. Zamora's governorship was a troubled one. He inherited a system in which both the curas and Indian officials resented the changes Ribera's regime had instituted. The curas missed their accustomed autonomy and had begun to chafe under the observation of administrators living in the stations. They also resented the redirection of mission production to La Plata and enforcement of strictures against commerce outside the Crown network. The Indians accused Zamora of a failure to observe *costumbres,* that is, the traditions of mission culture; they charged the administrators with such offenses as administering justice independent of local cabildos and forcing members of the Familia to work in the fields.[14] Zamora responded in kind, refusing to admonish his administrators and accusing his European detractors of engaging in extensive smuggling and exploiting Indian labor for personal gain. Ironically, all sides used the rhetoric of Indian mistreatment to justify their positions.

After years of trading insults with the governor in person and before the judges of Charcas, the curas boldly excommunicated Zamora in 1801 and encouraged the Indians to take action against the apostate. Zamora initially protested the curas' actions, but when faced with active Indian opposition, he decided to withdraw from the missions. At this point Juan Marasa, the cacique of San Pedro, seized the initiative by removing the governor's personal baggage, all fifty chests of it, to the San Javier mission and ordering Zamora to Santa Cruz. So ended what contemporary documents called the "tyrannical government of Don Miguel Zamora."[15]

These events demonstrated the power of the native leadership and their support by the mission population. Although the governor's excommunication furnished an immediate impetus, Marasa's forceful action and Zamora's capitulation reflect the caciques' power in the post-Jesuit missions. In fact, the failure of the curas and administrators to prove themselves worthy successors to the Jesuits diminished the power of European leadership in the missions, concomitantly enhancing the power of native leadership.

The governor's forced departure began a period of instability in the missions. Once aroused to take action against the governor, the Indians aired their grievances on a large scale. Most of the native hostility was directed at symbols of the New Plan. Spanish sources reported that Indians in the Mamoré stations sacked government storehouses and illicitly sold cacao, cotton, and other products on the Santa Cruz market.[16] Administrators became the special targets of the insurgents. Juan José Benites, the administrator of Exaltación, wrote of his harrowing experiences in this mission where Indians had threatened to kill him. As late as 1802 he was forced to live with the curas "to whom, after God, I owe my life for having rescued me from these hostile Indians."[17]

Another series of uprisings greeted Zamora's successor, Antonio Alvarez de Sotomayor. In 1804 Alvarez tried to restore order by jailing Pedro Ignacio Muiba, cacique of San Javier and one of the ringleaders of the 1801 disturbance. This ill-advised action caused an armed insurrection in Muiba's mission and a general abrogation of European authority in Loreto, Trinidad, San Pedro, and Exaltación. As had happened three years before, the Indians, under cacique Marasa's leadership, moved to prevent the governor from shipping his baggage out of the missions. Alvarez apparently weathered this crisis, but he continued his governorship on a much less confrontational plane until he departed in 1805.

The 1804 uprising appeared particularly ominous to Spanish observers. Reports penned by administrators in the area stressed the united opposition of the Indians, accusing Marasa of actively encouraging other caciques to follow his lead. The administrators were also disturbed by the Indians' behavior, claiming that they had ceased their work on mission-oriented activities and begun a series of drinking bouts, a preliminary to rebellion in the native tradition. Particularly worrisome to Crown functionaries was the account given to the Audiencia of Charcas by Andrés Urquieta, who was met by the cacique Estanislao Tilici on his arrival in Loreto. Rather than offering the traditional greetings, Tilici demanded to know why the Spaniard had come to his mission. When Urquieta answered that he was the new administrator in service to the governor, Tilici replied acerbically, "What governor? The cacique Juan Maraza [*sic*] is governor in Moxos."[18] This outburst was to earn Tilici a period of exile from his mission, but the message behind the cacique's assertion was a clear protest against the royal government in Moxos at a time when such protests were being voiced throughout the Indies.

Spanish officials proved unable to maintain their authority in this distant corner of the empire. Viceroys in Buenos Aires lived at too great a remove to influence events in Moxos significantly, and from the beginning of the nineteenth century, the Audiencia of Charcas was paralyzed by serious divisions of personality and politics. As Miguel Zamora fled the savanna in 1801, members of the court were embroiled in a struggle with the intendant of Cochabamba over his charges of sedition against the bishop of Santa Cruz. The judges were likewise at odds when the mission Indians rose against Governor Alvarez in 1804, in this instance debating the powers of the president of the Audiencia.[19]

The remainder of Moxos' colonial history continued the now well-established patterns: the Spanish officials attempted to establish a regime based on the points of the New Plan, and the Indians resisted all such actions. Pedro Pablo de Urquijo, who followed Alvarez as governor, took a hard line in enforcing the laws. He was ultimately met with armed resistance and took shelter in the royal warehouse at Trinidad in 1811. Again Juan Marasa played a leading role in events, this time allowing the governor to depart after lifting the siege at Trinidad and killing one of its leaders, Pedro Ignacio Muiba of San Javier.[20] With Urquijo's departure, the missions entered a period reminiscent of the years between Aymerich's death and Ribera's appointment. A series of interim governors served brief stints to little effect. Then, in the midst of his struggle against a patriot challenge to Spanish rule in South America, the viceroy in Lima appointed a new governor to Moxos, charged with returning order to the missions.

Rather than restoring order, however, Francisco Javier Velasco's governorship (1819–22) heightened the level of conflict in Moxos. Velasco, a colonel in the royalist army, sought to assert imperial prerogatives by directly challenging the caciques. Three years after he arrived on the savanna, Velasco confronted Juan Marasa, whose influence had been crucial since Governor Zamora's expulsion two decades before. Frustrated by the cacique's refusal to implement his orders, Velasco demanded Marasa's staff of office. When he was refused, Velasco shot the cacique dead in San Pedro, Marasa's home mission. The results were predictable and swift. The San Pedro Indians rose, forcing the governor and the curas into the royal storehouse. All were immolated when the insurgents set fire to the building, igniting the tallow supplies guarded there. With the governor's death, the San Pedro rebels sent envoys to other missions, encouraging a general uprising that effectively cut the missions off from the rest of the viceroyalty for a two-year period.[21] This uprising was put down only by the dispatch of a Spanish army from Santa Cruz in 1824, less than a year before the end of Spanish rule in South America.

ECONOMIC REDIRECTION

The departure of the Jesuits marked an opening of the missions' economies to secular penetration. Commercial relationships with the colonial core grew during the Jesuit century, but they were confined and mediated to the missions' advantage. After 1767, the missions felt greater pressure to produce for a market economy, to support themselves, and to turn a profit for the royal treasury. Economic demands reoriented mission economics toward export at the expense of local prosperity. Thus, despite the Jesuits' vaunted commercial emphasis, it was the Bourbon period that turned the missions toward a real market focus.

Jesuit exile renewed dreams of El Dorado in Moxos. The tangible attributes of mission culture presented an attractive target to those who had been excluded from the region by a century of Jesuit strictures. In the priests' places came two groups of Spaniards. The first had their roots in Santa Cruz, a city that had never totally relinquished its vision of the Gran Moxo. These men, tantalized by the reality of the missions' wealth and by fantasies born of their intermittent visits, imagined themselves the heirs to Jesuit treasure. They quickly volunteered for the newly created cura positions.[22] The second group had different origins and different ideas. Its members hailed from the metropolis or from the central Andean highlands and Pacific coast. They came to Moxos as representatives of the royal bureaucracy, charged with integrating the productive capacities of the missions into a wider market. Both groups favored bringing Moxos out of its Jesuit-age isolation, but they disagreed on the means. Cruceños felt that mission resources should be directed toward their city; their city's bishops and the curas living in the stations themselves presented this point of view. The bureaucrats put forward policies designed to increase revenues for imperial purposes. Their proponents occupied the position of governor and, after 1782, of administrator. The struggle between these two camps over Moxos' resources formed a major dynamic in the history of mission culture between 1767 and 1825.

The cruceños' links with the savanna were established many years before 1767. Sources from the Jesuit period contain numerous references to traders from the city who entered the missions — despite the priests' best efforts to exclude them — to barter with the neophytes.[23] After the Jesuit expulsion, cruceño influence in the missions was strengthened through the activities of the curas, many of whom apparently functioned as little more than agents for family commercial activities centered in Santa Cruz. As representatives of the Crown, Moxos governors opposed cruceño penetration of the mission economy and protested the intimate ties between the curas and their kin in the city. In 1778 José Franco, one of the interim governors who followed Antonio Aymerich y Villajuana, accused a nephew of the bishop of Santa Cruz of slaughtering cattle in Loreto at a precipitous rate for quick profits in tallow.[24] Ten years later, Governor Ribera informed the judges at La Plata that most of the curas who served in the Baures stations were sons of Santa Cruz and accused them of carrying on clandestine commerce with kinsmen who visited the missions.[25]

An examination of the activities of one cruceño who first came to Moxos as a member of Juan de Pestaña's expedition against the Portuguese shows that Ribera's accusation was not without merit. In 1767 Captain Lorenzo Chávez appears in the Concepción mission ledger for a debit of 850 pesos on the purchase of 27 hammocks and 200 varas of cotton cloth.[26] Eighteen years later, Chávez's name appears again, this time in a petition to the Audiencia asking that he be banned from Moxos. At this time Governor Ribera gives evidence that Chávez had maintained and expanded his initial contacts in the Baures region, regularly delivering trade goods and currency in exchange for cotton and cacao. Prominently mentioned in the indictment was Chávez's son, José Lorenzo, who served as a cura in the missions in the 1780s.[27]

During the entire Spanish period, this commercial orientation was typical of the curas' roles, for, despite their titles, these men were seldom motivated by spiritual concerns. For example, consider the first six curas who helped to usher out the Jesuits. Only one of these men, the Dominican Antonio de Peñalosa, was an ordained priest. The others were either seminarians, incomplete in their spiritual preparation, or laymen. Of the fifty-five men who served in the missions between 1767 and 1790, only twenty-two (40 percent) were actually ordained priests.[28] This is, of course, a striking contrast to their Jesuit predecessors and an anomaly for men charged with the spiritual lives of the mission Indians.

Records of the curas' periods of residence on the savanna point to another variation between the post-1767 arrivals and the departed Jesuits. Of the original six, only Friar Peñalosa resided at his original post in 1769. Rapid turnover of the curas and changes in their locations are trends that continue throughout the entire 1767–90 period. Between 1769 and 1773 only two of thirteen missionaries, one of these being Peñalosa, remained at their posts. Between 1773 and 1777 only one name recurs, and complete turnovers occurred in 1777–86 and 1786–90.[29] Compare these short periods of service with the Jesuit service records compiled in chapter 5. As we have seen, the governors accused the curas of entering the savanna intent on making quick profits from mission resources. While the service records do not substantiate the curas' profits, they do lend credence to the quick half of the charge.

More important than the contrast between Jesuit and cura service records, however, are the changes that occurred in mission land tenure, husbandry, and labor utilization after 1767. Here the European officials implemented a series of conscious policies designed to channel savanna resources toward Spanish markets, to turn mission products to cash. Aymerich's inventories, conducted in 1767 and 1768, show that the principal material resources of the missions were livestock, agricultural and pastoral products, and handicrafts. The secular regime saw these products as the basis of a new economic order.

During the early years of post-Jesuit mission history (ca. 1767–84), there were relatively few changes in traditional mission economic activities. Both governors and curas issued a series of optimistic appraisals of mission production, assuring their superiors that breaking the Jesuit monopoly would provide a bonanza for the colony and for the Indians.[30] However, as the governors and curas gained experience in the region, they realized that mission resources would never support their rosy assessments. Aymerich and his interim successors responded by consolidating the number of missions and by trying to direct all production to the royal warehouse in La Plata. The curas attempted to exploit traditional resources, especially cattle herds, for their own benefit and to open the missions to trade with Santa Cruz merchants.

This simple redirection of traditional production ended with the appointment of Lázaro de Ribera as governor in 1784. Ribera arrived in Moxos with what Alcides Parejas has called "a mind-set completely shaped by currents then fashionable in Europe and even having invaded Spain."[31] These "currents" were a belief in the virtues of administrative centralization and specialization and the validity of mercantilistic economic theory. As governor, Ribera attempted to translate his ideas into significant changes in mission operations.

Ribera inherited a system in apparent decline. The number of centers had shrunk from fifteen in 1767 to eleven a decade later, revenues were insufficient to meet expenses, and disagreements with the curas had mired his predecessors in paralyzing quarrels. However, the new governor was undaunted by the past. In fact he saw a potentially prosperous mission system. At the beginning of his tenure, Ribera wrote that tallow, cacao, and

Table 11: Mission Livestock, 1763–1803

Year	Cattle	Horses
1767	48,245	19,645
1773	30,277	11,702
1790	29,462	6,102
1796	50,015	9,091
1803	90,051*	12,666
1812	93,846	16,210

*This 80 percent increase seems unlikely within seven years; however, the sources give no clues as to why the anomaly exists.

Sources: Table 3; "I Autos originales de visitas 1773," ANB, ADM, Mojos 4, ff. 10–47; "Expediente que contiene las noticias de misiones," 1790, ANB, Audiencia de Charcas, Mojos IX, ff. 5v–40v; "Expediente que contiene las noticias de las misiones," 1796, ANB, ADM 14, ff. 153–90; "Razones originales de las misiones," 1803, ANB, ADM 17, ff. 183–253v; and Mojos y Chiquitos, 2 vols. (Lima: Biblioteca Ardina, 1988), 1:270.

cotton would form "the three great pillars upon which to build a prosperous mission edifice."[32]

Tallow, the first "pillar" cited by the governor, was a traditional commercial commodity in Moxos' pastoral economy. In the eighteenth century tallow was an important by-product of the cattle industry. Fat, removed from the carcass and boiled in covered kettles, emerged as a colorless liquid, which, when cooled and congealed, became the principal ingredient of candles and soap. But to erect an edifice on tallow, large numbers of cattle — much larger than those necessary to feed the mission Indians — would have to be slaughtered. Ribera, realizing that the curas' policy of rampant slaughter was foolish, refused to allow tallow production to endanger the stability of the herds. Although tallow remained an important part of mission revenues under the New Plan, the number of livestock actually increased in the years following Ribera's arrival, as shown in table 11.

As he stabilized the size of mission herds, Ribera reorganized mission agriculture. Cacao production and the land given over to its cultivation show a steady increase during the years after 1767. For example, production of both raw and processed cacao in San Pedro increased tenfold between 1772 and 1780. While this is the largest growth recorded, Magdalena and Concepción also show increases in production from 500 to 700 percent.[33] Land planted in cacao shows remarkable growth as well. In the dozen years following 1773, cacao tillage in Concepción increased from 8.34 hectares

Table 12: Selected Exports Produced in Moxos, 1807–20

Year	Cacao (lbs.)	Cotton Cloth (varas)	Tablecloths	Fine Handkerchiefs
1807	5,200	4,214	61	622
1816	12,100	6,918	18	224
1819	13,175	11,832	21	305
1820	9,100	3,471	58	246

Source: Mojos y Chiquitos, 2 vols. (Lima: Biblioteca Andina, 1988), 1:255–65.

(20.6 acres) to 33.0 hectares (81.5 acres). The largest of these fields covered 8.24 and 6.15 hectares (20.6 and 15.4 acres), great expanses given the small plots characteristic of traditional riverfront cultivation.[34]

While lagging behind cacao, savanna cotton production also increased after 1767. Since most of this fiber left the missions as woven textiles, yields are impossible to gauge from surviving records. However, land devoted to cotton crops, such as that at Concepción, increased: from 22.8 hectares (56.3 acres) to 40.93 hectares (101.1 acres) between 1786 and 1790.[35] Moreover, records of textiles shipped from the missions in the 1780s and 1790s suggest that a thriving cottage industry had developed to produce for highland markets. Production of *paños,* rectangular pieces of cloth one vara wide by 40 varas long, rose 30 percent between 1781 and 1786, and the production of the Magdalena mission in 1787 included: 600 paños, 300 pairs of undergarments, 125 tablecloths, 50 varas of cotton yard goods, 18 arrobas of spun cotton thread, and 20 arrobas of cleaned cotton.[36] The visita of 1790 shows that all eleven stations had weaving rooms, each with two to eight looms. Finished goods destined for export in 1790 varied from the small inventory of a pair of curtains at the Reyes storeroom to the 1026¾ varas of yard goods, 78 tablecloths with 1,116 napkins, two dozen pairs of cotton gloves, and 40 varas of fine broadcloth held at Concepción.[37] Records from the early nineteenth century show continued high levels of agricultural and cloth production, as summarized in Table 12.

The governor's actions also showed a flair for innovation. To rationalize mission livestock production, Lázaro de Ribera introduced more intensive patterns of animal husbandry, concentrating the animals into larger herds and employing larger numbers of Indian cowboys to manage them. He also tried to reduce the local use of tallow by encouraging the substitution of a lamp oil made from mocatu palm fruit.[38] Perhaps most imaginatively,

Ribera worked to lower the cost of cacao production through improved processing and transportation techniques. To cut spoilage in a tropical climate, the governor ordered a reduction in the time the cacao pods were dried before shipping, and he designed a watertight rawhide chest, which facilitated haulage by mule train and canoe. Then, rather than taking higher profits by maintaining prices, the governor lowered the price charged to buyers in an attempt to enlarge the total demand for the product. As a result of these innovations and the increased acreage devoted to the crop, cacao production rose from some 5,000 pounds per year over the period 1781–86 to 21,922 pounds for the single year 1787.[39]

Ribera and his successors stressed intensification and commercialization of traditional activities rather than the introduction of new ones. The governors were anxious to preserve the economic basis of mission culture, especially the subsistence infrastructure of communal herds and individually tilled food plots. In fact, they intended to capture some of the "private" production by setting up warehouses of European manufactures, which the administrators would use to barter exportable produce.[40] The governors also encouraged the continuance of skilled craft production. Employing the techniques and styles of the Jesuit period, mission artists produced large quantities of high-quality handicrafts, such as the painted crucifixion scene preserved on the 90-square-foot lenten curtain shown in plate 9 and the chest (*bargueño*) pictured in plates 10 and 11, identified by its place and date of fabrication on the back. To illustrate the progress of the missions under his governorship, Ribera prepared an accounting of the products exported from the missions in 1791–92. The list itemizes thirty-six separate commodities, including cacao, wax, coffee, tamarinds, sugar, sassafras, incense, balsam, cotton cloth, hats, sheets, gloves, cots, trunks, writing desks, luggage, pillows, leather gloves and boots, mats, combs, and cigarettes.[41] The number of exports rose to the extent that by 1794 mission products resold through the central warehouse in Chuquisaca comprised the majority of that province's sales to the Potosí mines.[42]

In the short term, Ribera's reforms had the desired effect. Refocused in their commercial orientation and redirected by resident administrators who insured the Crown's interests, the missions began to turn a profit. After requiring a decade of subsidies to support their operations, capped by a 480,000-real (60,000-peso) payment in 1778, the missions reported a 520,000-real (65,000-peso) surplus for the last three years of Ribera's governorship.[43] However, these sums came largely from replacing food crops and using ever-increasing amounts of Indian labor. The implementation of

Plate 9. Lenten Curtain from Spanish Period. Note the contrast between the images of two Jesuits attending to Christ and the secular Spanish figure on the lower right, adorned with devil's horns and spurs. Courtesy of Menil Collection, Houston, Texas.

Plate 10. Bargueño from Mission Concepción, 1790. Courtesy of Museo Nacional de Arte, La Paz.

DEL. PUEBLO. DELA.
CONCEPCION DEBAURES
AÑO DE 179o.

Plate 11. Verso of Bargueño from Mission Concepción, 1790. Inscription shows provenance and date of fabrication. Courtesy of Museo Nacional de Arte, La Paz.

the New Plan eroded the basis of mission culture, a reality quite evident to the native population. The unrest that followed the promulgation of Ribera's reforms demonstrates that the native population understood their effects.

Despite uncertainty as to the reasons why the curas came to the missions, the neophytes initially did not oppose their entry. One source claims that the Jesuits smoothed the transition of European mentors by giving the Indians detailed instructions on how to receive their replacements and preparing manuals on mission practices then in use.[44] While such documents would have proved quite useful to the curas, they were unnecessary for the Indians, whose knowledge of mission practices was part and parcel of their resilient culture.

This resilience appears most fundamentally in demographic trends. Observers of the Jesuit missions have long cited a declining population as characteristic of the post-1767 period. Governor Ribera calculated the mission population at twenty thousand in 1788 and claimed that this figure represented a ten thousand-Indian loss since 1767. While casting doubt on the exactness of the governor's statistics, Parejas accepts his assessment of sharp decline.[45] Despite traditional assertions of population loss, primary sources point to a remarkable stability in the size of mission populations during the Spanish period. Table 13, compiled from the counts made during periodic visitas to the stations, shows that the number of mission Indians in Moxos actually *increased* during the period of Spanish rule, at one point registering a population that was 17 percent larger than that left by the Jesuits.

Lying behind these population gains is a reversal of some of the trends defined in chapter 4. Table 8 shows that mission family sizes in the Jesuit century were below the level of population maintenance. Statistics from the Spanish period show a different pattern, one in which family sizes had increased significantly. The populations of the last third of the eighteenth century show significant increases in family sizes, over one-third if we compare the statistics of 1720–64 with those of 1773–1803. Extant documents give no explicit textual clues as to whether this difference represents an increased birthrate or a higher survival rate for babies born to mission couples. But an increase in the number of female children in these censuses,

Table 13: Mission Populations, 1767–1816

Year	Number of Missions	Population
1767	15	18,535
1773	13	17,191
1779	11	18,313
1788	11	20,000
1790–91	11	19,656
1796–97	11	20,502
1802–3	13	24,417
1810	12	23,026
1816	12	21,824

Source: Appendix.

ranging from 46.9 percent of the children enumerated in 1773 to 50.2 percent in 1790, suggests the onset of a higher birthrate resulting from an increasing childbearing cohort.

This population increase took place in what appears to be a period of "normal" demographic events. The Spanish period had its share of natural disasters and epidemic disease. Catastrophic floods occurred in 1773 and 1800, the former forcing the consolidation of San Javier with Trinidad and the latter contributing to the general uprising of the next year. Cool weather during the period 1792–95 diminished the harvest of cotton and food crops. Smallpox struck San Borja in 1798, and Ribera reported that malaria and dropsy were endemic in the missions. Nevertheless, the governor was impressed by the "general good health and physical fortitude of the native people."[46]

In fact, the population increase took place in a period when physical abuse and economic opportunity encouraged migration of mission Indians. One form of migration, usually in response to abuse, was sudden flight. Governor Aymerich wrote to the judges of Charcas that "in July of the past year of sixty-nine [1769] I was in route to San Pedro when I came upon some Canisiana people leaving the town and when I asked them their reasons, they responded 'because of their cura' . . . and they also told me that Itonomas had arrived in San Pedro carrying some chests that their cura intended to steal."[47] The themes of this letter are typical and recurring. Twenty years later Ribera cited flight as the principal cause for his assessment of a decreasing mission population. Spanish bureaucrats saw neo-

Table 14: Mission Family Sizes, 1773–1803

Year	Married Couples	Children	Children/ Couple
1773	4,560	8,536	1.8
1779	5,316	10,646	2.0
1786	2,724*	6,036	2.2
1790	4,250	9,648	2.3
1796	4,148	8,229	2.0
1803	5,735	10,174	1.8
1810	4,260	8,815	2.1

*Incomplete census, only four missions reported
Source: Appendix.

phytes deserting the mission in every possible direction — into the open grasslands, across the Guaporé into Brazil, into the sub-Andean forest — anywhere to escape the harsh rule of the curas.[48] While the governors accurately identified the flight itself, they misinterpreted its direction.

Mission culture, with its emphases on a settled life-style, surplus agriculture, and European production, made flight into the forest or grasslands unthinkable for the Indians. A more likely destination for those mission Indians who actually left Moxos were European settlements. Brazil offered an accessible escape, especially for Indians of the northern savanna. Evidence of the extent and direction of Brazil-destined flight comes from the scientific expedition to Amazonia made by Alexandre Rodrigues Ferreira (1783–92). When the expedition team reached the Guaporé, they found a group of mission Indian refugees, some who had come from as far away as Santa Ana, living in Brazil.[49] Ribera himself cites the case of a man named Esteban, majordomo of the weavers at Magdalena, who moved his family and fifteen others to Principe da Beira.[50] Such evidence suggests what students of the Paraguayan missions have demonstrated with more copious documentation, that skilled neophytes, such as Esteban, abandoned the missions and entered European settlements where they could ply their trades.[51]

There is also ample evidence of Indian migration to Spanish centers. By the 1780s there were savanna people living in Santa Cruz as agents of cruceño traders and as laborers on their haciendas. Governor Ribera reported his discovery of three groups of Indians from Exaltación working in

Santa Cruz for the merchants Antonio Mercado and Francisco Sándoval. A decade later, at least a small contingent of savanna neophytes lived in La Plata as well.[52] José Sivapaire, cacique of Loreto, spoke of the direction and the effect of this migration in his untutored Spanish: "many always going to this Chuquisaca, and few coming back."[53]

Taken as a whole, these demographic events support the conclusion first put forward in chapter 4, that somewhere in the middle of the eighteenth century, the aboriginal population of Moxos reached its nadir and began its gradual recovery. In the Jesuit century, the Indians reached an accommodation with the biological impact of European contact. The Spanish period marks the onset of the stable populations that characterized the remaining years of mission culture.

Basic sociopolitical patterns also demonstrate the resilience of mission culture in the Spanish period. By the 1790s the two-tiered structure of Familia and Pueblo had become so much a part of mission life that the Spanish administrators described it as a matter of fact. Governor Zamora wrote of the Familia as a "nobility" and contrasted it with the Pueblo or "plebeians" of San Pedro, each of which comprised roughly half the mission in 1792.[54] Indian leadership also remained intact at the top of mission society. The offices of cacique, lieutenant, and the cabildo positions appear in major documents of the period, including the visitas of the late eighteenth and early nineteenth centuries cited in table 13. In fact, the political leaders seem to have solidified their positions under the new regime. The recurrence of surnames among cabildo officeholders suggests the same sort of family alliances delineated for Reyes in 1773.[55] The powers of the caciques and their lieutenants were strengthened in various ways. Many accentuated their status by wearing Spanish dress. Accounts of the 1790s tell of Indian leaders and their dependents accoutred in silks and brocades, even affecting a military bearing with swords and medals. The same sources point to the cost of such ostentation, apparently supported with mission funds. And documents show that this status reached beyond the cosmetic. In San Pedro caciques had gained the right to succession by their sons. These heirs apparent prepared for their positions by receiving instruction in Spanish letters, sometimes traveling to La Plata for schooling.[56]

It was this political leadership that most prominently defended the substance of mission culture against challenges of the Spanish period. Strategies varied with time and circumstance, but the result was unflagging opposition to attempted inroads.

The post-Jesuit era began with the missions at a low ebb. The effects of mission support for the Portuguese war and the epidemics of the 1760s left the neophytes reduced in numbers and the community stores depleted. The loss of support from Jesuit corporate coffers would soon take an additional toll. Thus there was little margin for absorbing the shocks occasioned by the changes ordered by the curas and administrators. Protest began immediately and continued throughout this last half century of the colony.

Petitioning authorities emerged as the paramount strategy. The Indians became adept at exploiting the widening gap between the governors and the curas by appealing to one side for redress against the other. Until the 1790s, this normally meant petitioning the governor to rein in the curas, such as in the 1786 complaint against several curas who had transgressed mission "custom" by administering the lash without consulting the Indian cabildo.[57] In 1769 a scuffle between the cura of Exaltación, Cayetano Tudela, and three neophytes showed the Indians' skill at using the Spanish system of petition to thwart attacks on mission culture. Two sets of testimony, resulting from the governor's investigation, dispute the causes of the altercation. The first, given by the three Indians directly involved, stresses Tudela's violent temper and harsh punishments, which alienated the Indian community and eventually led to open resistance by the witnesses. A second version, taken from native witnesses to the struggle, focuses on the Indians involved, suggesting that they were spoiling for a fight.[58]

While the two accounts dispute guilt and innocence, they agree on the immediate background to the altercation. Tudela had a long-running disagreement with Carlos Ambasi over the ownership of two horses. Ambasi took advantage of Governor Aymerich's visit to Santa Ana to state his side of the case in a letter. This document makes clear a view of custom based on the traditions of the Jesuit era. Ambasi wrote of his great desire to see the governor and to tell him "how in the days of the *padres* [the Jesuits] all the Indians had their own mounts" and now Tudela was claiming that the entire mission remuda belonged to him.[59] Both versions of the quarrel also point to tensions between Tudela and the elite segment of the Indian population. All three of the Indians involved were members of the Familia—two were musicians, the third a carpenter. All spoke Castilian, and at least one, Ambasi, wrote in a clear hand.

The Indians successfully presented their case before the governor. Aymerich supported the Indians' contentions against the cura. He ordered Tudela to turn over the horses and refused to hear the cura's petition to exile

Ambasi and his allies. From the early days of the Spanish period in Moxos, native elites challenged attempts to change the bases of mission culture, and they often succeeded.

Protests intensified under the regimen of Ribera's New Plan, largely over its commercial intensification. Reports from the neophytes show how the demand for export crops strained mission resources. By 1790 cotton and cacao covered many fields in which manioc and maize once grew. The San Pedro Indians complained that they were forced to travel great distances to find gardens not devoted to cotton or cacao.[60] In Trinidad an Indian official testified that in his mission, only small, privately cultivated plots remained planted in food crops and that labor demands for exports reduced to one day a week the time available to work this land. The same official went on to describe the result of such policies in Loreto, where children combed the grasslands for roots and wild fruit to supplement meager stores of manioc and maize. Again the Indians gained a measure of redress as Ribera promised to allow them more food crop land.[61]

Not all protest was directed against Europeans. Events of the Spanish period sometimes pitted Indian groups against each other for control of local resources. Consolidation and division of traditional mission Indian populations were features of the Spanish period. Mission records show San Javier joined with Trinidad (1774), a contingent of fifty Moxo from Loreto forming an exemplary corps for a mission among the Yuracaré (1779), the abandonment of San Borja and its relocation at San Ignacio (1793), the movement of San Joaquín's population to Concepción (1794), and the division of Magdalena into two stations (1797). These actions mixed the separate linguistic groups that had maintained their autonomy in the Jesuit century. Documents from the 1770s and 1780s show Mure from San Simón in Loreto, Kayubaba from San Borja in San Ignacio, and Mobima from Magdalena in Trinidad.[62]

As traditional boundaries blurred, the more aggressive of the Indian groups moved onto lands claimed by other peoples. In 1773 the Indians of Santa Ana related that Canisiana from San Pedro had occupied two of their cacao fields. Governor Aymerich responded to the complaint by ordering the Canisiana to leave the fields while offering them gifts of wool and sugar as incentives.[63] Ten years later, with the disappearance of San Javier, the Canisiana moved into an area called Tamucu to cultivate fields claimed by the San Javier refugees. Realizing the futility of trying to reverse this land grab, Governor Ribera ordered the usurpers to compensate Tamucu's former owners with five hundred head of cattle.[64] The juxtaposition of traditional rivals also produced violence as ancient resentments boiled over. Governor Zamora, in a set of ordinances sent to all administrators in 1793, enjoined them to prevent the mistreatment of Indians who had recently changed stations. He specifically named Itonamas and borxanos (i.e. people from San Borja) as having been abused in the past.[65]

The open rebellions of the nineteenth century were, in a sense, the climax to three decades of stress. Spanish sources of the period explain the rebellions in terms of a deterioration of Indian living conditions. Writing from his perspective as the intendant of Cochabamba, Francisco de Viedma protested:

> The miserable Moxos y Chiquitos [Indians] are neither free nor able to reap the benefits of their labors. All their valuable manufactures are taken over by the administrators who underestimate their value, and for their work they receive only the rags which cover their bones; the same applies to their sustenance, with the exception of manioc and wild fruits, that are grown in those fertile lands; their other agricultural products, such as cacao, coffee, sugar and, more importantly, wax, which they produce with so much work, fatigue and even death, they are obliged to turn over to the administrators, because if they do not, they are punished.[66]

A part of this commentary was no doubt bound up in internecine bureaucratic warfare. Viedma had also suggested to Viceroy Nicolás de Arredondo that Moxos become part of his proposed new intendancy. But the kernel of the intendant's critique, an economic system that siphoned off savanna resources, cannot be explained away.

The Indian perspective sheds a different light on the causes of the rebellions. The native people appear less concerned with the increased intensity of exports and more concerned with the diminished intensity of imports to the missions. Spanish rule replaced an economic system in which mission production directly benefited the missions with one in which that production largely benefited the state. Returns from the Indians' labor, traditionally expressed in the distribution of European products, diminished after 1767, and both the Spaniards and the Indians knew it. Asked to explain the uprising of 1804, Loreto's administrator responded in the passive voice: "I have heard their [the Indians'] complaints that we give them nothing, and it is constantly true that they have found themselves in a miserable state of support."[67] That is, the governors and curas were giving little back for the labor and products they extracted. By diminishing the flow of European goods to the missions, Spanish administrators directly challenged one of the principal foundations of mission culture, the distribution of European manufactures for Indian labor.

This change in the terms of trade between the mission Indians and their European administrators lay at the heart of the nineteenth-century rebellions. Given the finite resources of the missions, the conflicting expectations of the two groups could not be accommodated during the Spanish period. And given the administrators' increased determination to extract a surplus from the missions after the implementation of Ribera's New Plan, the lines were drawn. Indians took advantage of rivalries between the governors and the curas to show their profound dissatisfaction with the Spanish regime. However, Spanish self-interest and internal divisions among the native people themselves prevented peaceful redress of grievances. When petition failed to produce the desired effect, open defiance resulted. Significantly, native violence vented itself on symbols of the economic restructuring: Indians menaced administrators and governors, expropriated stores of commodities, and destroyed fields filled with export crops.[68]

The Moxos revolts diminished Spanish power in the waning years of the colony. Inadvertently aided by the Wars of Independence, the mission Indians openly resisted threats to the bases of their culture. Skillful use of the Spanish legal system reversed some of the grossest instances of abuse, and force, or the threat of it, effectively paralyzed Spanish government on the savanna for periods of time. But neither petitions nor revolts could bring back the Jesuit century. The mission Indians could not revive a mission system independent of the economic and political influence of Santa Cruz and the Andean highlands.

VII MOXOS TO BENI: THE DISSOLUTION OF MISSION CULTURE

At the time the Bolivian Republic was created in 1825, mission culture existed as a vital force on the savanna. The people lived in their Jesuit-era settlements. Local political leaders held sway, as did traditional social patterns. And even though economic life showed the effects of a half-century of Bourbon rule with its emphasis on commercial production, communal patterns of landholding and livestock ownership remained in force. The first fifty years of Republican government would severely challenge all aspects of the status quo.

During this period, Moxos endured changes brought about by political and economic forces introduced from outside. The leaders of Republican Moxos, imbued with the liberal political and economic spirit of the age, saw Indian tradition — with its corporate approaches to property — as antithetical to development. They moved against it through national policy, encouraging white immigrants to come to the savanna and providing them with a legal basis for their alienation of community lands and animals.

The republic also encouraged the development of commerce and industry on the savanna for its own benefit. Enlarging the precedents set by their Bourbon predecessors, Bolivian bureaucrats and entrepreneurs expanded export agriculture and directed native labor power to cottage industry. However, it was the international economy that most deeply affected the foundations of mission culture.

An upsurge in the world's demand for tropical products pulled Moxos into the ambit of international capitalism in the middle of the nineteenth century. In the 1840s and 1850s, Indians living on the western savanna mobilized to supply cinchona bark for an emerging world pharmaceutical industry. And in the next decade, a voracious demand for latex gathered from the Amazonian rubber tree, *Hevea brasiliensis,* began to attract Moxos men for exploration of the Madeira River forest and for tapping and hauling of raw rubber.

This combination of state policy and capitalist economics altered all phases of life in the Moxos settlements. Republican legislation encouraged white immigration, and provided those immigrants with opportunities to exploit the native communities. The powerful attractions of the world economy proved even more disruptive. For as Indian men departed the savanna for the sub-Andean forest and middle Amazon, they left women and children behind to maintain mission culture.

Administration

Because Moxos remained isolated from the major theaters of the independence wars, its people were only tangentially affected by the sixteen years of armed struggle between patriot and royalist armies. Patriot guerrilla activity in the territory located between the savanna and Chuquisaca disrupted the Bourbon-instituted tribute system and likely resulted in a short-term refocusing of economic activity toward subsistence production. However, the final defeat of royalist forces in 1825 helped to intensify late colonial attempts to integrate the economy and people of Moxos into the newly declared Bolivian nation.

The evolution of early Republican politics profoundly affected the native people of Moxos. Bolivian leaders were determined to remedy what they regarded as shortcomings of the colonial years, among them the exploitation of Indians. However, economic realities forced them to adopt measures that preserved the essence of colonial policy. Bolivia's first president, Antonio José de Sucre, favored the promulgation of Simón Bolívar's abolition of Indian tribute in Peru and a fundamental reform of the relationships between the republic's aboriginal and European peoples. In fact, the constitution that brought the new republic into being specifically abolished hereditary privilege (article 149) and decreed uniform tax schedules (article 148).[1] Sucre proposed that the tribute tax, which had affected only the Indian communities, be abolished; to replace it he advocated what he called the *contribución directa* — a combination of a head tax paid by the entire population, ad valorem taxes on urban and rural property, and a tax on salaries—to support the national government.[2] Thus a tension was created between Bolivian statute and its case law: the latter upheld the colonial system of Indian communities and tribute that the former had challenged directly. While this tension played itself out principally in the highlands, tribute in the form of *temporalidades*, the colonial system of state-directed craft and agricultural labor, was perpetuated in Moxos for thirty years after independence.

The administrative history of Republican Moxos also preserves the traditional struggle between Santa Cruz and central authorities for the area's resources, and introduces a new legal framework that embodied nineteenth-century liberal concepts of property and government. The Bolivian Republic inherited the colonial jurisdiction of Charcas when it was created in 1825. Even though the exact boundaries of the new state would be in flux well into the twentieth century, Moxos became firmly fixed as its northeastern frontier. The Republican state initially established itself in Moxos by assigning it provincial status in the Santa Cruz Department and by preserving the secular administrator/sacred cura duality of the late colonial years. This emphasis on continuity in early Republican Moxos also appears in the retention of many of those who had held European offices during the colonial period. For while Sucre favored placing patriots in office throughout Bolivia, and established committees in each department (*juntas de notables*) empowered to identify supporters of the regime, his intentions were often frustrated by a dearth of qualified candidates.[3] For instance, Moxos' delegate to Bolivia's Constituent Assembly was a cura, Felipe Santiago Cortes, who had been a functionary in Trinidad since the 1811 uprising against Governor Urquijo.[4]

This administrative arrangement marked another phase in the historical struggle for Moxos between Santa Cruz and central authorities. As in the post-Jesuit years of the colony, the bishop of Santa Cruz continued to name curas for service in the "towns," now the preferred term for the savanna settlements. And with the overthrow of the colonial monopoly system, cruceños were free to enter the towns to trade with the native people. Merchants from the city immediately began to ply the river courses to traffic in cacao and cotton, supplying the traditional tools and trinkets that the native people had come to see as necessities. Apparently, at least a few cruceños established a more permanent economic presence by acquiring cattle herds in the 1820s and 1830s.[5] However, as in the colonial years, charges of abuse of the native people by those who viewed Moxos as an economic dependency of Santa Cruz produced a flood of protest and eventually a new administrative configuration.

On the seventeenth anniversary of Bolivian independence, August 6, 1842, President José Ballivián removed Moxos' administrative dependency on Santa Cruz by combining it with the area of Caupolicán in the Andean rain forest to form the new Beni Department. The presidential decree, a classic statement of liberal political ideology, justified changing the status quo ante on the basis of five considerations:

1. That the mission towns for the Mojos province find themselves reduced to a deplorable state of slavery, oppression, and misery, reaching extreme of demands, even upon the female population, for labor and services that cannot be carried out;

2. That the precious guarantees in favor of Bolivian citizens made in the several constitutions and laws of the Republic have not been observed among the poor inhabitants of these vast regions;

3. That the abundant resources that can establish the prosperity and richness of that province, and make it redound upon the rest of the Republic, find themselves obstructed by a very pernicious system of pauperizing and destructive colonialism which has been established;

4. That the governmental regimen to which the unhappy Indians of that province have been subjected is against the natural order, the enlightenment, the constitutional principles proclaimed by the Republic, and cannot continue without opprobrium on the government that authorizes it;

5. That it is the obligation of the government to secure the increase of the Republic's wealth, an object unobtainable without property, commerce and the other forms of industry.[6]

This lofty preamble led to a much more pragmatic set of articles establishing the Beni Department, extending all rights of citizenship to its inhabitants, and liberating women from forced personal service and any form of taxation. Most important to the welfare of the Moxos peoples were those articles dealing with the forms of property that the Republican state would recognize. Article 3 propounded individual property rights and extended them to all lands and housing sites in the region. Article 4 established a two-peso annual tax on all landholdings covered under article 3. Article 6 decreed that immigrants to the region could claim lands under the same stipulations as the native people. Article 7 ordered the sale of all public buildings except for the storehouses, employee quarters, and workshops.[7] These decrees directly contradicted the communal patterns of ownership that were part and parcel of mission culture. By favoring private over communal ownership and by instituting a system of tax payments as the basis for landholdings, Ballivián's decrees undermined the Indian conception of property rights. At the same time they opened Moxos to domination by those able to take advantage of new legal structures.

The August 6 decrees had set a precedent; further legislation would expand it. By the 1850s Bolivian leaders had expanded their definition of private property to include the privatization of cane fields and cacao groves in exchange for the payment of annual taxes. Finally, in 1856, the state ordered San Ignacio, Exaltación, San Joaquín, San Ramón, Magdalena, and Baures to sell off what were presumably the last of the Jesuit-age communal gardens. These sales, made in the name of developing the Beni, opened lands off the Mamoré core to immigrants and became the bases for their expansion in these areas later in the century.[8]

White Immigration

Also in the name of development, early Republican regimes instituted policies designed to increase Bolivia's population. Concerned with a perceived imbalance between the nation's population and its territorial extension, especially in the tropics, Bolivian officials sponsored a series of initiatives designed to boost native reproductive rates and attract immigration. As early as 1836 the government was on record as promoting an increased population for Moxos. In a series of instructions issued from Chuquisaca, the Santa Cruz administration offered tangible incentives, in the form of livestock, for the celebration of marriages. The bounty was open to both natives and immigrants who would establish legitimate unions in Moxos.[9]

While this legislation did not bring about the desired large-scale population redistribution, government policies and the opening of Moxos' economy to greater European participation after 1825 produced the first substantial white immigration to the savanna. Spanish surnames begin to appear on documents referring to the residents of the Moxos towns in the 1830s and 1840s. Passports issued by the Beni prefects after 1842 show whites residing on the savanna and traveling to Santa Cruz and the highlands, and a tally of the 1849 presidential election lists thirty Spanish surnames among sixty-eight men casting ballots.[10]

Between 1830 and 1855, the number of white inhabitants in Moxos increased from fifty-seven to 1,191, with the bulk of the migration occurring during the first fifteen years of this period.[11] The largest identifiable component of this immigration appears in the public sector. From 1833 to 1855, the number of government functionaries in the towns grew from twenty-three to ninety-four, shades of a modern bureaucracy.[12] By the end of this period, Moxos held the prefect and his three-member staff, five treasury officials, fifteen *administradores de temporalidades* and twenty-two assistants, sixteen police officers, a *juez de letras* and two assistants, three postal employees, a doctor and vaccinator, and thirteen curas with eleven coadjutors. This count does not include the twenty-five member national guard unit stationed at Trinidad in 1850.[13]

White immigration to Moxos also resulted from the high degree of political strife that characterized nineteenth-century Bolivia. Moxos' isolation from the highland centers fostered its use as a site for internal exile. The policy had become so much a part of the early Republican political scene that a contemporary British observer referred to the savanna as the Bolivian Siberia.[14] By mid-century exiles had reached conspicuous numbers. A visitor to Trinidad in 1852 opined that he had "never beheld such a rough-looking set, the very outcasts of the nation."[15] And this motley crew brought with it something of the fractiousness that afflicted Bolivian national politics in the mid–nineteenth century. Exiles continued their intense partisanship in Moxos, fighting pitched battles with those appointed by their enemies in the national government. Illustrative of this turmoil was Luís Valverde's tenure as prefect of the Beni Department. Between 1850 and 1851 he was forced to abandon his office twice before being killed in a third uprising, all sponsored by partisans of an opposing exile faction.[16]

In addition to fostering internal migration, Bolivia attempted to attract Europeans to its Amazonian territory. Departing from colonial precedent, the republic opened its boundaries to immigrants of all nationalities in 1826, but much to the disappointment of national leaders, this lowering of barriers had no measurable effect on immigration. Taking a more active approach to the issue, President Ballivián promoted European colonization of the Beni. Discussions conducted with the Belgian Colonization Company and the Company of French Guiana reached the point of formal accords, but in each case distance and expense prevented their implementation.[17] As with domestic policy, these attempts at stirring European immigration produced no significant changes in the gross population levels of the Bolivian east. However, a few foreigners did cross the Atlantic to try their luck in the distant interior; their arrival marked the beginning of an era of new economic and social relations in Moxos.

James C. Jones has called attention to the significance of increased white and mestizo immigration to Moxos after 1842, pointing to the escalating demands the immigrants made on savanna resources.[18] Records maintained by the Beni Prefecture show whites moving aggressively to control savanna capital and land. By the 1850s local treasuries had become sources of credit for the commercial ventures of Republican officials and merchants, principally for the purchase of cattle. A long history of nonpayment effectively changed many of these loans to grants.[19] During the next decade, land sales began in the Beni. In a movement corresponding to the great highland land grab fostered by the dictatorship of President Mariano Melgarejo, community lands in Trinidad, Magdalena, and Sécure (San Ignacio) were sold.[20] While the amount of land affected was small (less than 500 hectares changed hands), these transactions began to reach toward the potential promised by the liberal decrees that had established the Beni Department a quarter-century before.

COMMERCE AND INDUSTRY

If the Republican state disagreed with its colonial predecessor over the means for stimulating the economy and the distribution of its wealth, both the new nation and the former mother country favored the same end, increasing productivity. In Moxos, Bolivia inherited an economy commercially oriented by the last years of the colony and resting on an unsteady foundation of craft production and animal husbandry. This traditional productive capacity would decline steadily during succeeding decades, a result of unrealistic expectations, mismanagement, and the onset of world demand for tropical forest resources.

At the time of independence, the economy of Moxos bore the strong stamp of two legacies. The first was a residue of the El Dorado legend. From the vantage point of the highlands, Moxos looked like a land of great promise. One early Republican bureaucrat compiled a series of tables to illustrate the wealth of Loreto in 1829. By estimating the value of the town's assets from herding, textile production, and agriculture, Rursindo Vargas reached a figure of 159,320 pesos and projected a 10 percent annual return, a figure seven times greater than actual revenues in the 1830s.[21] Such optimistic evaluations could affect the appraisals of supposedly more sophisticated European observers as well. In his "Report on Bolivia," composed in 1827, the British commercial attaché Joseph Barclay Pentland singled out Moxos as one of only two areas in the country showing real commercial potential. While Pentland never visited the savanna, he was impressed by the area's cotton textiles and called Moxos a "land of fertile soils and numerous wild herds which would some day make the river networks of great commercial import."[22]

The second legacy came from the Spanish Bourbon economic policy of stressing production for export to the highland centers. Agriculture, Moxos' principal economic activity, concentrated on the cultivation of export crops, principally cacao, sugarcane, and cotton. The primary commercial craft production was weaving; other crafts included leather working, carving, furniture making, and painting. Cattle ranching employed large numbers of Indians, who moved with the herds to fresh and unflooded pastures, provisioned the resident populations, and collected hides and tallow for export. A less numerous but equally essential Indian merchant marine plied the river courses, moving goods and travelers between the savanna towns and toward the major Bolivian population centers.

Republican leaders decided that Moxos' potential could be realized both by expanding upon these legacies and by establishing new initiatives through good administration and careful investment. Bureaucrats assigned to the region were charged with increasing production. A set of instructions issued to Moxos administrators in 1836 expounds the government's desire to have the towns augment their contributions to the national treasury, citing "the notable difference between contemporary revenues and those contributed by the province before independence."[23] The document went on to prescribe such remedies as increasing the planting of export crops and improving the Indians' morale by reducing the use of corporal punishment. Contemporary documents record some success in bringing these reforms to life. One Republican administrator supervised a significant expansion of commercial agriculture in San Ignacio between 1828 and 1831; cotton acreage was doubled; the number of cacao bushes increased from 8,700 to 48,600; and similar changes took place with tamarind trees, banana trees, and coffee plants.[24]

Officials also addressed the transportation bottleneck that long had hampered Moxos' commerce. Determined to establish control over the existing transport infrastructure, departmental prefects established sched-

Table 15: Cattle and Horses in Moxos, 1825–46

Year	Cattle	Horses
1825	82,714	22,614
1830	124,150	25,369
1833	127,979	23,479
1846	129,528	—

Sources: "Estado gral. que demestra la existencia de ganados," Santa Cruz, 18/VIII/1825, ANB, MI 35, f.24; Alcide Dessalines d'Orbigny, *Descripción geográfica, histórica y estadística de Bolivia* (Paris: Librería de los Señores Guide y Compañia, 1845), 354; "Estado de la provincia de Mojos," Chuquisaca, 10/X/1833, ANB, MI 45, f.28; and José María Dalence, *Bosquejo estadístico de Bolivia* (La Paz: n.p., 1975), 244.

ules regulating the fees, crew sizes, and routes of native boats operating from the savanna towns. In addition, national and provincial governments sought alternatives to established traffic patterns. They commissioned expeditions designed to chart viable routes from the highlands to the headwaters of the Beni and Mamoré. In 1846 Prefect Rafael de la Borda fitted out a flotilla to explore the Mamoré-Madeira-Amazon network in search of markets for Moxos manufactures.[25]

Moxos' most durable asset was its livestock. The legendary size of the savanna herds of horses and cattle led the national government to regard these animals as an infinitely renewable resource. To pension veterans of the Wars of Independence, establish colonies in the lowlands, or simply raise cash for the treasury, the national government granted warrants to slaughter "its" cattle. Later in the century, this strategy was used to attract private investment in development projects such as George Earl Church's steam navigation company, which in 1870 gained the right to take eight thousand head of cattle "owned by the state" in the Beni.[26] The government also called upon its administrators in Moxos to furnish animals for a variety of public projects. Official correspondence of the 1820s and 1830s is filled with reports of the dispatch of horses to the army in Cochabamba, of cattle to feed the troops and civilians of Santa Cruz, and of cattle and horses to replenish the herds in Chiquitos.[27] Despite these ill-advised policies, savanna herd populations remained remarkably stable, as shown in table 15.

Reports written after 1846 provide a different picture of the savanna herds. Around 1848, a mysterious disease (one historian calls it *caderas*) attacked both cattle and horses. Writing of the disease in 1852, a North American visitor described its onset: "The animal does not lose his appetite,

Table 16: Cotton Textile Production, 1825–37

Year	Lienzo (varas)	Macana (varas)	Ponchos	Tablecloths
1825	1,046.5	410	124	30
1826	6,274.5	356	183	39
1827	2,922.0	149	629	18
1828	6,592.5	162	678	27
1829	7,709.2	605	240	—
1830	8,685.5	578	582	104
1837	1,094.0	19,828	290	12

Sources: Alcide Dessaunes d'Orbigny, *Descripción geográfica, histórica y estadística de Bolivia* (Paris: Librería de los Señores Guide y Compañia, 1845), 363, and "Demonstracion que se hase del caudal en especies," Trinidad, 28/V/1837, ANB, MI 67, f.29.

but gradually falls away, until his strength is entirely gone, when he lies down and eats the grass around him even to the roots with a most ravenous hunger."[28] While witnesses offer no estimates of the toll this disease took on the savanna herds, it must have been severe. In early 1850, Beni's prefect wrote to the national capital that Loreto, formerly the principal horse breeding center of Moxos, now lacked mounts even for the everyday activities of its citizens.[29]

Commercial agriculture, which occupied large numbers of native workers, generated substantial cash returns. For an idea of the diversity of this activity, consider the following list of products prepared in 1825: raw and processed cacao, tamarinds, beeswax, almond, copaiba and calaba oil, cascarilla, coffee, tobacco, vanilla, and indigo. Provincial accounts show that these products earned the treasuries an average annual return of 28,606 pesos in the six years between 1825 and 1830, with raw cacao providing the bulk of the revenues.[30]

Textile manufacture boomed in the early Bolivian Republic. Produced by native skill and encouraged by the protectionist trade policies of President Andrés de Santa Cruz (1829–38), Moxos textiles reached the levels of production illustrated in table 16.

The finished ponchos and tablecloths were "admired throughout the Republic" for their soft texture and fine decoration.[31] *Lienzo,* literally linen but actually finely woven cotton, and *macana,* a rough cotton fabric, comprise the lion's share of this textile production. These products were exported to the highlands as yard goods. The coarser cloth predominated as Moxos began to produce for the Bolivian mass market in the mid-1830s. This textile boom altered the nature of craft production in Moxos. Heightened demand for cotton cloth required a larger portion of the available labor force and effectively squeezed out other craft specialties. The fall of the Santa Cruz government and the introduction of cheap, imported fabrics in the Bolivian market undercut demand for domestically woven cottons, reducing Moxos' production by more than 50 percent by the end of the 1830s.[32] Bolivian administrators hoped to replace textile exports with other small manufactures. However, Moxos never regained the vibrant diversity of its commercial craft production. The disappointing revenues reported by Bolivian administrators well into the 1840s resulted, in large part, from the warping of productive capacity during a decade of textile boom.[33]

An inventory of the towns, conducted in 1844, shows the extent to which Moxos had altered its Jesuit inheritance.[34] While the churches held much of the plate accumulated during the Jesuit century—San Pedro's tally alone totaled nearly 1,800 pounds—the more perishable stocks of cloth, furniture, and books described in 1767 were gone. In addition, secular buildings rather than churches were now architecturally and organizationally preeminent. By the 1840s the *Casa Nacional* (government house) had overshadowed the church both in size and as the center of economic and political activity. Gone also were the well-stocked work shops—the foundries and carpentries—so prominent at the end of the Jesuit century. The inventory highlights the effects of seventy-five years of export orientation: the Moxos centers no longer resembled the missions of the past; both their orientation and their architecture call to mind a factory.

Traditional economic activity was both augmented and challenged by the demands of a world economy. The scientific and technological activities of the nineteenth century revealed industrial uses for natural products and set in motion extractive activities, which touched Moxos soon after Bolivian independence. The definitive synthesis of cinchona, the vegetable base for quinine, in 1820 touched off a scramble for this product in the mid-nineteenth century. Originally exported principally from the forests of southern Ecuador, several species of cinchona occur naturally in a long, narrow band along the eastern slopes of the Andes, an area one nineteenth-century traveler compared to "a green skirt which clothes these lofty mountains and protects their nakedness from the heavy east winds and beating rains."[35] Research on the chemical properties that made cinchona an effective remedy against tropical fevers revealed that a Bolivian species of the plant, *Cinchona Calisaya,* held the highest concentrations of quinine. Thus, collecting activities were redirected to the forests of Beni and Mamoré drainages, producing a virtual Bolivian monopoly of the cinchona market that would last until 1850.

During the 1840s and early 1850s, Bolivian sales of cinchona boomed, comprising some 10 percent of national income and rivaling silver as the country's chief export, a windfall to hard-pressed treasuries. In this period, collection expanded from the yungas forests near La Paz to the Caupolicán region, which drains into the Beni River of the western savanna.[36] It was during this period that international capitalism first touched Moxos.

In its natural state, cinchona grows interspersed with other trees rather than in large groves, which made for extensive exploitation. Identifying the trees in the rain forest was more time-consuming than collecting the *materia prima.* Transporting the cinchona also proved laborious. Most of the product followed traditional trade routes out of the forest to Cochabamba and La Paz, then went on to Arica for final export. As the boom reached Caupolicán, the need for laborers affected the Moxos towns. When Hughes Algernon Weddell, who became the world's authority on the plant in the nineteenth century, visited Caupolicán in 1853, he discovered that Moxos Indians were involved only peripherally in harvesting and packing cinchona in the forest. The Moxos people participated most actively in cinchona transportation. The western towns of Reyes and Santa Rosa became important bulking centers for dispatch of cinchona to the highlands, and savanna boatmen manned the first leg of the journey upriver to the end of the Beni's navigation.[37]

The boom ended with the depletion of *Cinchona Calisaya* and the emergence of competition from other producers. Quinine occurs in commercially exploitable concentrations only in the bark and small branches of the cinchona tree, an accident of nature that fostered felling the trees as the most efficient way of harvesting them. Bolivian attempts to limit this practice and thus preserve the species led to sporadic prohibitions against collecting bark and the establishment of monopolies with fixed export quotas. However, neither remedy prevented the exhaustion of Bolivian supplies. Colombia's emergence in the South American trade after 1855 signaled the end of the Bolivian domination of the cinchona market, a position further eroded by the beginning of plantation production from British Asia in the 1870s.[38]

Cinchona proved but a prelude to the second movement of international capitalism into Moxos. Knowledge of the properties of resins extracted from *Hevea brasiliensis* and other Amazonian species dates from the eighteenth century in Europe and from antiquity in the native tradition, yet until Charles Goodyear perfected the vulcanization process in 1839, rubber was used most extensively in the manufacture of waterproof garments. With Goodyear's discoveries, the potential uses of rubber expanded dramatically to include tires (bicycle and later automobile) and the belts, hoses, and fasteners that provided traction, lubrication, and cooling to the emerging machine age. As the only source for rubber's raw material, the Amazon became the center of intensifying exploitation in the mid-nineteenth century. Initially centered in Belém do Pará, at the river's mouth, the search for rubber moved rapidly into the South American interior. By 1870 the Madeira, with its heavy concentrations of rubber trees, had become fully integrated into the trade, bringing the boom to Moxos' back door.[39]

Most accounts of rubber production agree that Bolivia entered the trade in 1880, the year Edwin Heath discovered a practical river-borne transportation route along the Beni from Reyes to its confluence with the Mamoré.[40] While 1880 accurately fixes the onset of the boom in Bolivian territory, it overshoots Bolivians' involvement in it by some twenty years. For in a region of notoriously scarce labor, the Moxos towns provided an essential source of acclimated workers for the rubber trade on the Madeira.

Bolivia once claimed Amazonian territory nearly twice the size of that held by the contemporary republic. As late as 1867, the Beni Department included some four hundred kilometers along the west bank of the Madeira, from its headwaters to approximately 7° south latitude. During the 1860s, Bolivians actively participated in opening the Madeira to rubber gathering. But when the national government sold all of its claims above the junction of the Mamoré and Beni rivers (10° 20′ south latitude) to Brazil, Bolivian nationals could no longer claim ownership of the Madeira forests. Some retreated to rubber stands on the lower Mamoré and the middle Beni. However, there is ample evidence that Bolivian entrepreneurs remained actively engaged in gathering and shipping latex from their former claims on the Madeira, and that native people from the Moxos towns provided the principal labor supply for rubber activities on the river.

At the time the March 1867 Treaty of Amity, Limits, Navigation and Commerce was signed with Brazil, Bolivian influence on the Madeira was widespread. Franz Keller, who was commissioned by the Brazilian Empire to explore the river and assess the possibilities for a railroad around its rapids, made his initial contact with Bolivians on the Amazon eight months after the treaty went into effect. In Manaus, Keller and his party arranged for upriver navigation in the flotilla of an Italian merchant and his crew of eighty Moxo and Canisiana Indians. Keller was immediately struck by the appearance of these people who walked the streets of the town in their "singular clothing: straw hats made by themselves, and long shirts without sleeves, of the brown bark of the turury-tree." Keller explained the presence of these distinctive outlanders in economic terms, claiming that the boatmen could earn ten times their Bolivian wage by working these long-distance journeys, and he cites a resultant "endless current of emigration from Bolivia to Brazil, in spite of all the reclamations of the former."[41]

Entering the Madeira, the party discovered its rubber forests largely exhausted until the middle reaches of the river. Here they found Bolivian entrepreneurs and Moxos workers tapping the rubber stands (*barracas*). Near Crato (ca. 7° 30′ south latitude), Keller reported some ten or twelve Bolivian rubber gatherers (*seringueiros*), "each of them working with twenty or thirty Mojos Indians, who will make them rich men in a few years."[42] In the same vicinity, the party visited a place called Tres-Casas, where "Bolivian rubber gatherers and a number of Mojos Indians employed themselves in the extraction of rubber sap."[43]

Subsequent descriptions of the area reveal similar experiences. In 1869 an Italian missionary, Jesualdo Maccheti, covered the then-used route from Reyes to the Madeira — a portage from the Beni to the Yacuma River and down the Yacuma to the Mamoré — with a crew of Moxo and Canisiana boatmen. Just past the last of the Madeira falls, he discovered the camp of a cruceño recorded only as Avelino N. (so cited presumably to protect an international interloper from exact identification). Maccheti reported that the upper Madeira was filled with barracas, most of them Bolivian, and that the work force of the camps consisted entirely of Bolivian, that is, Moxos, Indians.[44]

English accounts from the 1870s document the importance of the Madeira as a continuing focus of Bolivian and Moxos activity in the pre-1880 rubber boom. In 1873 C. Barrington Brown visited the Bolivian consulate at San Antonio on the upper Madeira and reported that Moxos Indians were well distributed in the region. A year later Edward Mathews, traveling upriver toward the Madeira rapids, described passing a steady stream of

Moxo and Baure people on their way to the rubber zones downstream.[45] And, in an ironic twist of history, Henry Wickham, the exporter of Amazonian rubber seeds that eventually sprouted in British Asia, had a Bolivian rival named Ricardo Chávez. Before Wickham's successful "rubber snatch" of 1876, Chávez had unsuccessfully shipped seeds to London from his base at Carapanatuba on the Madeira, where he had established himself with two hundred Moxos Indians.[46]

The actions of Bolivian administrators echo the message of these accounts by addressing the impact of population loss. As early as 1861 Beni prefects had attempted to stem the migrant tide by issuing orders, such as those dictated by José Manuel Suárez, restricting the Indians' ability to leave their towns, change their employers, or enter into a labor contract of longer than three months' duration. Similar regulations addressed the fees, obligations, and activities of Moxos' boatmen. A decade later, the prefect decreed a ten-peso assessment for each native laborer taken to the Madeira rubber fields and expressly prohibited the contracting of Trinidad Indians, claiming that they were needed for public projects then underway at the capital.[47] The prefects apparently had reasons for their decrees, as British travelers repeated local assertions of significant rises in the price of beef in the 1860s and a 30–40 percent wage increase in the first half of the next decade.[48]

Although fragmentary, these accounts clearly document a significant Bolivian participation in the rubber boom before 1880. Cruceño entrepreneurs were involved in the Madeira trade, and it was Moxos' native peoples who became the most important component of the regional labor pool. Boatmen from the Beni towns virtually monopolized the Madeira traffic, regularly paddled their crafts to Manaus, and occasionally made the five thousand-kilometer round-trip to Belém. Moxos people also entered the extractive process, attaching themselves to Bolivian and Brazilian patrons or finding themselves forced into the barracas. This involvement had a marked effect on the Indians' lives.

INDIAN COMMUNITIES

Alcide Dessalines d'Orbigny paid an extensive visit to Moxos as it entered the Republican era. The French savant's observations and his publication of quantitative data collected by Bolivian administrators provide a convenient baseline for examining the last half-century of mission culture.

Table 17: Population Changes in Moxos, 1828–31

Year	Births	Deaths	Net Change
1828	1,572	1,075	497
1829	1,540	1,122	418
1830	1,591	1,122	469
1831	1,385	2,798	(1,413)
TOTALS	6,088	6,117	(29)

Source: Alcide Dessalines d'Orbigny, *El hombre americano* (Buenos Aires: Editorial Futuro, 1944), 49, 53.

Orbigny found thirteen Moxos settlements, which he referred to as missions, in 1832: Loreto, Trinidad, San Javier, San Pedro, San Ignacio, Santa Ana, Reyes, Exaltación, San Ramón, San Joaquín, Magdalena, Concepción, and Carmen. Using the then recently compiled, but even today unpublished, census of 1830, he recorded 22,833 native people and 57 whites (all single males) resident, with the natives broken down as follows: 5,708 married couples, 434 widowers, 5,197 males under age 14, 533 widows, and 5,303 females under age 12.[49] Again referring to locally compiled data, Orbigny detailed a short history of life events in early Republican Moxos, depicting the population stability characteristic of the post-Jesuit years (see table 17).

Orbigny's observations of Moxo society further underscore continuities with the past. He found that the majority of the population did not speak Spanish but communicated with administrators and visitors using interpreters. He recognized the existence of the Familia and Pueblo, the two traditional social units, and referred to the caciques as "all-powerful" (*todopoderoso*) men, to whom their villagers showed great respect. Displaying his skills as an ethnologist, Orbigny pointed to the survival of pre-Jesuit customs such as infant betrothal, to syncretic observances such as a ban against men riding horses while their wives were ill, and colorful subtleties such as the different rowing styles of Itonama (short strokes), Kayubaba (long strokes), and Baure (standing).[50] In summarizing his experiences, Orbigny found that the Jesuit-age heritage of the Moxos towns remained strong:

From the Paraguayan example one would generalize that the conservation of Jesuit institutions under different governors, as has taken place for the past 65 years, would have destroyed the Moxos missions; but, in 1832, one finds still intact, under other men, with different customs and a much reduced standard of living, all the administrative and religious institutions which the Jesuits left on their expulsion from the province in 1767.[51]

Had Orbigny returned fifty years later, his sharp eye would have discerned a situation more akin to the Paraguay he described in 1832. For by 1880 a combination of events and processes—population decline, political marginalization, and economic exploitation—stemming from white immigration and the demands of the world economic system had eroded the institutions of mission culture significantly.

Demographic Trends

Figure 5 charts available population statistics for the first half-century of Republican Moxos.

If we set aside the populations reported for 1846 and 1860, both of which are of questionable reliability,[52] figure 5 points to two trends in Moxos' population in the period. First, it shows remarkable stability between 1826 and 1867. Extracting the data for 1846 and 1860 produces a mean population of 22,742 for the eight remaining years, with a tight standard deviation of 5.2 percent (1,198) around the mean.

This stability was supported by demographic characteristics of the Moxos people. Resistance to European disease, a trait developed by the end of the Jesuit century, was reinforced under the period of Spanish rule, allowing the native people to maintain their numbers in the face of continued epidemics. The last year in table 17, 1831, shows the impact of an outbreak of smallpox in the towns, devastating for the year but sustainable even in the brief period shown. Outbreaks of smallpox and fevers appear in the records for 1845, 1849, 1850, and 1858. While the results may have been severe in the short term, they do not appear to have had a lasting impact.[53] Moreover, both adult females and girls outnumber their male counterparts during the Republican years 1826, 1830, 1846, and 1854—all the years for which such statistics are enumerated.

The second trend illustrated in figure 5 began in the late 1860s. Sometime after 1867, the population of Moxos began to decline. It had declined 18 percent by 1874, and 29 percent by 1882. The reasons for this decline have been discussed previously: the displacement of handicraft industry in the 1840s; livestock diseases beginning in the 1850s; the attacks on community property, culminating in the sale of lands in the 1860s; and, most

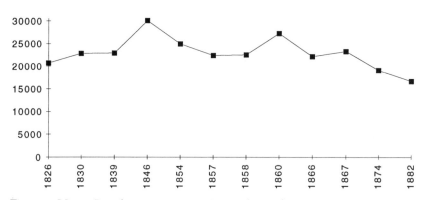

Figure 5. Moxos Populations, 1826–82. *Source:* Appendix.

important, the movement of Moxos peoples into the rubber zones in the 1860s and 1870s all had a cumulative effect on population levels.

The quantitative impact of the rubber boom on Moxos can only be implied. Pablo Macera's compilation of tribute records for the period 1854–74 documents a marked decline in Moxos' tributary population (*originarios*) at the end of the period. Between 1867 and 1874, 2,228 originarios left the tax rolls, a marked contrast to the rest of the period when this group showed demographic stability.[54] Edward D. Mathews estimated that the Beni lost an average of one thousand men per year between 1862 and 1872. He knew where these men had gone: "the reason for the decline of the Indian population [in Moxos] is to be found, without doubt, in the baneful effects to Bolivia of the rubber-collecting trade of the Madeira and Purus rivers."[55] While the English observer's numbers may not be entirely accurate, his sense of direction was flawless. The removal of large numbers of adult males from Moxos had a profound effect on the population's ability to maintain itself. In his study of California Indians during the gold rush, Albert L. Hurtado ascribes population decline among the state's native peoples to their removal from traditional communities into circumstances that did not favor reproduction, citing female prostitution and male mine labor among others.[56] The Amazonian rubber boom exerted similar centrifugal forces in Moxos after 1860.

Society

The society of mission culture relied on the extended family networks derived from aboriginal and European traditions. The Familia/Pueblo structure described in chapter 4 provided a mechanism for spouse exchange, brokering political power, and maintenance of the separate linguistic groups that resided in the settlements. This extended family structure deteriorated during the Republican period; as a result, the governors became separated from the governed. Orbigny uses the expression "hereditary classes" to identify the Familia and Pueblo in 1832, giving the impression that these social classifications were immutable. While a close examination of extant documents reveals that his impression is not entirely accurate, it does support a description of a more rigid social organization than that of the Jesuit century.

Surviving fragments of the 1830 Bolivian national census contain town-level counts for Concepción, San Joaquín, and Santa Ana.[57] When juxtaposed with the 1773 Reyes census, these documents delineate several aspects of social change. By 1830 occupation rather than status had become the operative variable for describing the population. Such an organization was in keeping with a succession of regimes that for nearly fifty years had stressed the importance of commercial production. It also probably represents a decreased emphasis on the discrete groups that had composed the original mission settlements.

Although the occupations of town residents duplicate those shown in Reyes for 1773, two significant differences emerge from comparing the lists. First, the 1830 censuses show that a very few families held a near monopoly on some of the Familia occupations. For instance, in Santa Ana all six members of the Tavauni family were musicians, and the town's shoemakers were all Tamalanis and Viviis. These examples help to explain why Orbigny contended there were hereditary classes. Second, the censuses for all three towns show that large segments of the populations were classified as engaged in two occupations. Without exception, adult women appear as spinners (*hilares*). While this enumeration may reflect a change in the categories used by the census takers, it also reflects a mass incorporation of women into the commercial segment of the economy, standing in marked contrast to the 1773 document where women appeared only as wives or widows. Also, within the parcialidades (linguistic groups), all men were classified as farmers (*labradores*). While the number of men designated as labradores ranged from 42 percent of the total population in Santa Ana to 62 percent in Concepción, in each of the towns this category claimed a very large portion of the population. These statistics show that the work force had evolved from a number of small segments in 1773 to a small elite and large peasantry in 1830.

The 1830 censuses also document a contraction of the elite. The compilations show no townwide officers other than the cacique and, in the cases of Concepción and Santa Ana, his lieutenants. This stands in marked contrast to Reyes, where a mission of 648 individuals had six central officers; each parcialidad had its own leadership as well. The evolution of the Moxos communities from missions to towns seems to have fostered a merging of formerly discrete hierarchies, with a single lineage or family gaining ascendancy over its rivals.

But even as they bested their Indian rivals, the native elites faced a series of challenges unknown to their forefathers. The growth of a state bureaucracy, especially the corregidores who resided in the towns and depended on a percentage of the revenues they collected for their own maintenance, presented the caciques with serious rivals for local influence. Although reformers proposed appointing caciques to corregidor positions, lists of departmental officials record only one instance in which this was done.[58]

By the 1850s caciques functioned in a diminished role, manipulated by white administrators and visiting merchants. Manipulation occurred as whites began to attach local products for their own ends. In 1852 José Luís Osorio, the Bolivian corregidor of Loreto, sent his son to Exaltación to buy cacao at below-market prices. To accomplish his task, Osorio tapped Exaltación's chain of command, approaching the corregidor, who in turn summoned the town's cacique, Domingo Abaroma. Then, at the insistence of the corregidor, Abaroma received one hundred pesos from Osorio and the order to procure the cacao from his people.[59] Caciques also were forced to participate in a continuous demand for native labor. Rather than bidding for labor power, Bolivian merchants often turned to caciques for help in manning their boat crews. Again, the corregidores served a crucial role, passing labor requirements to the caciques and delivering the paddlers to the merchants.[60]

The increasingly conflicted position of native leadership is consistent with events occurring contemporaneously in the Andean highlands. In the Chayanta region of Potosí, those responsible for collecting Indian tribute found themselves squeezed between Republican officials who demanded revenues and a native populace that increasingly resisted their efforts.[61] In Moxos the caciques often retreated into the background. Franz Keller relates the fate of the cacique from Exaltación who, in the 1860s, was tricked into buying two gold watches from an itinerant merchant. Unable to deliver the purchase price, "he was so pestered and dunned by his creditor that, in despair of otherwise satisfying him, he sold off his house and his herds, and all he possessed; and he now lives, a ruined man, in as poor and wretched a condition as the meanest in the Pueblo."[62]

In the Republican era Moxos native leadership was marginalized as the social structure became progressively more stratified, more elitist, and more homogenized. There is also evidence that traditional social patterns had become irrelevant. At the end of the 1850s, Matías Carrasco, a man with years of experience in the region, noted the decline of the parcialidades. He ordered the corregidores to revive them and to name new officials, as a means of providing for the subsistence needs of the native population.[63] While enlightened, Carrasco's orders came too late to revive what had been a vibrant institution.

Labor

The Republican period corresponds to an erosion of the terms of trade between Moxos' native people and the outside world. Despite his praise of the Indians' industry and physical well-being, Orbigny observed that they were oppressed by their administrators and curas, who demanded six days of hard work each week on state projects. He concluded with intended irony, "never have I seen more slavery and despotism operating under a free government."[64]

In addition to perpetuating the temporalidades, the Republican state assessed local resources to support its programs in the area. In an attempt to defray the costs of its growing bureaucracy, the state required each town to contribute between 300 and 500 pesos in cash each year. Later assessments included quotas of cattle, soap, sugar, and cane alcohol (*aguardiente*).[65]

Until 1842 Moxos' labor system conformed to the compulsory production of products for the state (*temporalidades*) carried over from the colony. This system placed individuals or groups of laborers on piecework quotas and established delivery dates for turning over their products — principally cacao, cotton thread, and finished cotton cloth — to administrators. Remuneration came in the form of goods provided by the state and distributed locally through its representatives rather than the caciques. In 1832 the government's yearly contribution consisted of 400 cakes of salt, 200 lengths of woolen cloth, 2,000 pounds of iron, 400 knives, an unspecified quantity of paper, a sack of wheat flour, and 70 pounds [*sic*] of wine for the mass.[66]

Executive decrees of the 1840s, beginning with Ballivián's charter for the Beni Department, railed against the temporalidades and decreed the institution of free labor. The numerous prohibitions against the temporalidades, however, shows the durability of the system. Indeed, accounts from the mid-nineteenth century describe an evolution from the temporalidades to even more pernicious labor systems. In 1844 Prefect Rafael de la Borda outlined the terms of a new relationship between the state and Moxos' workers. Indians who worked in state enterprises would not be paid in cash; instead they would run accounts at the state warehouse, where deliveries would be credited against withdrawals.[67] This system amounted to nothing less than debt peonage, a system easily manipulated by those who kept the accounts. Seven years later, a North American visitor reported his boatmen's complaints about this manipulation of exchange, stating that Bolivian authorities made every effort to keep cash out of the Indians' hands.[68]

Under the demands of the rubber boom, labor systems changed yet again. Now the objective was not to control available laborers on the savanna but to draw them away from it. The Moxos peoples began to enter the Madeira barracas in search of alternatives to the increasingly repressive economic and social conditions of the mid-nineteenth century. The incessant canoe traffic reported by European travelers in the 1860s bears witness to a veritable folk movement into the rubber zones. However, a free market never furnished the number of workers the rubber trade needed; coercion quickly became the dominant form of labor consignment.

Legal documents accuse a local official, Damón Barberi, of establishing a corporation for rubber gathering on the Madeira in 1871: "to fulfill his objectives [he] forced more than two hundred 'benianos' [i.e., native people] to enter Brazil against their will."[69] In his defense, Barberi never objected to this characterization of his enterprise, contesting only the government's contention that it violated the law. This case illustrates two salient points about the procuring of Moxos workers for the rubber boom after 1870: first, native people were taken against their will; second, the perpetrator was often a government official.

The local form of coercion operated under the term *enganche* (enlistment). Recruiters, sometimes the operators themselves but more often independent entrepreneurs, entered the towns and enlisted workers on the strength of cash advances and promises of quick riches. James C. Jones records surviving oral histories of the recruiters' methods: "In those years the pound sterling circulated hereabouts, there were no bills; the contratistas [contractors] would sometimes offer a hat-full of the white coins to entice people to go with them to collect rubber."[70] Local officials often conspired with the recruiters, adding powers of persuasion and sometimes naked force to the enterprise. In 1870, 250 men from Trinidad were contracted forcibly to the agents of a Brazilian company, with the complicity of the departmental prefect.[71]

Conditions in the rubber zones were uniformly brutal. Scenes from Werner Herzog's film *Fitzcarraldo* illuminate the atrocities and human suffering that characterized the workers' lives in the forests. A Brazilian official sent to investigate conditions on the Madeira in 1884 testifies to the veracity of Herzog's images. Julio Pinkas reported, with marked relief, that most of the laborers in the area were Moxos Indians rather than subjects of the Brazilian Empire. He reported that these people worked under appalling conditions and were kept in the barracas by debt peonage and physical force.[72] Adding to the misery of camp life is the poignant testimony of a resident of San Ignacio, who recounted the tales he had heard as a youth:

The collectors suffered very much; some died of yellow fever. People were truly slaves in those years. . . . How the Ignacianos had to submit and endure it! I remember well the Ignacianos who returned and told of their experiences to the north, even though I was quite young then. They would gather here in San Ignacio to drink and sing — the seringueiros had their songs, you know. They would often cry as they recalled their sufferings in the forests, where there was no cattle, no fresh beef. They were forced to eat monkeys and badgers.[73]

The effects of population decline, social dislocation, and economic exploitation destroyed the vitality of mission culture. Evidence of the unraveling of the system appears throughout the Republican era, but it increased after 1840 and accelerated markedly during the period 1860–80. Most obvious in the testimonies of travelers to the region, Moxos' decline also appears in the breakdown of social harmony that had characterized mission culture from its inception.

Indian resistance to Republican rule followed the patterns established in the Spanish period. In 1833 the Indians of Santa Ana rose against misrule, killing the Creole corregidor. The results were swift and severe. The central government sent troops who quelled the revolt, executed its leaders, and carried off half the town's silver plate.[74] Such a ruthless response to their resistance demonstrated to the Indians that Bolivian leaders possessed both the will and the resources to enforce "law and order." Other than occasional participation in the struggles stirred by exile factions in the 1840s, this ended armed opposition to Republican authority. However, judicial records of the same period note a significant increase in individual violence against white immigrants. In 1843, 1847, and 1849, Indians from Trinidad, San Ignacio, and San Pedro stood trial for homicides involving Bolivian officials or immigrant entrepreneurs.[75] Gabriel René-Moreno observed this breakdown in what he calls the "bland joviality" of the Indians under the demands the highland immigrants brought to Moxos after 1842. While he does not specifically refer to mission culture, this great nineteenth-century Bolivian historian recognized that the rupture of internal peace in the region marked the end of an age in the area.[76]

As early as 1847, an outside observer noticed a remarkable imbalance in the savanna populations. On his search for viable routes to the Amazon, José Agustín Palacios reported that the towns he visited held a superabundance of widows, a phenomenon he attributed to the risks inherent in the Indians' dedication to river navigation.[77] Whether the Bolivian explorer actually saw widows or merely women "widowed" by their husbands' prolonged voyages is unclear. However, by this date, the increased demands occasioned by merchant traffic and the transportation of cinchona on the western savanna had caused dislocation.

Two decades later, visitors' observations had become less ambiguous and more pessimistic. Descriptions of Exaltación, a town lying close to the rubber zones, speak of misery and depopulation. Keller, writing in 1868, describes a population reduced to the point that the corregidor proved unable to raise a crew of paddlers, even to serve a cash-paying expedition. He was shocked at what was clearly decline: "large grass-grown streets bordered by mouldering house-posts, showing the former importance of the place."[78] Mathews reiterates his predecessor's impressions and adds his own. He claimed that by 1874 Exaltación had virtually ceased to exist as a town. In its place he found a series of hamlets, one inhabited by the former cacique, scattered along the river. Mathews' report of an encounter with a group of "savage" Pacaguara in the Madeira rapids, whose headman was a runaway from Exaltación, confirms this atomized image of Moxos society. The Englishman concludes his observations on the town with an estimate that, at the time of his visit, women outnumbered men five or six to one, a claim also made with different ciphers for Carmen and Trinidad.[79]

This accelerated decline of mission culture in the mid-nineteenth century reflects the experience of native people throughout Latin America. The Mexican *Reforma,* despite its abolition of privileges for the church and the military, had the effect of placing the Indian population at the mercy of the state. Here, as communal landholdings were disestablished, government policy encouraged land speculation and large estate formation, and the church, traditionally the defender of Indian corporations, lacked the strength to stand up for them.[80] The Moxos experience adds additional support, if additional support were needed, to E. Bradford Burns's formulation of "the poverty of progress." Under the aegis of modernization, the Latin American republics replaced the colonial compromise between native and European customs — mission culture in Moxos — with a policy emphasizing individual property rights and the primacy of exports to the world market.[81] Under the challenge of Republican legislation and the world market, traditional societies across Latin America disintegrated.

After two hundred years of vitality, mission culture collapsed in the mid-nineteenth century. The onset of international capitalism in Moxos provided the final shock to the system. However, events of the 1870s should not be viewed as a dramatic break with the past. Commercial exploitation of savanna agriculture, begun in the Spanish period, eroded the peoples' subsistence base as did the outbreak of epidemic livestock disease after 1850. Republican state policies, particularly the opening of the savanna to white immigration, alienated communal property and substantially reduced native political power. And concurrent changes in the organization of Indian society made it less cohesive.

Under Republican rule, the native people saw a steady decline in their returns for participation in the system. The traditional terms of trade, labor power for manufactures, tilted to the Indians' disadvantage under the regime of the temporalidades and took another turn for the worse with the onset of debt peonage. Unlike in the colonial years, the native people faced governors both determined and sufficiently powerful to enforce changes in the status quo. Thus cinchona and rubber gathering took place at the end of a hundred-year continuum of economic decline and political marginalization. The rubber boom, which completed the process of native dispossession begun under Spanish administration, marks the end of mission culture in Moxos.

CONCLUSIONS

With the quincentenary of Columbus's first voyage, scholars and the general public have begun to consider the significance of the onset of continuous contact between Europeans and native Americans. While current debate has called these events into question, it has not obscured their importance. The encounter of two separate biological and cultural traditions, each separated from the other by tens of millennia, and the new societies that grew out of their contact lay the foundations for the growth of institutions in the American colonial period and beyond. The mission, a significant variant of these new societies, has been the focus of this book.

A series of themes significant to both the history of the Bolivian Amazon and the general field of American mission studies can be developed from examining the period of mission culture in Moxos. As I have used the term here, mission culture subsumes a multifaceted approach to reconstructing the Moxos experience. It defines an interplay of natural, aboriginal, and European elements, each contributing to a set of modes that guided life in the region for two centuries. While mission culture fused these elements into a single amalgam, it now seems useful to discuss the significance of a series of separate components.

JESUIT ENTERPRISE

The Society of Jesus forms such an important part of colonial historiography that some will likely read this book as another chapter in the Jesuit experience. Mission activities in Moxos illuminate Jesuit strategies in establishing the centers and in providing them with the material and human resources that enabled their century of existence. In addition, comments on the activities of the priests and brothers reopen questions about their motivations and the whole raison d'être of the American missions.

The Jesuit approach to missionary activity emphasized central direction and support. Even though the solitary explorations of such well-known missionaries as Eusebio Kino and Samuel Fritz are a part of the Jesuit tradition, these "freelances" were very much the exception to the accumulated record of practice. In Moxos, the initial reconnoiter of the savanna was directed by a survey instrument collecting data on the area and its people for the benefit of central authorities in Lima. Provincial officials, not priests in the field, made the decision to authorize the commitment of resources, and it was the Province of Peru that took the responsibility for procuring them.

Central direction also guided the Jesuit approach to the establishment and maintenance of the centers. The rules and precepts of the Society ordered certain activities, among them an emphasis on the learning of local languages and the regular reports modern historians have found so useful. Peruvian experience suggested that missions isolated from secular society were far preferable to those that tried to coexist alongside Spanish centers. Local regulations, such as those formulated by Diego Francisco Altamirano, laid out prescribed methods of conversion, education, even mission architecture. However, as other writers have pointed out, these strategies arose from the exigencies of work on the frontier, and most of the other orders evolved similar mission methodologies.[1]

The most striking feature of Moxos' central support, and of a particularly Jesuit approach, is the development of an investment strategy for the missions. By earmarking capital and land for Moxos, the Province of Peru provided an income stream for the missions' material needs. Pesos earned in the core economy of the viceroyalty subsidized the recruitment of European operatives, provided tools and supplies for Indian use, and purchased sumptuary goods for missions churches. This support, rather than what the missions themselves produced, made the Moxos operation flourish. In opposition to the usual pattern of capital flow, the center supported the periphery. The Jesuits, themselves fond of military metaphors, excelled as quartermasters; this gave them a competitive advantage over other missionary orders, whose mendicant orientation effectively reduced all support to the annual Crown stipend.

While Lima provided a reliable supply network, field missionaries supplied the skill and energy that established a European presence in Moxos.

This book has not focused on the activities of individual Jesuits. Although it describes dedicated and skillful individuals, it adds no new names to the pantheon of missionary heroes. Instead it concentrates on the operatives as a group and uncovers a number of tendencies that help to explain the direction of the Jesuit enterprise. A social history of the Moxos Jesuits emphasizes: a corps of diverse origin, with Peruvian Creoles, peninsular Spaniards, and continental Europeans as well represented; a predominance of priests in the field staff, with lay brothers providing much-needed technical skills; and service records of extraordinary duration, both in terms of years of residence and permanence in single missions. As the supply system did, these characteristics gave the Jesuits an edge over other orders in attracting men fit for the rigors of mission life and in establishing a European work force experienced in the language and habits of the various native peoples.

Finally, evidence from Moxos provides a new slant on the long debate over the ultimate intent of the Jesuit system. The Jesuits traditionally have been accused of creating paternalistic systems, making themselves indispensable, and not preparing Indian neophytes for lives outside their tutelage. This succession of paternalism, dependency, and collapse has become almost canonical in mission history, with the former quality used to explain the latter two. Certainly the Moxos Jesuits shared the colonial ethos of their time, one of guiding benighted people to enlightenment. However, the weight of evidence supports a policy of accommodation as characteristic of Jesuit activities on the savanna. The missionaries integrated themselves with aboriginal structures of government, society, and even religious ritual. A model of indirect rule, similar to that practiced in the European colonization of Asia, seems more apt than paternalism for describing the Moxos experience. And just as India did not collapse in the wake of British departure, neither did mission culture disappear with Jesuit exile.

SECULAR POLICY

As Herbert E. Bolton and his students first demonstrated for the North American Southwest, Iberian missions functioned as accessories to the colonial state. By the end of the sixteenth century, Iberian America was clearly divided between a core region and a periphery, each with its own set of modes and institutions. While the core became the domain of the encomienda and the city, the presidio and the mission developed as representatives of European populations on the periphery. Moxos was one of six Jesuit mission systems that, together with Franciscan, Agustinian, Dominican, and Capuchin missions, fixed the poorly defined margin of Spanish claims in the South American interior. As such, it became part of an imperial policy designed to define the territory, hispanize its native inhabitants, and protect both against rival claimants.

For most of the Jesuit century, this charge involved the contact and conversion activities of the missionaries. The colonial state authorized and sponsored the Jesuit enterprise through its exercise of the Patronato Real and its financial support from royal treasures. Moxos missionaries proved an economical investment for the Crown. Unlike in the Southwest, the Moxos missions never worked alongside military garrisons. Tradition, proximity to Spanish centers, lack of formidable rivals, and the perhaps perceived value of the territory all may have mitigated against sending military forces to the South American frontier. However, a shift in European alliances and the continuous westward advance of Portuguese explorers changed Spanish perceptions in the eighteenth century.

The territorial ambitions of both Iberian empires led to increased rivalries across the interior of South America. Tensions along the Guaporé, culminating in hostilities in 1760, established Moxos as a theater of war. For the first time, neophytes were asked to bear the obligations of citizenship in the Spanish Empire by sheltering and provisioning a Spanish army as well as by participating actively in the campaigns. This rupture of eighty years of isolation from large-scale contact with the European world proved traumatic for the missions, absorbing their attentions, reducing their populations, and emptying their storehouses.

As hostilities ended, Charles III decreed Jesuit exile and with it a deepening of Moxos' connections with the Spanish world. The introduction of Bourbon imperial policy to the savanna translated into changes in the relationship between the missions and the Peruvian core. Under the Jesuits, the center had subsidized the periphery; when the priests departed, the tables turned. Commercially viable activities became the order of the day: cotton textiles replaced feather weaving; cacao cultivation pushed manioc gardens far from central settlements; additions to sumptuary inventories ceased. This reorientation, bound up in the provisions of Lázaro de Ribera's New Plan, turned the missions into revenue producers for the Crown, but at the expense of mission prosperity.

Independence heightened late colonial challenges to mission culture.

Intent on instituting the liberal ideology of the day, successive Republican regimes disestablished communal claims to property at the same time as they retained the tributary system of the temporalidades. They also intensified the commercial orientation of the area, linking traditional production, such as textiles, to the fluctuations of the national market. As they looked for sources of revenues, policymakers made ill-advised use of savanna resources, granting cattle in payment of debts or as inducements to develop the area. In their attempts to integrate Moxos into the Bolivian nation, the same men encouraged its first large-scale white immigration. Republican policy, coupled with the effects of labor displacement from the Amazonian rubber boom, provided the final, insurmountable obstacle to mission culture. Nevertheless, two hundred years of history in Moxos was not simply legislated out of existence; the native tradition only grudgingly complied.

NATIVE TRADITION

The Indian peoples of Moxos became the primary bearers of mission culture. The native world of the savanna was characterized by various ethnic groups distributed according to their numbers and their martial skills. The most powerful groups lived on the riverfronts, Moxos' prime acreage, while weaker peoples inhabited the lesser river courses and open grasslands. This riverine orientation was the most salient characteristic of the savanna variant of tropical forest culture.

Despite their significant losses to European diseases and Spanish slavers, the native people continued to prosper in the mid-seventeenth century. Moxos' relatively large populations offered an appealing target for a missionary enterprise. Equally important, its surplus agricultural technology enabled the simultaneous European and native occupation of the savanna without drastic changes in traditional modes of subsistence, a situation unlike that encountered in the largely frustrated missionary attempts in Baja California and the South American Chaco.[2]

The Jesuit mission system in Moxos was not established overnight. Fifteen years passed between the first sustained contacts and the foundation of Loreto in 1682. But once this initial mission was in place, the system expanded rapidly. James Axtell has challenged students of the missions to take the Indian point of view on reasons for native participation.[3] In Moxos, native tradition encouraged Indian participation by defining a tenacious attraction to territory. Occupation of the riverfronts was a survival imperative; fleeing them meant marginalization. Thus Jesuit establishment of mission stations on the sites of former Indian villages insured a level of native participation. The Indians also saw tangible benefits resulting from allying themselves with the Jesuits. The missionary presence offered all Indians protection against cruceño slavers; it offered some protection against depredations by more powerful native adversaries. Finally, the Indians quickly discovered that the Jesuits provided dependable access to a wide variety of European manufactures, which revolutionized their lives.

Crossing the mission threshold did not entail leaving the native world behind. This would have defied both logic and experience. Nevertheless, until the 1980s, studies of mission life continued to imply that the missionaries reproduced a European culture and were little influenced by the culturally distinct populations among whom they lived. The Moxos experience offers a different interpretation of mission history, one characterized by the active participation of native people in mission affairs. Here accommodation rather than compulsion ruled the missions.

This is not to say that the Indians continued their former lives in new clothes. Important and painful changes took place. Perhaps the most painful change was the concentrating of formerly dispersed villages into central locations. Concentration exposed the native people to the full weight of epidemic disease as well as to cohabitation with former aboriginal rivals. However, as demographic analysis of the Jesuit century has shown, mission populations underwent a transformation during this period and emerged from it with significant resistance to disease. Mission culture also had a pronounced effect on the Indians' economic activities. A system of clocks and regimens, without a basis in the natural rhythms of the savanna, ordered days and seasons. European craft specialists (the Familia) emerged in the missions, supported by the subsistence activities of others. And finally, community-based labor patterns — tending mission herds, tilling the communal gardens, erecting church buildings — demanded time and energy beyond subsistence.

Native modes found clear expression in a number of mission modes. Agricultural technology, where manioc and maize constituted the dietary staples and where traditional ways of site selection and earth preparation remained the rule, governed the cultivation of new crops such as cotton and cacao. Politics and social structure, too, continued to follow established patterns. Traditional leaders continued to exercise real authority in cooperation with the missionaries. While the Familia emerged as an economic and political elite, it retained its links with the diverse ethnic groups that made up the majority of the mission populations. The evidence for accommodation in the Jesuit century is so clear that readers may be tempted to view this period as a golden age. I would urge, however, that this vision be rejected since it is sustainable only in comparison with the post-Jesuit years. This period, 1767–1880, was one of increasing challenges to mission culture and its traditional posture of accommodation.

The Spanish years in Moxos began a reorientation of the mission economies and a substantial change in the balance of trade between the missions and the Andean core. It was this latter trend that most deeply affected the native people. The decline in returns for their labor as they were manipulated by a closed system (the temporalidades) helped to impoverish mission culture. Living standards dropped as the curas and administrators demanded more work on commercially productive activities. And the loss of Jesuit subsidies reduced access to material goods that the Indians had come to regard as essential. Thus Republican rule must be seen as a continuation of declining returns and impoverishment among the native people.

The mission Indians resisted these changes with a variety of strategies. As long as they believed they had a chance of success, they attempted to redress their grievances by petitioning authorities. Citing both the traditions of mission culture and recent violations of those traditions, the Indians appealed to local and regional officials for help. When petitions failed, so did the *Pax Jesuitica*. During the early nineteenth century there were sporadic revivals of intra-Indian rivalries and active rebellions against Spanish authorities. The rebellions served as a purge, expelling particularly noxious offenders, but achieving their ends only when the European presence on the savanna was small. A substantial European force, such as that dispatched from Santa Cruz against the rebellion of 1823–24, invariably quelled the uprisings. In the Republican period, this force came to reside permanently on the savanna itself. When rebellion failed, flight remained the only strategy of resistance. And once its adherents had fled, mission culture ceased to be a vital force in the functioning of the Moxos towns.

The mission was never intended as a permanent institution. Both in theory and in practice, it marks a middle phase in the continuum between a pagan and uncivilized world and a Christian and enlightened one. One study of the North American experience defines three purposes advanced by advocates of the Protestant missions there: the introduction of piety, learning, and industry.[4] The desired result was an Indian population fully integrated with its white counterpart, a vision compatible with the nineteenth-century Bolivian ethos. Thus defined and established, the mission had no relevance off the frontier. Mission culture became irrelevant when, in the mid-nineteenth century, the western Amazonian frontier passed Moxos by. As the history of the gold rush in California and the Canadian far west has shown, Indian traditions were overwhelmed when white immigrants demanded Indians' land and their labor power.[5]

Nevertheless, mission culture changed Moxos' native people forever. Because of the missions, future generations received a biological and cultural heritage very different from that of Amazonian peoples not contacted by the priests and brothers. The history of mission culture in Moxos does not suggest a melting pot, a gradual absorption of native people into the mainstream of the colony or the Bolivian nation. It is more accurately the account of a struggle for Indian survival, a struggle that continues five hundred years after Columbus's arrival on American shores set it in motion.

APPENDIX:
Sources of Demographic Data on
Moxos Settlements, 1683–1882

YEAR AND SOURCE

1683 Diego de Eguiluz, *Historia de la misión de Mojos* (Lima: Imprenta del Universo de C. Prince, 1884), 13.

1684 "Lettra Annua," *Revista de archivos y bibliotecas nacionales* 3, no. 5 (1900): 191.

1691 Eguiluz, *Historia de la misión de Mojos*, 16–43.

1692 "Memorial de Francisco de Rotalde," in *Historia de la Compañía de Jesus en la provincia de Paraguay*, ed. Pablo Pastells, 9 vols. (Madrid: V. Suárez, 1912–49), 6:75.

1696 "Lettra Annua," ARSI, Peru 18, f. 168.

1700 Diego Francisco Altamirano, *Historia de la misión de los Mojos* (La Paz: Imprenta "El Comercio," 1891), 34, 67–71.

1713 Guillermo Furlong Cardiff, *Cartografía histórica argentina* (Buenos Aires: Comisión Nacional Ejecutiva de Homenaje al 150 Aniversario de la Revolución de Mayo, 1963), map XXV.

1717 "Breve noticia de las misiones," in *Historia de la Compañía de Jesus en la provincia de Paraguay*, 6:57–58.

1720 "Catalogus missionum," ARSI, Peru 21, f. 175.

1723 "Carta a SM," in *Historia de la Compañía de Jesus en la provincia de Paraguay*, 5:348.

1736 "Catalogus Reductionum," ARSI, Peru 5, ff. 65–65v.

1748 "Catalogo de las misiones," in *Historia de la Compañía de Jesus en la provincia de Paraguay*, 7:746–48.

1752 "El Gobernador Cap. de Santa Cruz de la Sierra," AGI, Charcas 474.

1764 *Memorias de los virreyes que han gobernado el Perú*, 6 vols. (Lima: Librería de Felipe Bailly, 1859), 4:4–5.

1767 Gabriel René-Moreno, *Catálogo del Archivo de Mojos y Chiquitos,* 2d ed. (La Paz: Librería Editorial "Juventud," 1973), 15.

1773 "I Autos originales de visitas," 1773, ANB, ADM 10v–47v.

1779 "Padron del obispado de Sta Cruz," 1779, ADLP, Limites con Bolivia, no. 517.

1786 "I Testimonio del expendiente de la visita del pueblo de Loreto . . . ," ANB, ADM 11, ff. 1–46, 1–64, 1–32, 1–82v.

1788 Alcides Parejas, *Historia de Moxos y Chiquitos a fines del siglo XVII* (La Paz: Instituto Boliviano de Cultura, 1976), 64.

1790–91 "Expedientes de visitas," 1790–91, ANB, Audiencia de Charcas, Mojos IX.

1796–97 "XX Expediente que contiene las visitas," ANB, ADM 14, ff. 146–90.

1802–3 "XIX Razones originales," 1802–3, ANB, ADM 17, ff. 183–251v.

1810 "XXXIX Extractos sacados de Moxos," 1810, ANB, ADM 18, ff. 18–73.

1816 José Chávez Suárez, *Historia de Moxos,* 2d ed. (La Paz: Editorial Don Bosco, 1986), 483.

1826 "Estado que manifiestan las riquezas," 1826, ANB, MI 14, f. 18.

1830 Alcide Dessalines d'Orbigny, *Descripción geográfica, histórica y estadística de Bolivia* (Paris: Librería de los Señores Guide y Compañía, 1845), 299.

1839 "Demonstración de las dotaciones," 1839, ANB, MI 74, f. 31.

1846 Pablo Macera, *Bolivia, tierra y población,* 1825–1936 (Lima: Biblioteca Andina, 1978), 5–6.

1854 Ibid., 106.

1857 Ibid.

1858 Ibid.

1860 Quintín Quevedo, *Pequeño bosquejo de la provincia de Mojos en el Departamento del Beni* (La Paz: Imprento Paceña, 1861), n.p.

1866 Pablo Macera, *Bolivia, tierra y población, 1825–1936,* 106.

1867 Ibid.

1874 Ibid.

1882 Ibid., 45.

NOTES

INTRODUCTION

1. R. B. Cunninghame Graham, *A Vanished Arcadia: Being Some Account of the Jesuits in Paraguay, 1607 to 1767* (London: Heinemann, 1901), and Philip Caraman, *The Lost Paradise: The Jesuit Republic in South America* (New York: Seabury Press, 1976).

2. Bolton's essay, "The Missions as a Frontier Institution in the Spanish American Colonies," first appeared in 1917. It was reprinted most recently in *Bolton and the Spanish Borderlands,* ed. John Francis Bannon (Norman: University of Oklahoma Press, 1964); his exhortation comes from p.188.

3. Magnus Mörner, *The Political and Economic Activities of the Jesuits in the La Plata Region: The Hapsburg Era* (Stockholm: Victor Petersens Bokindustri, 1953).

4. For important examples of these new approaches, see Robert Reid Archibald, *The Economic Aspects of the California Missions* (Washington, D.C.: Academy of Franciscan History, 1978); Erik D. Langer and Robert H. Jackson, "Colonial and Republican Missions Compared: The Cases of Alta California and Southeastern Bolivia," *Comparative Studies in Society and History* 20, no.2 (Apr. 1988): 286–311; and Cynthia Radding, *Las estructuras socio-económicas de las misiones de la Pimería Alta 1768–1850* (Hermosillo: Instituto Nacional de Antropología e Historia, Centro Regional del Noroeste, 1979).

5. William Denevan, "Aboriginal Drained-Field Cultivation in the Americas," *Science* 169 (1970): 647–54, and "The Aboriginal Population of Amazonia," in *The Native Population of the Americas in 1492,* ed. Denevan (Madison: University of Wisconsin Press, 1976), 205–34.

6. Francisco J. Eder, *Breve descripción de las reducciones de Mojos,* trans. and ed. Josep M. Barnadas (Cochabamba: Historia Boliviana, 1985).

7. Donald W. Lathrap, *The Upper Amazon* (New York: Praeger, 1970), 77.

8. James C. Jones, "Conflict between Whites and Indians on the Llanos de

Moxos, Beni Department: A Case Study in Development from the Cattle Region of the Bolivian Oriente" (Ph.D. diss., University of Florida, 1980), and J. Valerie Fifer, *Bolivia: Land, Location and Politics since 1825* (Cambridge: Cambridge University Press, 1972). For a description of the rubber firm archives, see "Centro de Documentación e información de la Universidad del Beni," in *Simposio sobre las misiones jesuitas en Bolivia* (La Paz: Ministerio de Relaciones Exteriores y Culto, 1987), 215–36.

CHAPTER I

1. Adolfo Muñoz Reyes, *Nuevo geografía de Bolivia* (La Paz: Academia Nacional de Ciencias de Bolivia, 1977), 438–58.

2. "Descripcion de varias plantas de la provincia de Moxos," Loreto, 1789, BPR 2769. This manuscript has now been published as part of *Moxos descripciones exactas e historia fiel de los indios, animales y plantas de la provincia de Moxos en el virreinato del Perú por Lázaro de Ribera 1786–1794* (Madrid: Ministerio de Agricultura Pesca y Alimentación, Ediciones el Viso, [1989]).

3. See especially William Denevan, *The Aboriginal Cultural Geography of the Llanos de Mojos of Bolivia* (Berkeley and Los Angeles: University of California Press, 1966). A Spanish-language edition of this work appears as *La geografía cultural aborigen de los Llanos de Mojos* (La Paz: Editorial Juventud, 1980).

4. Although the primary analysis of these data was done by G. Kingsley Nobel, for the purposes of this work, see Donald W. Lathrap's interpretation of Nobel's work in *The Upper Amazon* (New York: Praeger, 1970), 74–75.

5. Erland Nordenskiöld, *L'archéologie du bassin de l'Amazone* (Paris: Les Editions G. van Oest, 1930).

6. Lathrap, *The Upper Amazon*, 127, and Gordon R. Willey, *An Introduction to American Archaeology* (Englewood Cliffs, N.J.: Prentice-Hall, 1971), 419.

7. Willey, *An Introduction to American Archaeology*, 420–21.

8. Max Portugal Ortiz, *La arqueología de la región del Río Beni* (La Paz: Editorial Casa de la Cultura "Franz Tamayo," 1978), 112–13.

9. Denevan, *Aboriginal Cultural Geography*, esp. 80, 84, 90–92.

10. Bernard Dougherty and Joracio A. Calandra, "Prehispanic Human Settlement in the Llanos de Moxos, Bolivia," in *Quarentary of South America and Antarctic Peninsula*, ed. Jorge Rabassa, 2 vols. (Rotterdam: A. A. Balkema, 1983), 2:181, 191–92.

11. "Relacion de la provincia de Mojos," in *Documentos para la historia geográfica de la República de Bolivia*, ed. Manuel V. Ballivián. 2 vols. (La Paz: J. M. Gamarra, 1906), 1:296–300.

12. Lorenzo Hervás y Panduro. *Catálogo de las lenguas de las naciones conocidas*, 2 vols. (Madrid: Imprenta del Real Arbitro de Beneficiencia, 1800), 1:246.

13. Ibid., 1:252, and "Carta del Governador de Sta. Cruz de la Sierra," Santa Cruz, 8/1/1764, AGI Charcas 474, ff.8–8v.

14. "Expediente relativo a diversos asuntos de las misiones de Mojos," n.p., 1715, BNL 1715/C58.

15. Diego Francisco Altamirano, *Historia de la misión de los Mojos* (La Paz: Imprenta "El Comercio," 1891), 199.

16. "Expediente relativo a diversos asuntos de las misiones de Mojos."

17. "Consultas hechas a S.M. por Don Juan de Lizarazu presidente de Charcas sobre su entrada a Moxos o Toros," in *Juicio de límites entre el Perú y Bolivia,* ed. V. M. Mautua, 12 vols. (Barcelona: Imprenta de Henrich y Compañía, 1906), 9:170.

18. Annua de la Provincia del Perú del año de 1596," *Monumenta Peruana,* ed. Antonio de Egaña (Rome: APUD Institutum Historicum Societatis Ieus, 1954–), 6:426–34.

19. Denevan, *Aboriginal Cultural Geography,* 116–17, and *The Native Populations of the Americas in 1492,* ed. Denevan (Madison: University of Wisconsin Press, 1976), 212.

20. Clark L. Erickson, "Sistemas agrícolas prehispánicos en los Llanos de Mojos," *América indigena* 40, no.4 (Oct.–Dec. 1980): 735.

21. Julian H. Steward and Louis C. Faron, *Native Peoples of South America* (New York: McGraw-Hill, 1959), 177–78, 252–53.

22. Leslie Gill, *Peasants, Entrepreneurs and Social Change* (Boulder, Colo.: Westview Press, 1987), 25.

23. Alcide Dessalines d'Orbigny, *L'homme american* (Paris: Chez Pitios-Levrault, et Cie., 1839), 200.

24. "Annua de la Provicia del Perú del año de 1596," ARSI, Peru 12, f.143, and Pedro Marbán, *Arte y vocabulario de la lengua Moxa* (Lima: Imprimase El Conde, 1701), 329.

25. "Carta de los PP," Provincia de los Moxos, 20/IV/1676, ARSI, Peru 6, f.200v, and "Annua de la Provincia del Perú del año de 1596," f.143v.

26. See Denevan, *Aboriginal Cultural Geography,* 99–101, for a detailed description of aboriginal cultivars.

27. "Annua de la Provincia del Perú del año de 1596," f.143v, and "Carta del Gov. de Santa Cruz, D. Juan de Mendoza a la Rl Audiencia de La Plata," Provincia de los Mariquionos, 1603, ANB, Reales Cédulas 816.

28. Thierry Saignes, *Historia de un olvido* (La Paz: CERES, Instituto Francés de Estudios Andinos, 1986), 8–26.

29. "Relación de la provincia de los Mojos," 1:297.

30. Willey, "Ceramics," in *Handbook of South American Indians* (Washington, D.C.: U.S. Government Printing Office), 142–43. For an early description of savanna pottery, see "Relación de la provincia de los Mojos," 1:320, and "Annua de la Provincia del Perú del año de 1596," f.143.

31. "Annua de la Compañía de Jesús-Tucumán y Perú-1596," in *Relaciones geográficas de Indias,* ed. Marcos Jiménez de la Espada (Madrid: Ediciones Atlas, 1965), 2:95.

32. "Carta de los PP," f.200v.

33. "Relación de la provincia de los Mojos," 1:350.

34. Francisco J. Eder, *Breve descripción de las reducciones de Mojos,* trans. and ed. Josep M. Barnadas (Cochabamba: Historia Boliviana, 1985), 85.

35. Diego Francisco Altamirano, *Historia de la misión de los Mojos* (La Paz: Imprenta "El Comercio," 1891), 107–9, 136.

36. "Relación de la provincia de los Mojos," 1:298, 350.

37. "Informe de P. Antonio de Orellana al P. Provincial Martín de Jaregui," Loreto, 18/X/1682, ARSI, Peru 20, f.16v.

38. Eder, *Breve descripción de las reducciones de Mojos,* 107.

39. Another result of these early expeditions was the fixing of Moxos, however vaguely, in the European cartographic tradition. Its location, east of the Andes and roughly paralleling Lake Titicaca in latitude, was placed on charts at least as early as 1589. Diego Mendez's map, *Peruviae Auriferae Regionis typus,* includes a Moxos and a Moxos River near 14° south latitude. See *Atlas de Bolivia* (La Paz: Instituto Geográfico Militar, 1985), 35.

40. Major sources for the Spanish entries across the Chaco are Rui Díaz de Guzmán, *La Argentina* (Buenos Aires: Librería Huemel, 1974); Ulrich Schmidel, *Viaje al Río de la Plata* (Buenos Aires: Cabaut y Cía Editores, 1903); and "Relación de los casos en que el Capitán Nufrio (sic) de Chavez a servido a Su Magestad desde el año de qunientos quarenta," in *Colección de documentos relativos a la historia de América y particularmente a la historia del Paraguay,* ed. Blas Garay, 2 vols. (Asunción: Talleres Nacionales de H. Kraus, 1899), 1:336–40.

41. For a copiously documented account of the foundations of Santa Cruz and its early economy, see José María García Recio, *Análisis de una sociedad de frontera: Santa Cruz de la Sierra en los siglos XVI y XVII* (Sevilla: Publicaciones de la Exema, Diputación Provincial de Sevilla, 1988).

42. The original of Andión's account has been lost, but a condensed version appears in "Annua de la provincia del Perú del año de 1596," 6:426–34.

43. "Carta de la Real Audiencia a SM," Potosí, 24/III/1609, ADLB, D1-1-102,

no.491, and "Carta a la Real Audiencia de La Plata," Santa Cruz, 1603, ANB, Reales Cédulas 807.

44. See especially Mario Góngora, *Los grupos de conquistadores en Tierra Firme* (Santiago: Universidad de Chile, 1962).

45. "Capitulaciones formadas entre el Governador de Santa Cruz D. Lorenzo Suarez de Figueroa y el Capital Gonzalo Solis Olguin," San Lorenzo, 10/IX/1590, ADLP, Límites con Bolivia, no.124.

46. "Memoria jurada de D. Joseph Cayetano Hurtado Dabila," San Lorenzo, 27/III/1617, AGI, Charcas 158. For an example of these expeditionary documents, see "Relacion de la entrada de Gonzalo de Solis Holguin a Moxos," San Lorenzo de la Frontera, 4/I/1620, AGI, Charcas 27.

47. "Reparticion de los indios que se traugeron," Provincia de los Mojos, Pueblo de Curobosa, 28/X/1667, ANB, Mojos Complementario, IV ff.43–47.

48. See, for instance, *Actas capitulares de Santa Cruz de la Sierra, 1634–1640* (La Paz: Universidad Boliviana Gabriel René Moreno, 1977), 88–89, which mentions taking native people out of the region for sale in Charcas as an additional cause of native depopulation.

49. David G. Sweet, "A Rich Realm of Nature Destroyed: The Middle Amazon Valley 1640–1750" (Ph.D. diss., University of Wisconsin, 1974), 120–21.

CHAPTER 2

1. Fernando de Armas Medina, *Cristianización del Perú, 1532–1600* (Sevilla: Escuela de Estudios Hispano-Americanos, 1953), 15–39.

2. "Carta annua 1603," ARSI, Peru 12, ff.350–350v, and "Carta annua 1609," ARSI, Peru 13, ff.71–71v.

3. "Carta annua 1592," ARSI, Peru 12, ff.143–44.

4. See "Carta annua 1596," ARSI, Peru 12, ff.143–44, and "Informes hechas por Juan de Lizarazu sobre el descubrimiento de los Mojos," in *Juicio de límites entre Perú y Bolivia,* ed. Victor M. Maurtua, 12 vols. (Barcelona: Imprenta de Henrich y Compañía, 1906), 9:150–55.

5. "Relacion de lo sucedido en la jornada de los Mojos en el ano de 1667," ARSI, Peru 20, f.135v.

6. I acknowledge my debt to Diane Langmore, who used Weberian terminology to describe generations of Victorian-age missionaries to Papua. See her *Missionary Lives Papua, 1874–1914* (Honolulu: University of Hawaii Press, 1989), 206.

7. Antonine Tibesar, *Franciscan Beginnings in Colonial Peru* (Washington, D.C.: Academy of Franciscan History, 1953), 43.

8. For accounts of the early Jesuit expeditions into Moxos, see Diego de Eguiluz, *Historia de la misión de Mojos* (Lima: Imprenta del Universo de C. Prince, 1884); Castillo's entry appears on 4–5.

9. "Carta de los PP que residen en la mision de los Moxos para el P. Hernando Cavero de la Comp. de Jesus, Provincial de esta provincia del Peru," Provincia de Moxos, 20/IV/1676, ARSI, Peru 20, ff.201–5.

10. Eguiluz, *Historia de la misión de los Mojos*, 7. See also Diego Francisco Altamirano, *Historia de la misión de los Mojos* (La Paz: Imprenta "El Comercio," 1891), 52, and "Carta de los PP," f.200v.

11. Eguiluz, *Historia de la misión de los Mojos*, 10.

12. "Carta del Padre Antonio de Orellana sobre el origen de las misiones de Mojos," in *Juicio de límites entre Perú y Bolivia*, 10:14.

13. Eguiluz, *Historia de la misión de los Mojos*, 25, and Altamirano, *Historia de la misión de los Mojos*, 58.

14. Eguiluz, *Historia de la misión de los Mojos*, 23.

15. "Carta del P. Francisco Javier al P. Hernando de Tardio," Mojos, 18/VII/1696, ADLP, Límites con Bolivia, no.282; "Carta del P. Franco. de Borja al P. Provincial," Mojos, 20/V/1697, ADLP, Límites con Bolivia, no.296; and "Carta del P. Misionero Juan de Espejo al P. Provincial Diego de Eguiluz," San José, 28/XI/1696, ADLP, Límites con Bolivia, no.281.

16. Nicolás de Armentía, *Relación de las misiones franciscanas de Apolobamba* (La Paz: Tip. Artística, 1905), 75, and José Chávez Suárez, *Historia de Moxos*, 2d ed. (La Paz: Editorial Don Bosco, 1986), 249–52.

17. "El Padre Diego Francisco Altamirano," in Altamirano, *Historia de la misión de los Mojos*, 5–18.

18. Altamirano, *Historia de la misión de los Mojos*, 88.

19. Ibid., 85.

20. Ibid., 83–85.

21. "Carta annua 1702," ARSI, Peru 18b, ff.246–47.

22. Altamirano, *Historia de la misión de los Mojos*, 138–39. The Moxos Jesuits lost a second priest, Balthasar de Espinosa, who died trying to establish a mission among the Mobima of the southwestern savanna in 1709.

23. Ibid., 96–97, 142.

24. Ibid., 100–101.

25. "Annua 1728," ARSI, Peru 18, f.167.

26. "Annua 1731," ARSI, Peru 18, f.186, and "Annua Littera Provincia Peruanae 1746–1748," ARSI, Peru 18, f.188v.

27. "Annua 1730," ARSI, Peru 18, f.178v.

28. "Annua 1728," f.167v, and "Annua Littere Peruvius Provincias 1749," ARSI, Peru 18, f.233.

29. "Carta del P. Superior de la misión de los Mojos," Trinidad, 24/VIII/1723, in *Historia de la Compañía de Jesús en la provincia de Paraguay*, ed. Pablo Pastells, 9 vols. (Madrid: V. Suárez, 1912–49), 6:285–86; "Diario del viaje hecho por el governador de Santa Cruz," 11/XI/1760, in ibid., 8:739; and Rubén Vargas Ugarte, *Historia de la Compañía de Jesús en el Perú*, 4 vols. (Burgos: Imprenta de Aldecoa, 1963–65), 3:75–76.

30. "Carta del Padre missionero Joseph de Vargas al P. Francisco Javier," San Miguel de Parabas, 24/XI/1696, ADLP, Límites con Bolivia, no.277, and "Carta de Pedro Marban al Padre Provincial," Loreto, 13/VII/1696, BNL, 1715/C58.

31. José Gonçalves da Fonseca, "Primeira exploração dos rios Madeira e Guaporé em 1749," in *Memórias para a história do extincto estado do Maranhão*, ed. Candido Mendez de Almeida, 2 vols. (Rio de Janeiro: n.p., 1874), 2:354–55. On the folk movement of Portuguese into Moxos, see Francisco Mateos, "Avances portugueses y misiones españolas en la América del Sur," *Missionalia Hispánica* 5, no.15 (1948): 501.

32. Artur C. F. Reis, *Limites e demarcações na Amazonia brasileira*, 2 vols. (Rio de Janeiro: Imprenta Nacional, 1947), 2:18; "Carta de Franco de Melo Palleta [*sic*] al Gov. de Santa Cruz," Exaltación, 5/VII/1723, AGI, Charcas 159; and Basilio de Magalhães, *Expansão geográfico do Brasil colonial* (São Paulo: Companhia Editorial Nacional, 1935), 223.

33. Manoel Felix's account appears in Robert Southey, *History of Brazil*, 2d ed., 3 vols. (New York: Greenwood Press, 1969), 3:320–33.

34. David M. Davidson, "Rivers and Empire: The Madeira Route and the Incorporation of the Brazilian Far West, 1737–1808" (Ph.D. diss., Yale University, 1970), 55–56.

35. José Maria de Souza Nunes, *Real forte Príncipe da Beira* (Rio de Janeiro: Fundação Emílio Odebrecht, 1985), 101–4, 124, 134.

36. This version of the Luso-Spanish conflict on the Mamoré comes from the documents reproduced in *Historia de la Compañía de Jesús en la provincia de Paraguay*, 8:655–66, 793, 795, 921–23. See also Leandro Tormo Sanz, "La campaña de Moxos contra los Portugueses del Brasil," *Revista de la Universidad Autónoma "Gabriel René Moreno*," 9, no.18 (July–Dec. 1962): 6–28, for his use of the same sources in a more extensive way.

37. "Ynforme de Don Antonio Porlier," Madrid, II/1767, ADLB, D1-1-101, No. 650, f.2v.

38. Manuel de Amat y Junient, *Memoria de gobierno* (Sevilla: Escuela de Estudios

Hispano-Americanos, 1947), 276, and "Preguntas sobre el expediente de Mojos," n/1, 19/VIII/1769, AGI, Lima 1054, f.1v.

39. Nunes, *Real forte Príncipe da Beira*, 138.

40. Amat y Junient, *Memoria de gobierno*, 280–81.

41. "Cuaderno de cuentas recividas y escritas," San Pedro, 18/X/1766, ANB, Audiencia de Charcas, Mojos II, f.9.

42. "Autos originales de visitas practicadas, primer por el governador interino D. Leon Gonzalez de Velasco, en el año de 1773," San Pedro, 27/XI/1773, ANB, ADM, ff.30–31v.

43. "Aymerich y Villajuana escritas a M.Y.S. Juan Vintorino Martines," Loreto, 11/VIII/1768, ANB, Audiencia de Charcas, Mojos IV, f.58.

44. "Carta de Alonso Verdugo," San Lorenzo, 8/I/1764, AGI, Charcas 474, f.15r.

45. "II Correspondencia epistolar y de oficio," Loreto, 5/X/1767, ANB, ADM 1, ff.78v–79.

46. "Diario de Lorenzo Miranda de su viaje a San Borja," Loreto, 16/III/1768, ANB, MYCH, Mojos 1, ff.295v–296v.

47. Despite Josep Barnadas's questioning of these figures, published in my thesis, in his excellent introduction to Francisco J. Eder's *Breve descripción de las reducciones de Mojos,* ed. Barnadas (Cochabamba: Historia Boliviana, 1985), lxxx, I stand by the version given in "Carta de D. Juan Leonardo a SM," Oruro, 12/VII/1768, BNL, 1762/C229, and "Provincia de los jesuitas en el Peru," BNL, F459.

48. Vargas Ugarte, *Historia de la Compañía de Jesús en el Perú,* 3:140–42, and Barnadas, "Introducción," in Eder, *Breve descripción de las reducciones de Mojos,* lxxx.

CHAPTER 3

1. Robert Southey, *History of Brazil,* 2d ed., 3 vols. (New York: Greenwood Press, 1969), 3:329.

2. Francisco J. Eder, *Breve descripción de las reducciones de Mojos,* trans. and ed. Josep M. Barnadas (Cochabamba: Historia Boliviana, 1985), 355–58.

3. "Diario del viaje hecho por el Governador de Santa Cruz en 1760," in *Historia de la Compañía de Jesús en la provincia de Paraguay,* ed. Pablo Pastells, 9 vols. (Madrid: V. Suárez, 1912–49), 8:742.

4. "Autos originales de visitas practicadas primera por el Governador interino D. Leon Gonzales de Velasco," San Pedro, 27/III/1773, ANB, ADM 4, ff.11–11v, and "Autos originales de visitas," Magdalena, 21/III/1773, ANB, ADM 4, f.11v. The sketch, rendered by Alcide Dessalines d'Orbigny appears in Mario J. Buschiazzo,

Architectura en las misiones de Mojos y Chiquitos (La Paz: Imprenta de la Universidad Mayor de San Andres, 1972), 12.

5. "II Correspondencia epistolar y de oficio," Loreto, 20/X/1767, ANB, ADM 1, f.84v; "Carta del Obispo de Santa Cruz a SM," Mizque, 28/II/1719, AGI, Charcas 375; and Eder, *Breve descripción de las reducciones de Mojos,* 33.

6. "Linderos de los pueblos de Mojos," in *Juicio de límites entre el Perú y Bolivia,* ed. Victor M. Maurtua, 12 vols. (Barcelona: Imprenta de Henrich y Compañía, 1906), 9:34.

7. Eder, *Breve descripción de las reducciones de Mojos,* 355.

8. Rubén Vargas Ugarte, *Historia de la Compañía de Jesús en el Perú,* 4 vols. (Burgos: Imprenta de Aldecoa, 1963–65), 3:50a.

9. For details of these inventories, see the documents cited in table 3.

10. For descriptions of these churches, see "Expediente relativo a diversos asuntos de las misiones de Mojos," 1696, BNL, 1715/C58, and "Testimonio de las diligencias actuadas," San Pedro, 8/X/1767, ANB, ADM 1, f.23.

11. "Linderos de los pueblos de Mojos," 9:42.

12. "Carta del Obispo de Santa Cruz a SM," Mizque, 28/II/1719, AGI, Charcas 375.

13. Buschiazzo, *Architectura en las misiones de Mojos y Chiquitos,* 25, 34–35.

14. José de Mesa and Teresa Gisbert, *Bolivia: monumentos históricos y arqueológicos* (Mexico: Instituto Panamericano de Geografía y Historia, 1970), 94, and Franz Keller, *The Amazon and Madeira Rivers* (Philadelphia: J. B. Lippincott and Co., 1875), 188.

15. Southey, *History of Brazil,* 3:328, and Diego de Eguiluz, *Historia de la misión de Mojos* (Lima: Imprenta del Universo de C. Prince, 1884), 32–33.

16. The inventories appear as "Ynbentarios de los bienes de Loreto, Trinidad, San Javier, San Pedro, Santa Ana, Exaltacion, Magdalena, San Ygnacio y Reyes," ANB, ADM 1, ff.7–68, and "Inventario de los bienes pertenecientes a la iglesia y a la comunidad de los pueblos de San Borja, San Nicolas, San Simon, San Martin y la Concepcion," ANB, ADM 1, ff.172–201.

17. For a fuller discussion of the Moxos book collections, see my "Missionary Libraries on the Amazonian Frontier: The Jesuits in Moxos, 1680–1767," *Journal of Library History* 18, no.3 (Summer 1983): 292–303.

18. Valerie Fraser, *The Architecture of Conquest: Building in the Viceroyalty of Peru, 1535–1635* (Cambridge: Cambridge University Press, 1990).

19. "Carta de Pedro Marbán a SM," San Lorenzo, 25/VII/1698, AGI, Lima 407.

20. "Carta del P. Phelipe del Castillo al Sr. Presidente," Cadiz, 25/IV/1736, AGI, Contratación 5548, f.2v.

21. Magnus Mörner, *The Political and Economic Activities of the Jesuits in the Rio de la Plata Region: The Hapsburg Era* (Stockholm: Victor Petersens Bokindustri, 1953), 100–101.

22. "Real Cedula 1736," Madrid, 1736, AGI, Contratación 5548; "Relacion de todos los religiosos que destos reynos han pasado a las yndias," Cadiz, 17/X/1737, AGI, Indiferente General 2797; and "Real Cedula 1747," Aranjuez, 27/V/1747, BNL, 1747/C880.

23. Jay F. Lehnertz, "Lands of the Infidels: The Franciscans in the Central Montaña of Perú, 1709–1824" (Ph.D. diss., University of Wisconsin, 1974), 294.

24. "Ynventarios de los bienes de Loreto, Trinidad, San Javier, San Pedro, Santa Ana, Exaltacion, Magdalena, San Ygnacio y Reyes," f.38.

25. Robert Reid Archibald, *The Economic Aspects of the California Missions* (Washington, D.C.: Academy of American Franciscan History, 1978), 161–83, and Mardith Keithly Schuetz, "The Indians of the San Antonio Missions" (Ph.D. diss., University of Texas, 1980), 246–49.

26. Nicholas P. Cushner, *Jesuit Ranches and the Agrarian Development of Colonial Argentina, 1650–1767* (Albany: State University of New York Press, 1983), 164.

27. Diego Francisco Altamirano, *Historia de la misión de los Mojos* (La Paz: Imprenta "El Comercio," 1891), 9, and "Expediente obrado acerca del remate de la hacienda de Chalguani," La Plata, 20/IX/1768. ANB, Audiencia de Charcas, Mojos III, f.14v.

28. "Expediente obrado acerca del remate de la hacienda de Chalguani," f.14v.

29. "Traslado de la ynposicion de un censo," Lima 20/X/1698, AGNP, Compañía de Jesús, Censos, legajo 8, and "Testamento del General D. Juan de Murga," Lima 25/II/1725, AGNP, Compañía de Jesús, Cuentas Generales, legajo 100.

30. The practice of Church investment in censos has been well documented. For New Spain, see Michael P. Costeloe, *Church Wealth in Mexico: A Study of the Juzgado de Capellanías in the Archbishopric of Mexico, 1800–1856* (Cambridge: Cambridge University Press, 1967). For Peru, see Brian Hamnett, "Church Wealth in Peru: Estates and Loans in the Archdiocesis of Lima in the Seventeenth Century," *Jahrbuch für geschichte von staat, wirtschaft und gesellschaft lateinamerikas* 10 (1973): 113–32.

31. "Visita del P. Leonardo de Baldivia a las haciendas de Challuani y Habana," Lima, 1751, AGNP, Compañía de Jesús, Varios, legajo 120.

32. Barnadas, "Introdución," in Eder, *Breve descripción de las reducciones de Mojos,* lviii.

33. "Libro de la hacienda de San Antonio de Motocache," Motocache, n.d.

AGNP, Compañía de Jesús, Cuentas de Haciendas, legajo 87, f.1, and "Testimonio de el ymbentario del colegio del noviciado de la Compañía de Jesús, Año de 1767," in Luís Antonio Eguiguren, *Las Huellas de la Compañía de Jesús en el Perú* (Lima: Librería y Imprenta Gil, 1956), 56.

34. "Testimonio de el ymbentario del colegio del noviciado de la Compañía de Jesús, Año de 1767," 57.

35. "Libro de la hacienda de San Antonio de Motocache," Motocache, 1709, ff.1v–2v.

36. "Libro de la hacienda de San Antonio de Motocache," Motocache, 1/VIII/1713, f.9; Motocache, 14/IX/1720, f.19v.

37. "Libro de rezivos y gastos de San Jacinto," San Jacinto, 31/I/1712, AGNP, Compañía de Jesús, Cuentas de Haciendas, legajo 93, ff.424–43.

38. "Libro de la hacienda de San Antonio de Motocache," Motocache, 31/XI/1710, f.6v. Motocache, 15/XI/1718, f.19.

39. "Testimonio del ymbentario del colegio del noviciado de la Compañía de Jesús, Año de 1767," 59–60; "Censo de 22U718 p. de principal a favor de las misiones de Moxos," Lima, 22/III/1725, AGNP, Compañía de Jesús, Hojas Sueltas, legajo 126, nos.11, 12, 16; "Libro de la hacienda de San Antonio de Motocache," Motocache, 6/V/1724, ff.27v, 29; and "Inventario de la hacienda de vina de Humay, Los Reyes, 23/XII/1739, ANB, ADM 1, f.98.

40. For studies of Jesuit agriculture in Mexico, see Herman W. Konrad, *A Jesuit Hacienda in Colonial Mexico: Santa Lucía, 1576–1767* (Stanford, Calif.: Stanford University Press, 1980); for Colombia, see Germán Colmenares, *Haciendas de los jesuitas en el Nuevo Reino del Granda, siglo XVIII* (Universidad Nacional de Colombia, 1969); for Peru, see Cushner, *Lords of the Land* (Albany: State University of New York Press, 1980).

41. John Lynch, *Spain under the Hapsburgs*, 2 vols. (Oxford: Oxford University Press, 1969), 2:216.

42. "Inventario de la hacienda de vina de Umay," Reyes, 23/XIII/1739, ff.98–101.

43. "Razón o resumen general," in *Memorias de los virreyes que han gobernado al Perú*, 6 vols. (Lima: Librería de Felipe Bailly, 1859), 4:2–3.

44. Cushner, *Lords of the Land,* 136–37.

45. For an excellent survey of the literature and some new evidence as well, see Kendall W. Brown, "Jesuit Wealth and Economic Activity within the Peruvian Economy: The Case of Colonial Southern Peru," *The Americas* 44, no.1 (July 1987): 25, 43.

CHAPTER 4

1. For a clear statement of this purpose, see "A los reverendos PP Jesuitas," in *Cartas edificantes y curiosas escritas de las misiones estranjeras, y de levante por algunos misioneros de la Compañía de Jesus,* ed. Diego Davin, 16 vols. (Madrid: Imprenta de la viuda de Manuel Fernández, 1755), 7:118.

2. See Sherburne F. Cook and Woodrow Borah, *Essays in Population History,* 3 vols. (Berkeley and Los Angeles: University of California Press, 1971–79); Noble David Cook, *Demographic Collapse, Indian Peru 1520–1620* (Cambridge: Cambridge University Press, 1981); and *The Native Populations of the Americas in 1492,* ed. William M. Denevan (Madison: University of Wisconsin Press, 1976).

3. Sherburne F. Cook, *Population Trends among the California Mission Indians* (Berkeley and Los Angeles: University of California Press, 1940), 16–17.

4. Recent studies of sedentary agriculturalists show young populations characterized by relatively high rates of natality. See Francisco M. Salzano and Sidia M. Callegari-Jacques, *South American Indians* (Oxford: Clarendon Press, 1988), 46–54, which shows modern agricultural Amerindians as having 6.5 live births per completed family.

5. Francisco J. Eder, *Breve descripción de las reducciones de Mojos,* trans. and ed. Josep M. Barnadas (Cochabamba: Historia Boliviana, 1985), 341. See also Diego Francisco Altamirano, *Historia de la misión de los Mojos* (La Paz: Imprenta "El Comercio," 1891), 46, and "Relacion de la provincia de los Mojos," in *Documentos para la historia geográfica de la República de Bolivia,* ed. M. V. Ballivián, 2 vols. (La Paz: J. M. Gamarra, 1906), 1:335.

6. Jane M. Rausch, *A Tropical Plains Frontier* (Albuquerque: University of New Mexico Press, 1984), 72.

7. Mardith Keithly Schuetz, "The Indians of the San Antonio Missions" (Ph.D. diss., University of Texas, 1980), 178.

8. Cook, *Population Trends among the California Mission Indians,* 17.

9. Schuetz, "The Indians of the San Antonio Missions," 157.

10. David James Owens, "A Historical Geography of the Indian Missions in the Jesuit Province of Paraguay: 1609–1768" (Ph.D. diss., University of Kansas, 1977), 242.

11. Eder, *Breve descripción de las reducciones de Mojos,* 359.

12. For the most accessible list, see ibid., 332, 335. See also Antonio de Egaña, *Historia de la iglesia en la América española,* 2 vols. (Madrid: Biblioteca de Autores Cristianos, 1966), 2:397; "Letras annuas 1697–1699," ARSI, Peru 18b, ff.216–216v; "Carta de D. Francisco Antonio Argomosa," San Lorenzo, 6/II/1737, in *Historia de*

la Compañía de Jesús en la provincia de Paraguay, ed. Pablo Pastells, 9 vols. (Madrid: V. Suárez, 1912–49), 7:279; Rubén Vargas Ugarte, *Historia de la Compañía de Jesús en el Perú,* 4 vols. (Burgos: Imprenta de Aldecoa, 1963–65), 3:76; and "Carta de Alonso Verdugo," San Lorenzo, 8/I/1764, AGI, Charcas 474, f.15v.

13. Leandro Tormo Sanz, "Historia demográfica de las misiones de Mojos," *Missionalia hispánica,* 35–36, no.103–8 (1978–79): 297.

14. Cook, *Population Trends among the California Mission Indians,* 25.

15. Altamirano, *Historia de la misión de los Mojos,* 83–89.

16. Pablo Hernández, *Organización social de las doctrinas guaraníes de la Compañía de Jesús,* 2 vols. (Barcelona: Gustavo Gili, 1913), 1:107.

17. Robert Southey, *History of Brazil,* 2d ed., 3 vols. (New York: Greenwood Press, 1969), 3:329, and "El Gobernador Capitan General de Santa Cruz de la Sierra ynforma del estado de las misiones de Mojos," San Lorenzo, 8/1/1764, AGI, Charcas 474, f.14. I also should point out that the previously cited studies of the San Antonio and Paraguayan missions show similar tendencies of redundancy in native political leadership. See Schuetz, "The Indians of the San Antonio Missions," 256, and Owens, "A Historical Geography of the Indian Missions in the Jesuit Province of Paraguay," 302–3.

18. Diego de Eguiluz, *Historia de la misión de Mojos* (Lima: Imprenta del Universo de C. Prince, 1884), 54. See also "Carta de P. Franco. Xavier Granado al P. Xptoval de Rojas," Moxos, 26/IV/1699, BNL, 1716/C63, which describes a celebrated shaman who delighted in donning a crown of thorns and carrying a cross during Holy Week.

19. Owens, "A Historical Geography of the Indian Missions in the Jesuit Province of Paraguay," 324.

20. "Carta del P. Agustín Zapata al P. Fernando de Tardio," San Javier, 9/II/1697, BNL, 1716/C63, and Alcides Parejas, *Historia de Moxos y Chiquitos a fines del siglo XVIII* (La Paz: Instituto Boliviano de Cultura, 1976), 38.

21. The Reyes census appears as "I Autos originales de visitas practicadas, primera por el governador interino D. Leon Gonzales de Velasco," Reyes, 2/V/1773, ANB, ADM 4.

22. "Correspondencia epistolar y de oficio," Loreto, 20/X/1767, ANB, ADM 1, f.85v.

23. For examples for the missions as a whole and for Loreto in particular, see "Relacion de las misiones de Moxos," n.p., 1713, ARSI, Peru 21, f.179, and "Correspondencia epistolar y de oficio," f.85v.

24. "Relación de la provincia de los Mojos," 1:324.

25. Eder, *Breve descripción de las reducciones de Mojos,* 284.

26. For descriptions of the traditional Indian dress in the missionary age, see ibid., 78–81, and Altamirano, *Historia de la misión de los Mojos,* 44.

27. J. Fred Rippy and Jean Thomas Nelson, *Crusaders of the Jungle* (Chapel Hill: University of North Carolina Press, 1936), 94–95.

28. Tormo Sanz, "El sistema comunalista indiano en la región comunera de Mojos-Chiquitos," *Comunidades* 1, no.1 (Jan.–Apr. 1966): 109.

29. "Relacion de las misiones de los moxos de la Compa. de JhS en la Prova. del Peru el ano de 1713," 1713, ARSI, Peru 21, ff.178v–179.

30. Eder, *Breve descripción de las reducciones de Mojos,* 295–96.

31. On the mission fiestas, see ibid., 96, and "Carta del P. Francisco Xavier al P. Fernando Tardio," San Javier, 18/VII/1696, BNL, 1716/C63.

32. "Carta de Antonio Aymerich a SM," Loreto, 20/X/1767, ANB, MYCH, Mojos 1, f.93, and Eder, *Breve descripción de las reducciones de Mojos,* 283.

33. Vicente L. Rafael makes a similar observation on Spanish missions among the Tagalog speakers of the Philippine Islands in his *Contracting Colonialism: Translation and Christian Conversion in Tagalog Society under Early Spanish Rule* (Ithaca, N.Y.: Cornell University Press, 1988), 166.

34. Eguiluz, *Historia de la misión de Mojos,* 51.

35. Eder, *Breve descripción de las reducciones de Mojos,* 320, 323.

36. Ibid., 321.

37. Rogers Becerra Casanovos, *Retablos coloniales del Beni* ([Trinidad]: n.p., 1984), section of plates.

38. Samuel Claro, "La música en las misiones de Moxos," *Revista musical chilena* 22, no.108 (July/Sept. 1969): 23–24.

39. For descriptions of mission agriculture, see "Testimonio de dos cartas," Loreto, 6/I/1768, ANB, ADM 2, f.4v, and Eder, *Breve descripción de las reducciones de Mojos,* 73–74.

40. "Lettre du Pere Nyel, missionnaire de la Compagnie de Jesus, au Pere Dez," 26 May 1705, in *Lettres édifiantes et curieuses écrites par des missionaires de la Compagnie de Jésus,* 34 vols. (Paris: Chez N. Le Clerc, 1702–76), 8:145–46; translation by Marcia Jebb.

41. Eder, *Breve descripción de las reducciones de Mojos,* 272–73.

42. Ibid., 91, 105.

43. Southey, *History of Brazil,* 3:330–31.

44. "Cartas que resultan a Dn. Felix León," San Ignacio, 17/X/1795, ANB, ADM 14, f.56, and "Autos seguidos de visitas al pueblo de Santa Ana," Santa Ana, 12/X/1773, ANB, ADM 3.

45. "Breve noticia de las misiones de Mojos en Obispado de Santa Cruz de la Sierra," in *Historia de la Compañía de Jesús en la provicia de Paraguay,* 8:66.

46. Hervás y Panduro, *Catálogo de las lenguas de las naciones conocidas,* 2 vols. (Madrid: Imprenta del Real Arbitro de Beneficiencia, 1800), 1:253–54.

47. Amy Turner Bushnell, "Ruling 'the Republic of Indians' in Seventeenth-Century Florida," in *Powhatan's Mantle,* ed. Peter Wood et al. (Lincoln: University of Nebraska Press, 1989), 136–37.

48. Alfred Métraux, "The Revolution of the Ax," *Diogenes* 25 (Spring 1959): 28–40.

49. Benjamin Keen and Mark Wasserman, *A Short History of Latin America* (Boston: Houghton Mifflin Co., 1980), 98–99.

50. On San Antonio, see Schuetz, "The Indians of the San Antonio Missions"; on California, see Ignacio del Río, *Conquista y aculturación en la California jesuítica 1697–1768* (Mexico: Universidad Nacional Autónoma de México, 1984).

CHAPTER 5

1. Rubén Vargas Ugarte, *Historia de la Compañía de Jesús en el Perú,* 4 vols. (Burgos: Imprenta de Aldecoa, 1963–65), 1:112, 168.

2. Pedro Borges Morán, *El envío de misioneros a América durante la época española* (Salamanca: Universidad Pontífica, 1977), 539.

3. See the figures given by Antonio Vázquez de Espinoza, *Compendium and Description of the West Indies,* trans. Charles Upson Clark (1628; Washington, D.C.: The Smithsonian Institution, 1942); Cosme Bueno, *Descripción del Peru* [Lima, 1771?] (Note: the Peruvian sections of this work were published as Bueno, *Geografía del Perú virreinal (siglo XVIII)* (Lima: n.p., 1951); and Antonio de Alcedo, *Diccionario geográfico-historico de las indias occidentales o América.* 5 vols. (Madrid: En la Impr. de B. Cano, 1786–89).

4. Antonine Tibesar, "The Alternativa: A Study in the Spanish-Creole Relations in 17th Century Peru," *The Americas* 11 (Jan. 1955): 280 and passim, and Jay F. Lehnertz, "Lands of the Infidels: The Franciscans in the Central Montaña of Peru, 1709–1824" (Ph.D. diss., University of Wisconsin, 1974), 327–30.

5. See, for example, Borges Morán, *El envío de misioneros a América,* 48.

6. "Real Cedula 1715," Madrid, 1715, BNL, 1715/C58.

7. Lino Gómez Canedo has pointed out that the early Franciscan missions to the Indies also had an international flavor, with Flemings, Frenchmen, Italians, Danes, and even Scotchmen entering service in the first half of the sixteenth century.

However, by 1550 this trend had completely disappeared. See Gómez Canedo, *Evangelización y conquista* (Mexico: Porrúa, 1977), 60.

8. Fernando de Armas Medina, *Cristianización del Perú (1532–1600)* (Sevilla: Escuela de Estudios Hispano-Americanos, 1953), 81–82.

9. Antonio Astrain, *Historia de la Compañía de Jesús en la asistencia de España,* 7 vols. (Madrid: Administración de Razón y Fé, 1902–25), 5:547, and "Carta de P. Mayr a su cuñado," in *Cartas e informes de misioneros jesuitas extranjeros en hispanoamérica,* ed. Mauro Matthei, 3 vols. (Santiago: Universidad Católica de Chile, 1968–72), 2:222.

10. The French original and its subsequent extractions and translations appear as *Lettres édifiantes et curieuses écrites par des missionaires de la Compagnie de Jésus,* 34 vols. (Paris: Chez N. Le Clerc, 1702–76); *Allerhand so lehr-als geist-reiche Brief Schrifften und Reis-Beschreibungen, welch von denen Missionariis der Gesellschaft Jesu aus beyden Indien, und andern über Meer gelegenen Ländern, seit An. 1642* (Augspurg und Grätz: In Verlag Philipp, Martin, und Johann Veith, 1728); *Travels of the Jesuits into Various Parts of the World: Compiled from Their Letters by Mr. Lockman,* 2 vols. (London: J. Noon, 1743); *Lettere edificcanti, i curiose, scritte delle missioni strangiere d'alcuni missionarj della Compagnia di Gesu* (Venezia: Appresso Antonio Mora, 1752); *Cartas edificantes y curiosas escritas de las missiones estranjeras, y de levante por algunos misioneros de la Compañía de Jésus,* ed. Diego Davin, 16 vols. (Madrid: Imprenta de la viuda de Manuel Fernández, 1755).

11. "Lettre du pere Stanislaus Arlet au Réverénd Pere General de la même compaignie," in *Lettres édifiantes et curieuses écrites par des missionaires de la Compagnie de Jésus,* 8:39–51.

12. Vicente D. Sierra, *Los Jesuitas germanos en la conquista espiritual de hispanoamérica* (Buenos Aires: Institución Cultural Argentino-Germano, 1944), 63–72.

13. Vargas Ugarte, *Historia de la Compañía de Jesús en el Perú,* 2:170.

14. This manuscript composes the entire contents of ARSI, Peru 22.

15. Borges Morán, *El envío de misioneros a América,* 538–39.

16. Astrain, *Historia de la Compañía de Jesús en la asistencia de España,* 7:365–66.

17. Theodore Edward Treutlein, "Jesuit Travel to America (1678–1756) as Recorded in the Travel Diaries of German Jesuits" (Ph.D. diss., University of California, 1934), 61.

18. "Carta de P. Mayr a su cuñado," 2:222–30.

19. Borges Morán, *El envío de misioneros a América,* 408, 419.

20. "Carta de P. Mayr a su cuñado," 2:229.

21. Maynard Geiger, "Biographical Data on the California Missionaries," *California Historical Society Quarterly* 44, no.4 (Dec. 1965): 291–310.

22. Lehnertz, "Lands of the Infidels," 348–49.

23. Ibid., 350, and Geiger, "Biographical Data on the California Missionaries," 297–303.

24. "Carta de los PP que residen en la mision de los Moxos para el P. Hernando Cavero de la Comp. de Jesus, Provincial de esta provincia del Peru," Provincia de Moxos, 20/IV/1676, ARSI Peru 20, ff.202–3.

25. Joseph del Castillo, "Relación de la provincia de Mojos," in *Documentos para la historia geográfica de la República de Bolivia,* ed. M. V. Ballivián (La Paz: J. M. Gamarra, 1906), 313.

26. "Informe del P. Antonio de Orellana al P. Provincial Martin de Jaregui," Loreto, 18/X/1687, ADLP, Límites con Bolivia, no.283.

27. "Carta de P. Domingo Mayr a su Provincial," in *Cartas e informes de misioneros jesuitas extranjeros en hispanoamérica,* 3:220.

28. "Carta del RP Francisco Javier Dirheim al RP Pedro Mantelo," in *Cartas e informes de misioneros jesuitas extranjeros en hispanoamérica,* 3:295.

29. For descriptions of the effects of disease, see "Carta del P. Juan de Espejo al P. Provincial Diego de Eguiluz," Sant Joseph, 20/IV/1697, ADLP, Límites con Bolivia, no.281; "Carta del P. Miguel Sanchez al Prov. Alonso Mesia," Loreto, 19/IX/1713, ADLP, Límites con Bolivia, no.350; and Vargas Ugarte, *Historia de la Compañía de Jesús en el Perú,* 3:116.

30. This sketch of Garriga's life comes from data in ARSI, Peru 6–8, and from Enrique Torres Saldamando, "El Padre Antonio Garriga," *Revista de artes y letras* [Santiago de Chile] 17 (1890): 412–24.

31. The best source for Eder's biography is Josep M. Barnadas's "Francisco Javier Eder," in Francisco J. Eder, *Breve descripción de las reducciones de Mojos,* trans. and ed. Barnadas (Cochabamba: Historia Boliviana, 1985), lxv–lxxxi.

32. Barnadas, "The Catholic Church in Colonial Spanish America," in *The Cambridge History of Latin America,* ed. Leslie Bethell, 8 vols. (Cambridge: Cambridge University Press , 1984–86), 1:515. This utopian impulse evolved from the vision of the earliest Iberian missionaries to Mexico. See Eric Wolf, *Sons of the Shaking Earth* (Chicago: University of Chicago Press, 1959), and John Leddy Phelan, *The Millenial Kingdom of the Franciscans in the New World* (Berkeley and Los Angeles: University of California Press, 1956).

33. "Relacion de las misiones de los Moxos de la Comp. de JhS en la Prova. del Peru el año de 1713," ARSI, Peru 21, f.176.

34. José de Acosta, *De procuranda indorum salute* (Madrid: Ediciones España Misionera, 1952), 46–47.

35. Eder, *Breve descripción de las reducciones de Mojos,* 362.

36. Astrain, *Historia de la Compañía de Jesús en la asistencia de España,* 3:159–61, and Vargas Ugarte, *Historia de la Compañía de Jesús en el Perú,* 1:99–100.

37. Félix Zubillaga, "Métodos misionales de la primera instrucción de San Francisco de Borja para la América española (1567)," *Archivum historicum Societatis Iesu* 12, no.1–11 (Jan.–Dec. 1943): 60–61.

38. "Ordenes de ynstrucion 1676," n.p., 8/XII/1676, ARSI, Peru 20, ff.214–17.

39. For treatment of the Jesuit experience in Juli, see Norman Meiklejohn, *La iglesia y los lupaqas de Chucuito durante la colonia* (Cusco: Centro de Estudios Rurales Andinos "Bartolomé de las Casas," 1988).

40. This quote comes from the 1888 Spanish translation of Eder's work entitled *Descripción de la provincia de los Mojos en el reino del Perú,* trans. Nicolás Armentía (La Paz: El Siglo Industrial, 1888), 174. The same information, in a less abstracted form, appears in Eder, *Breve descripción de las reducciones de Mojos,* 362–63.

41. Lorenzo Hervás y Panduro, *Catálogo de las lenguas de las naciones conocidas,* 2 vols. (Madrid: Imprenta del Real Arbitro de Beneficiencia, 1800), 1:252.

42. "El Gov. Capp. General de Santa Cruz informa del estado de las miciones de Mojos," Sn. Lorenzo, 8/I/1764, AGI, Charcas 474, f.8.

43. Diane Langmore, *Missionary Lives, Papua 1874–1914* (Honolulu: University of Hawaii Press, 1989), 206.

44. In examining the conversion of highland Indians in Peru, Sabine MacCormack has observed that early texts, such as those prepared by Domingo de Santo Tomás, did include native terms for Christian concepts. She attributes a later suppression of this practice to the Europeans' failure to achieve a grasp of native culture. See MacCormack, " 'The Heart Has Its Reasons': Predicaments of Missionary Christianity in Early Colonial Peru," *Hispanic American Historical Review* 65, no.3 (Oct. 1985): 443–66.

45. "Relacion de las missiones de los Moxos de la Comp. de JhS en la Prova. del Peru el año de 1713," ff.175v–176, and Eder, *Breve descripción de las reducciones de Mojos,* 376.

46. For Jesuit accounts of native music and dance in religious services, see Diego de Eguiluz, *Historia de la misión de Mojos* (Lima: Imprenta del Universo de C. Prince, 1884), 32, and Eder, *Breve descripción de las reducciones de Mojos,* 286–91.

47. For instance, see James Axtell, *The Invasion Within* (New York: Oxford University Press, 1985), 179.

48. See ibid., 179–217. Also see Robert F. Berkhofer, *Salvation and the Savage* ([Lexington]: University of Kentucky Press, [1965]), 16–43.

49. For reference to lay brothers working in arts and offices, see "Carta del P. Agustin Zapata al P. Joseph de Buendia," San Javier, 20/VIII/1696, ADLP, Límites

con Bolivia, no.287; José de Mesa and Teresa Gisbert, *Bolivia: monumentos históricos y arqueológicos* (Mexico: Instituto Panamericano de Geografía y Historia, 1970), 94–96; and Vargas Ugarte, *Historia de la Compañía de Jesús en el Perú,* 3:72, 127.

50. "Carta de los PP," f.203v.

51. "Carta del P. Miguel de Yrigoyen al P. Provincial," San Pedro, 22/IV/1753, ARSI, Peru 21a, f.149v.

52. Stephen Neill, *A History of Christian Missions* (Hammondsworth: Penguin Books, 1964), 203.

53. J. H. Parry, *The Spanish Seaborne Empire* (New York: Alfred A. Knopf, 1966), 171.

54. "Carta de P. Domingo Mayr a su Provincial," 3:245.

55. Urs Bitterli, *Cultures in Conflict,* trans. Ritchie Robertson (Stanford, Calif.: Stanford University Press, 1989), 47.

CHAPTER 6

1. The decree appears in Luís Antonio Eguiguren, *Las huellas de la Compañía de Jesús en el Perú* (Lima: Librería y Imprenta Gil, 1956), 7–8.

2. "Consulta del Consejo y minuta del Real Decreto sobre el gobierno espiritual y temporal de las misiones de Mojos y Chiquitos, 1772," in *Juicio de límites entre el Perú y Bolivia,* ed. Victor M. Maurtua, 12 vols. (Barcelona: Imprenta de Henrich y Compañía, 1906), 10:84–91.

3. Alcides Parejas, *Historia de Moxos y Chiquitos a fines del siglo XVIII* (La Paz: Instituto Boliviano de Cultura, 1976), 47–48. The decree that defined the position of the governors of Moxos also confirmed Herboso's reglamento: "Consulta del Consejo y minuta del Real Decreto sobre el gobierno espiritual y temporal," 10:91.

4. "Testimonio del cuaderno de autos obrados sobre la visita practicado el Dr. D. Pedro de Rocha," La Plata, 1/VII/1769, ANB, Audiencia de Charcas, Mojos IV, ff.1–36.

5. "XVII Testimonio de cinco cartas," Loreto, 29/IX/1769, ANB, ADM 3, f.3v.

6. "Expediente de las diligencias seguidas por Antonio Aymerich sobre el ilicito comercio," Loreto, 5/III/1770, ANB, Audiencia de Charcas, Mojos V, ff.1v–3v.

7. Guillermo Furlong Cardiff, "Lázaro de Ribera y su cartilla real," *Humanidades* 34 (1954): 16–17.

8. For a discussion of these events from an imperial perspective, see John Lynch, *Spanish Colonial Administration, 1782–1810: The Intendant System in the Viceroyalty of the Río de la Plata* (London: University of London/The Athlone Press, 1958).

9. Brooke Larson has developed this theme of the new professional bureaucrats in the highlands, especially Francisco de Viedma; see her *Colonialism and Agrarian Transformation in Bolivia* (Princeton, N.J.: Princeton University Press, 1988), esp. 246–58.

10. Parejas, *Historia de Moxos y Chiquitos a fines del siglo XVIII,* 62.

11. Ibid., 65–66.

12. "Cartilla de instrucción para Mojos, 1786," in *Mojos y Chiquitos,* 2 vols. (Lima: Biblioteca Andina, 1988), 1:75–77.

13. Lynch, *Spanish Colonial Administration, 1782–1810,* 297. Ribera's tenure in Paraguay was troubled, as Lynch documents, but he managed to rescue his career as intendant of Huancavelica and then of the Province of Lima.

14. "Autos seguidos contra los licenciados," Loreto, 9/I/1793, ANB, Audiencia de Charcas, Mojos IX, ff.26v–27v, and "Testimonio de la carta escrita," Santa Ana, [1793?], ANB, Audiencia de Charcas, Mojos VIII, f.1v.

15. This summary of Zamora's governorship comes from "Resumen sobre el tiranico gobierno de Dn. Miguel de Zamora, con los yndios Mojos," 1800, ADLP, Límites con Bolivia, no.797, and "Expediente que trata sobre las ilicitas extraciones," Santa Cruz, 12/IX/1802, ANB, Audiencia de Charcas, Mojos XVIII, ff.2v–3v.

16. "Expediente que trata sobre las ilicitas extraciones," f.2v.

17. "IV Expediente que contiene el ultimo estado en que hallaba la Prova. de Moxos por el año de 1802," Exaltacion, 8/VIII/1803, ANB, ADM f.30.

18. The administrators Antonio de Landivar of Exaltación and Manuel Delgadillo of Loreto have their testimonies preserved as "Declaraciones de los administradores," San Pedro, 5/II/1806, ANB, Audiencia de Charcas, Mojos XX, s/f.

19. Lynch, *Spanish Colonial Administration, 1782–1810,* 254–56.

20. José Chávez Suárez, *Historia de Moxos,* 2d ed. (La Paz: Editorial Don Bosco, 1986), 477–78, and Antonio Carvalho Urey, *Pedro Ignacio Muiba: el héroe.* 3d ed. (Trinidad: n.p., 1977), 41–42.

21. Chávez Suárez, *Historia de Moxos,* 486–87.

22. Fernando Sanabria Fernández, *En busca de el dorado: La colonización del oriente boliviano por los cruceños* (Buenos Aires: Imprenta López, 1958), 157–58.

23. Parejas, *Historia de Moxos y Chiquitos a fines del siglo XVIII,* 98; Leandro Tormo Sanz, "El Padre Julián Aller y su relación de Mojos," *Missionalia hispánica* 13, no.38 (1956): 380; José María García Recio, *Análisis de una sociedad de frontera: Santa Cruz de la Sierra en los siglos XVI y XVII* (Sevilla: Publicaciones de la Exema, Diputación Provincial de Sevilla, 1988), 389–90.

24. "Carta de D. Jose Franco a SM," La Plata, 14/VII/1778, ADLP, Límites con Bolivia, no.436.

25. "El informe del governador de Mojos," San Pedro, 17/X/1787, ANB, ADM 7, ff.4v–5.

26. "III Inventarios de los bienes pertenecientes a la Iglesia y la comunidad de Concepcion," Concepción, 15/III/1768, ANB, ADM 1, f.193.

27. "Testimonio de las diligencias practicadas por el governador de Moxos," San Pedro, 30/X/1786, ANB, Audiencia de Charcas, Mojos X, f.28. For additional comments on Lorenzo Chávez's life, see Sanabria Fernández's "Notas Adicionales" in the 1973 version of René-Moreno's *Catálogo del archivo de Mojos y Chiquitos,* 523.

28. The fifty-five curas appear in a series of inventories and visitas that stretch across the entire period: "II Correspondencia epistolar y de oficio, Loreto, 20/X/1767, ANB, ADM 1, f.83v; "Testimonio del cuaderno de autos," La Plata, 1/VII/1769, ANB, ADM 1, ff.1–36; "I Autos originales de visitas, 1773," ANB, ADM 4, ff.10–47; "Autos del licenciado Fernando Salas," Santa Cruz, 10/IX/1777, ANB, Audiencia de Charcas, Mojos V, ff.4v–5; "Testimonio del expediente de la visita a las misiones," 1786, ANB, ADM 11, ff.1–46v; "Expediente que contiene relaciones de visitas," 1790, ANB, Audiencia de Charcas, Mojos IX, ff.5–40v.

29. Ibid.

30. "Carta de Francisco, Obispo de Santa Cruz a SM," Loreto, 28/VIII/1768, ANB, Audiencia de Charcas, Mojos V, ff.8v–9, and "IV Expediente sobre dos cartas," Loreto, 28/VIII/1768, ANB, ADM 3, ff.IV–2v. Interestingly, these two documents (now separated in the archive although obviously prepared together), reflect two estimates of mission production. The curas' estimate, summarized in the bishop's letter, was 16,400 pesos per annum; that of Governor Aymerich was 19,400 pesos.

31. Parejas, *Historia de Moxos y Chiquitos a fines del siglo XVIII,* 61.

32. "Expediente obrado por el administrador general de misiones," La Plata, 26/VIII/1786, ANB, Audiencia de Charcas, Mojos XIII.

33. "I Autos originales," San Pedro, 27/XI/1773, ANB, ADM 4, f.29v, and "Documentos de la cuenta que presenta Don Joaquin de Artachu," Cochabamba, 6/X/1783, ANB, Audiencia de Charcas, Mojos VIII, f.11.

34. "I Autos originales," Concepción, 28/II/1772, ANB, ADM 4, f.43, and "I Testimonio del expediente de la visita del pueblo de Concepcion," Concepción, 6/VI/1786, ANB, ADM 11, f.4.

35. "I Testimonio del expediente de la visita del pueblo de Concepcion," Concepción, 6/VI/1786, ff.3v–4, and "Expediente que contiene las noticias de misiones," Concepción, III/1790, ANB, Audiencia de Charcas, Mojos IX, f.29.

36. Daniel J. Santamaría, "La economía de las misiones de Moxos y Chiquitos (1675–1810)," *Ibero-Amerikanisches archiv* n.s. 13, no.2 (1987): 283–84.

37. "Expediente que contiene las noticias de misiones," Reyes, VIII/1790; Concepción, III/1790, ANB, Audiencia de Charcas, Mojos IX, ff.8, 29.

38. Santamaría, "La economía de las misiones de Moxos y Chiquitos (1675–1810)," 279–81, and Parejas, *Historia de Moxos y Chiquitos a fines del siglo XVIII,* 119.

39. Santamaría, "La economía de las misiones de Moxos y Chiquitos (1675–1810), 281–82.

40. "Testimonio de las diligencias practicadas por el Gov. de la Provincia de Moxos," San Pedro, 30/X/1786, ANB, Audiencia de Charcas, Mojos X, f.26v.

41. "Carta de Don Lázaro de Rivera, Gobernador de Mojos, al Conde de Floridablanca," in *Juicio de Límites entre el Perú y Bolivia,* 10:270–71.

42. Larson, *Colonialism and Agrarian Transformation in Bolivia,* 234.

43. Santamaría, "La economía de las misiones de Moxos y Chiquitos," (1675–1810)," 272. Santamaría points out that this surplus eventually returned to the region to cover the deficits of the Chiquitos missions.

44. Rubén Vargas Ugarte, *Historia de la Compañía de Jesús en el Perú,* 4 vols. (Burgos: Imprenta de Aldecoa, 1963–65), 3:131–32.

45. Both Ribera's estimate and Parejas's commentary appear in Parejas, *Historia de Moxos y Chiquitos a fines del siglo XVIII,* 64.

46. Santamaría, "La economía de las misiones de Moxos y Chiquitos (1675–1810)," 267. On bad weather see "Las escases de cosecha en Mojos, 1795–1796," in *Mojos y Chiquitos,* 2 vols. (Lima: Biblioteca Andina, 1988), 1:152.

47. "Autos seguidos por el governador de Mojos D. Antonio Aymerich contra las personas de los Yndios," ANB, Audiencia de Charcas, Mojos IV, f.56v.

48. For reports of flight, see "Carta de Manuel Nicolas, Obispo de Santa Cruz," Punata, 9/VI/1798, ADLP, Límites con Bolivia, no.436, and "Autos originales de visitas," Loreto, 20/XII/1773, ANB, ADM 3, f.17v.

49. Thekla Hartmann, *A contribuição inconografia para o conhecimento de índios brasileiros do século XIX* (São Paulo: Edição do Fondo de Pesquisas de Museu Paulista da Universidade de São Paulo, 1975), 26–27.

50. "Correspondencia y oficios," Loreto, 26/VIII/1786, ANB, ADM 6, ff.IV–2.

51. José Luís Mora Merida, "La demografía colonial paraguaya," *Jahrbuch für geschichte von staat, wirtschaft und gesselschaft lateinamerikas* 11 (1974): 63–66.

52. On the Indians as merchants' employees, see "II contiene cinco cartas," Santa Cruz, 30/X/1784, ANB, ADM 9, f.2, and "XXI Auto contra la libertad," San Pedro, 2/XI/1786, ANB, ADM 6, ff.2v–3, 4. The accounts show that twenty mission Indians from Exaltación came to work in a store in La Plata owned by Don Angel Gutiérrez between 1802 and 1806. The same records show payment for burial of ten

"Indios de Moxos" in La Plata between 1801 and 1802. "Expediente No. 25," La Plata, 15/II/1802, ANB, Audiencia de Charcas, Mojos XVIII.

53. Sivapaire actually said, "siempre todo mucho camina para este [*sic*] tierra Chuquisaca, de este Chuquisaca no viene harto, poquito no mas." "VIII sobre el aumento de las missiones [*sic*]," Loreto, 30/XI/1792, ANB, ADM 13, ff.1–IV.

54. "XXXVIII, San Pedro," San Pedro, 24/IX/1792, ANB, ADM 10, ff.4v–5.

55. "Autos originales de visitas," Loreto, 13/V/1773, ANB, ADM 4, ff.2–6.

56. "XXVII Ano 1792, sobre Juan Copareari," San Pedro, 17/V/1792, ANB, ADM 11, ff.7–7v.

57. "Autos seguidos contra los licenciados," Loreto, 9/I/1786, ANB, Audiencia de Charcas, Mojos IX, ff.26v–27.

58. "Autos seguidos por el gobernador de Mojos, D. Antonio Aymerich contra las personas de los indios," Loreto, 9/XI/1769, ANB, Audiencia de Charcas, Mojos IV, ff.10–11, and "Autos seguidos por el governador de Mojos," Exaltación, 13/XI/1769, ANB, Audiencia de Charcas, Mojos IV, ff.6–8.

59. "Autos seguidos por el governador de Mojos," Loreto, 9/XI/1769, f.1.

60. "XXVII Relacion de D. Lazaro de Ribera," San Pedro, 24/IX/1792, ANB, ADM 10, ff.5–5v, and "XII Razon de los existencias," San Pedro, 3/X/1796, ANB, ADM 14, f.148v. This latter document points out that cotton grew where rice lay some ten years before.

61. "VII sobre el cumiento [*sic*] de las misiones de Mojos," Trinidad, 8/XII/1792, ANB, ADM 13, f.20v.

62. "XVI Expediente que contiene las cartas," Loreto, 12/XI/1770, ANB, ADM 2, f.8; "XVI Expediente que contiene las cartas," Loreto, 7/I/1771, ANB, ADM 2, ff.16–16v; "XII Expediente sobre la concorporacion," San Pedro, 15/V/193, ANB, ADM 13, ff.7–8v; "Sobre el aumento de las misiones," Loreto, 1/XII/1792, ANB, ADM 13, f.2; and "Carta de Manuel Nicolas, Obispo de Santa Cruz," Punata, 9/VI/1798, ADLP, Límites con Bolivia, no.436.

63. "I Autos seguidos de visitas al pueblo de Santa Ana," Santa Ana, 12/XI/1773, ANB, ADM 3.

64. "Expediente que contiene el informe de la fundacion de San Javier," Narasaquixi, 29/VIII/1796, ANB, ADM 14, f.5.

65. "Cartas que resultan a Dn. Felix Leon," San Ignacio, 17/X/1795, ANB, ADM 14, f.56.

66. Francisco de Viedma, *Descripción geográfica y estadística de la provincia de Santa Cruz de la Sierra,* 3d ed. (Cochabamba: Editorial "Los Amigos del Libro," 1969), 202.

67. "Declaraciones de los administradores," San Pedro, 5/II/1806, ANB, Audiencia de Charcas, Mojos XX.

68. For evidence of the destruction of cacao, cotton, and cane crops, see "Expediente que trata sobre las ilicitas extraciones," San Pedro, 10/XII/1802, ANB, Audiencia de Charcas, Mojos XVIII, f.11v, and "XIX Razones originales," Loreto 21/I/1803, ANB, ADM 17.

CHAPTER 7

1. Simón Bolivar, *Proyecto de constitución para la República Boliviana* (Caracas: Academia Nacional de la Historia, Lagoven, S.A., 1978), 145.

2. William Lee Lofstrom, *El Mariscal Sucre en Bolivia* (La Paz: Editorial e Imprenta Alenkar Ltda., 1983), 334–35.

3. Ibid., 77, 80–82.

4. Antonio Carvalho Urey, "Síntesis histórica del Beni," in *Monografía de Bolivia*, 4 vols. (La Paz: Biblioteca del Sesquicentenario de la República, 1975), 4:35.

5. Fernando Sanabria Fernández, *En busca de el dorado: la colonización del oriente boliviano por los cruceños* (Buenos Aires: Imprenta López, 1958), 19.

6. Manuel Limpias Saucedo, *Los gobernadores de Mojos* (La Paz: Escuela Tipográfica Salesiana, 1942), 3.

7. Ibid., 4.

8. Felix Reyes Ortiz, *Anuario administrativo y político de Bolivia, 1856* (La Paz: Imprenta del Vapor, 1856), 104, and Carvalho Urey, *Beni ensayo de interpretación histórica* (Trinidad: n.p., 1983), 33.

9. "Instrucciones que se observan para el gobierno de la provincia de Mojos, 1836," Chuquisica, 3/X/1836, ANB, Mojos y Chiquitos II, f.117.

10. "Correspondencia con los gobernadores de Moxos," Chuquisaca, 13/II/1835, ANB, MI 69, f.10a; "Razon de los pasaportes espedidos por esta comisaria mayor," Trinidad, 31/XI/1849; "Lista de los ciudadanos que han emetido sus votos para Presidente de la Republica," Concepción, San Joaquín, Magdalena, Santa Ana, 1849, ANB, MI 130, f.25.

11. White population counts appear in Alcides Dessalines d'Orbigny, *Descripción geográfica, histórica y estadística de Bolivia* (Paris: Librería de los Señores Guide y Compañía, 1845), 296; Pablo Macera, *Bolivia, tierra y población, 1825–1836* (Lima: Biblioteca Andina, 1978), 1; and Reyes Ortiz, *Anuario administrativo y político de Bolivia, 1856*, 150.

12. "Razón nominal de los señores empleados de la lista civil que tiene esta provincia," Mojos 28/VI/1837, ANB, MI 67, f.28; "Relación ecsata que remite al Prefecto del Departamento del Beni," Concepción, 2/XI/1843, ANB, MI 96, f.48;

and "Cuadro que manifiesta la relacion nominal de los empleados," Trinidad 5/VII/ 1855, ANB, MI 155, f.38.

13. William Lewis Herndon and Lardner Gibbon, *Exploration of the Valley of the Amazon,* 2 vols. (Washington, D.C.: A.O.P. Nicholson, Public Printer 1854), 2:242.

14. J. Valerie Fifer attributes this observation to J. A. Lloyd in 1853 (Fifer, *Bolivia: Land, Location, and Politics since 1825* [Cambridge: Cambridge University Press, 1972], 100).

15. Herndon and Gibbon, *Exploration of the Valley of the Amazon,* 2:249.

16. Limpias Saucedo, *Los gobernadores de Mojos,* 83–92.

17. Janet Groff Greever, *José Ballivián y el oriente boliviano* (La Paz: Empresa Editora Siglo Ltda., 1987), 63–84. Greever's analysis of the colonization accords points out that, in each case, the companies were to exercise extensive powers over the native people of Moxos, suggesting that, despite the rhetoric of the 1842 declaration, the Ballivián regime was more interested in economic development than in citizens' rights.

18. James C. Jones, "Conflict between Whites and Indians on the Llano de Moxos, Beni Department: A Case Study in Development from the Cattle Regions of the Bolivian Oriente" (Ph.D. diss., University of Florida, 1980), esp.103–7.

19. "Relacion nominal de los deudores al Tesoro Publico del Departamento del Beni," Trinidad, 29/XI/1856, ANB, MH 141, f.29.

20. "Cuadro demonstrativo de tierras sobrantes y de comunidades vendidas 1866–1869," Trinidad, 1869, ANB, MH 1870, ff.3, 48. See also Zulema Lehm Ardaya, "Diagnostico de la situación actual de los indígenas de Trinidad y areas cercanas," in *Simposio sobre las misiones jesuitas en Bolivia* (La Paz: Ministerio de Relaciones Exteriores y Culto, 1987), 208.

21. "Cuenta q. presenta el Admor. del pueblo de Loreto Cno. Rursindo Vargas," Loreto, 31/XII/1829, ANB, MI 62, f.27.

22. Joseph Barclay Pentland, "Report on Bolivia, 1827," in *Camden Miscellany,* ed. J. Valerie Fifer, 4th ser., vol.13 (London: Offices of the Royal Historical Society, 1974), 228–29.

23. "Instrucciones que se observan para el gobierno de la Provincia de Mojos, 1836," Chuquisaca, 3/X/1836, ANB, Mojos y Chiquitos II, 112.

24. Orbigny, *Descripción geográfica, histórica y estadística de Bolivia,* 213.

25. Limpias Saucedo, *Los gobernadores de Mojos,* 32.

26. Franz Keller, *The Amazon and Madeira Rivers* (Philadelphia: J. B. Lippincott and Co., 1875), 184–85.

27. For a sample of the correspondence, see "Carta de Antonio de Velasco al Yntendiente de Santa Cruz," Santa Cruz, 28/I/1827, ANB, MI 18, f.21; "Correspon-

dencia con los gobernadores de Mojos," Chuquisaca, 28/II/1835, ANB, MI 69, f.10a; and "Instrucciones que se observan para el gobierno de la Provincia de Mojos," Chuquisaca, 3/X/1836, ANB, Mojos y Chiquitos, II, f.114.

28. Herndon and Gibbon, *Exploration of the Valley of the Amazon,* 240.

29. "Carta de Luis Valverde," Trinidad, 26/III/1850, ANB, AI 134, f.36.

30. The 1825 list appears as "Estado que demuestra las producciones del Departamento en sus cuatro partidos," Santa Cruz, 26/X/1825, ANB, MI 35, f.24. Financial statistics are presented in Orbigny, *Descripción geográfica, histórica y estadística de Bolivia,* 364.

31. Orbigny, *Viaje a la América meridional,* trans. Alfredo Cepada, 4 vols. (Buenos Aires: Editorial Futuro, 1945), 4:1314.

32. "Demonstracion que se hase del caudal en especies," Trinidad, 29/V/1838, ANB, MI 67, f.28.

33. For reports on declining revenues, see "Estado que manifiesta la quiebra que han padecido los productos de las administraciones de los Pueblos de Mojos," Trinidad, 2/III/1839, ANB, MI 74, f.31, and "Demonstracion de la diferencia en el ingreso de los productos en especie de la provincia de Mojos," Trinidad, n.d., ANB, MI 67, f.28.

34. The inventories assay the property of Exaltación, Trinidad, Santa Ana, Reyes, and San Pedro and appear as "Ynventarios de los bienes de Yglesia de Mojos No. 432," ANB, MI 101, f.23.

35. Herndon and Gibbon, *Exploration of the Valley of the Amazon,* 1:193.

36. José Antonio Ocampo, *Colombia y la economía mundial 1830–1910* (Bogotá: Siglo Veintiuno, 1984), 271–73. See also José María Dalence, *Bosquejo estadística de Bolivia* (La Paz: [s.n.], 1975), and Herbert S. Klein, *Bolivia: The Evolution of a Multi-Ethnic Society* (New York: Oxford University Press, 1982), 121.

37. Hughes Algernon Weddell, *Voyages dans le nord de la Bolivie et dans les parties voisines de Pérou* (Paris: V. Masson, 1849); J. Valerie Fifer, "The Empire Builders: A History of the Bolivian Rubber Boom and the Rise of the House of Suárez," *Journal of Latin American Studies* 2, no.2 (1970): 118; and "N. 12 al Sor. Ministro del E. del D. de lo Ynterior y del Culto," Trinidad 31/I/1856, ANB, MI 158, f.17.

38. Clements Markham, *Travels in Peru and India* (London: John Murray, 1862), 36–38, and Ocampo, *Colombia y la economía mundial 1830–1910,* 273.

39. To date, the most reliable discussion of the boom and bust of rubber in the area comes from Barbara Weinstein, *The Amazon Rubber Boom 1850–1920* (Stanford, Calif.: Stanford University Press, 1983), 52–53.

40. Antonio Vaca Díez, *Memorial que presenta al Delegdo Nacional en el Madre de Dios, Acre y Purús* (La Paz: Imprenta y Litografía de "El Nacional" de Isaac V.

Vila, 1894), 34; Fifer, *Bolivia,* 110; and Limpias Saucedo, *Los gobernadores de Mojos,* 223.

41. Keller, *The Amazon and Madeira Rivers,* 42.

42. Ibid., 47.

43. Keller, "Report of José and Francisco Keller, Made to the Imperial Government of Brazil," in George Earl Church, *Explorations Made in the Valley of the Madeira from 1749 to 1868* (n.p. Published for the National Bolivia Navigation Company, 1875), 6.

44. Jesualdo Maccheti, *Diario del viaje fluvial de padre Fray Jesualdo Maccheti* [La Paz]: Imprenta El Siglo Industrial, 1869), 52–54.

45. C. Barrington Brown and William Lidstone, *Fifteen Thousand Miles on the Amazon and Its Tributaries* (London: Edward Stanford, 1878), 348–50, and Edward D. Mathews, *Up the Amazon and Madeira Rivers, through Bolivia and Peru* (London: Sampson Low, Marston, Searle and Rivington, 1879), 85, 94.

46. Warren Dean, *Brazil and the Struggle for Rubber* (Cambridge: Cambridge University Press, 1987), 16.

47. Evidence for all these regulations comes from Limpias Saucedo, *Los gobernadores de Mojos,* 151–54, 162–63, 170, and 199–200.

48. See Keller, *The Amazon and Madeira Rivers,* 78, for beef prices, and Mathews, *Up the Amazon and Madeira Rivers, through Bolivia and Peru,* 160–61, for wage rates.

49. Orbigny, *Descripción geográfica, histórica y estadística de Bolivia,* 299.

50. Citations for Orbigny's observations are, in order: *Viaje a la América meridional,* trans. Alfredo Cepada, 4 vols. (Buenos Aires: Editorial Futuro, 1945), 4:1446; *Descripción geográfica, histórica y estadística de Bolivia,* 187; and *Viaje a la América meridional,* 4:1313, 1316–17, 1341–42, 1357–58.

51. Orbigny, *Viaje a la América meridional,* 4:1445.

52. The 1846 count stems from the results of a national census conducted in that year and includes an unspecified number of native people from areas outside the savanna, in Caupolicán. The 1860 figure is clearly some sort of estimate, since each population recorded appears in the source rounded to the nearest hundred.

53. For reports of disease, see Limpias Saucedo, *Los gobernadores de Mojos,* 43 (for 1845) and 71 (for 1850); "Al Sor. Ministro del Estado," Trinidad, 9/IV/1851, ANB, MI 137, f.27 (for 1849); and "Al S. S.H. el Secret. Gral d S. E. el Presidente de la Republica," Trinidad, 5/I/1858, ANB, MI 163, f.31 (for 1858).

54. Macera, *Bolivia, tierra y poblacion, 1825–1836,* 106.

55. Mathews, *Up the Amazon and Madeira Rivers, through Bolivia and Peru,* 132.

56. Albert L. Hurtado, *Indian Survival on the California Frontier* (New Haven, Conn.: Yale University Press, 1988), 209–10 and passim.

57. The census fragments appear with the same title, "Estado q. manifiesta el No. de almas que tiene esta Paroquia y demas q. se espresa," San Joaquín, 1830, ANB, MI 35, f.24; Santa Ana, 31/XII/1830, ANB, MI 32, f.25; Concepción 31/XII/1830, ANB, MI 32, f.25.

58. "Plan de las reformas que la Provincia de Mojos pide en su actual ruinoso estado," Cochabamba, 18/VI/1839, ANB, MI 74, f.31, and "Cuadro que manifesta la relacion nominal de los empleados," Trinidad, 5/VII/1855, ANB, MI 155, f.38.

59. "Juicios contre Jose Luis Osorio," Exaltación, VIII/1852, ANB, MI 143, f.25.

60. "No. 20 al H.S. Ministro de E. del Pespacho de Hacienda," Trinidad, 6/VII/1856, ANB, MH 141, f.29.

61. Tristan Platt, "The Andean Experience of Bolivian Liberalism, 1825–1900: Roots of Rebellion in 19th Century Chayanta (Potosí)," in *Resistance, Rebellion, and Consciousness in the Andean Peasant World,* ed. Steve J. Stern (Madison: University of Wisconsin Press, 1987), 213 and passim. See also the treatment of nineteenth-century events in Yura territory of southern Potosí in Roger Neil Rasnake, *Domination and Cultural Resistance* (Durham, N.C.: Duke University Press, 1988), 151–65.

62. Keller, *The Amazon and Madeira Rivers,* 187.

63. Limpias Saucedo, *Los gobernadores de Mojos,* 154–55.

64. Orbigny, *Viaje a la América meridional,* 4:1312.

65. "Comunicaciones con el gobernador de Moxos," Chuquisaca, 30/X/1833, ANB, MI 69, f.10a, and "A los Corregidores," n.p., 13/I/1837, ANB, MI 62, f.27.

66. Orbigny, *Descripción geográfica, histórica y estadística de Bolivia,* 338.

67. Limpias Saucedo, *Los gobernadores de Mojos,* 44.

68. Herndon and Gibbon, *Exploration of the Valley of the Amazon,* 2:227.

69. *Documentos que comprueban la conducta nada honrosa de D. Damón Barberi Prefecto del Beni* (Santa Cruz: Imprenta de Cayetano R. Daza, 1872), 3, 12–13.

70. Jones, "Conflict between Whites and Indians on the Llano de Moxos, Beni Department," 113.

71. Rogers Becerra Casanovos, *El Imperio del caucho: perfil del noroeste boliviano* (Trinidad: n.p., 1984), 60. Beni historians are particularly insistent on the use of force by local officials. See also Carvalho Urey, *Beni ensayo de interpretación histórica* (Trinidad: n.p., 1983), 34–35.

72. A synopsis of Pinkas's report appears in John Hemming, *Amazon Frontier* (Cambridge, Mass.: Harvard University Press, 1987), 277.

73. Jones, "Conflict between Indians and Whites on the Llano de Moxos, Beni Department," 113–14.

74. Carvalho Urey, "Síntesis histórica del Beni," 37–38.

75. "Al Sr. Ministro de Estado del Despacho del Ynterior," Trinidad, 8/IV/1842,

ANB, MI 137, f.27; "Testimonio de varias piezas de la causa criminal seguida contra los naturales de la Provincia de Mojos," Cochabamba, 15/IV/1847, ANB, MI 120, f.32; and "Razon del estado de las causas criminales pendientes en el juzgago de letras de la capital del Beni," Trinidad, 27/II/1846, ANB, MI 115, f.37.

76. Gabriel René-Moreno, *Catálogo del Archivo de Mojos y Chiquitos*, 2d ed. (La Paz: Librería Editorial "Juventud," 1973), 75.

77. José Agustín Palacios, *Exploraciones de don José Agustín Palacios realizados en los ríos Beni, Mamoré y Madeira y el lago Rogo-aguado, durante los años 1844 al 47* (La Paz: Editorial del Estado, 1944), 65.

78. Keller, *The Amazon and Madeira Rivers*, 80–82.

79. Mathews, *Up the Amazon and Madeira Rivers, through Bolivia and Peru*, 59, 121, 160–61; Keller, "Report of José and Francisco Keller, made to the Imperial Government of Brazil," 52; and René-Moreno, *Catálogo del Archivo de Mojos y Chiquitos*, 74.

80. David Bushnell and Neill Maccaulay, *The Emergence of Latin America in the Nineteenth Century* (New York: Oxford University Press, 1988), 209.

81. E. Bradford Burns, *The Poverty of Progress* (Berkeley and Los Angeles: University of California Press, 1980), 9, 12, and passim.

CONCLUSIONS

1. For example, see Lino Gómez Canedo, *Evangelización y conquista* (Mexico: Porrúa, 1977), who points to the Franciscans' dedication to instruction in native languages and their preference for work among the young (157–59, 170–71).

2. For useful studies of missions in these areas, see Ignacio del Río, *Conquista y aculturación en la California jesuítica 1697–1768* (Mexico: Universidad Nacional Autónoma de México, 1984), and Erik D. Langer and Robert H. Jackson, "Colonial and Republican Missions Compared: The Cases of Alta California and Southeastern Bolivia," *Comparative Studies in Society and History* 20, no.2 (Apr. 1988), esp. 289, 293.

3. James Axtell, *After Columbus* (New York: Oxford University Press, 1988), 49–50.

4. Robert F. Berkhofer, *Salvation and the Savage* ([Lexington]: University of Kentucky Press, [1965]), 15.

5. See Albert L. Hurtado, *Indian Survival on the California Frontier* (New Haven, Conn.: Yale University Press, 1988), 100 and passim, and Robin Fisher, *Contact and Conflict: Indian European Relations in British Columbia, 1744–1890* (Vancouver: University of British Columbia Press, 1977), 96–97.

BIBLIOGRAPHY

UNPUBLISHED SOURCES

Archivo de Límites de Bolivia, La Paz (ADLB)

Archivo de Límites del Perú, Lima (ADLP) Límites con Bolivia

Archivo General de Indias, Sevilla (AGI)
    Audiencia de Charcas
    Audiencia de Lima
    Contratación
    Indiferente General
    Mapas y Planos
    Patronato Real

Archivo General de la Nacion del Perú, Lima (AGNP)
    Sección Compañía de Jesús

Archivo Nacional de Bolivia, Sucre (ANB)
    Audiencia de Charcas
    Mojos y Chiquitos (MYCH)
    Archivo de Mojos (ADM)
    Documentos de la Corte Suprema de Justicia
    Ministerio de Hacienda (MH)
    Ministerio del Interior (MI)

Archivum Romanum Societatis Ieus, Rome (ARSI) Peru

Biblioteca Nacional de Perú, Lima (BNL)

Biblioteca del Palacio Real, Madrid (BPR)

Biblioteca Nacional, Madrid (BN) Papeles de América

Acosta, José de. *De procuranda indorum salute.* Madrid: Ediciones España Misionera, 1952.

Actas capitulares de Santa Cruz de la Sierra, 1634–1640. La Paz: Universidad Boliviana Gabriel René Moreno, 1977.

Alexandre de Gusmão e o Tratado de Madrid. Ed. Jaime Cortesão. 5 vols. Rio de Janeiro: Ministério das Relações Exteriores, Instituto Rio-Branco, 1950–63.

Almaráz, Félix D. *The San Antonio Missions and Their System of Land Tenure.* Austin: University of Texas Press, 1989.

Altamirano, Diego Francisco. *Historia de la misión de los Mojos.* La Paz: Imprenta "El Comercio," 1891.

Archibald, Robert Reid. *The Economic Aspects of the California Missions.* Washington, D.C.: Academy of American Franciscan History, 1978.

Arlet, Stanislaus. "Lettre du pere Stanislaus Arlet, de la Compagnie de Jésus, au réverénd Pere General de la même Compagnie." In *Lettres édifiantes et curieuses écrites par des missionaires de la Compagnie de Jésus,* 8:39–51.

Armas Medina, Fernando de. *Cristianización del Perú, 1532–1600.* Sevilla: Escuela de Estudios Hispano-Americanos, 1953.

Armentía, Nicolás de. *Relación de las misiones franciscanas de Apolobamba.* La Paz: Tip. Artística, 1905.

Astrain, Antonio. *Historia de la Compañía de Jesús en la asistencia de España.* 7 vols. Madrid: Administración de Razón y Fé, 1902–25.

Axtell, James. *After Columbus.* New York: Oxford University Press, 1988.

——. *The Invasion Within.* New York: Oxford University Press, 1985.

Bangert, William V. *A History of the Society of Jesus.* St. Louis: The Institute of Jesuit Sources, 1972.

Barnadas, Josep M. "The Catholic Church in Colonial Spanish America." In *The Cambridge History of Latin America,* ed. Leslie Bethell, 8 vols., 1:511–40. Cambridge: Cambridge University Press, 1984.

——. "Introducción." In Francisco J. Eder, *Breve descripción de las reducciones de Mojos,* xxi–ciii.

Becerra Casanovos, Rogers. *El Imperio del caucho: perfil del noroeste boliviano.* Trinidad: n.p., 1984.

——. "Orígenes y natualeza de las danzas y música moxeñas." In *Simposio sobre las misiones jesuitas en Bolivia,* 67–75.

——. *Reliquías de moxos.* La Paz: Casa de la Cultura F. Tamayo, 1977.

——. *Retablos coloniales del Beni.* [Trinidad]: n.p., 1984.

Berkhofer, Robert F. *Salvation and the Savage.* [Lexington]: University of Kentucky Press, [1965].

Bitterli, Urs. *Cultures in Conflict.* Trans. Ritchie Robertson. Stanford, Calif.: Stanford University Press, 1989.

Block, David. "Missionary Libraries on the Amazonian Frontier: The Jesuits in Moxos, 1680–1767." *Journal of Library History* 18, no.3 (Summer 1983): 292–303.

Bolton, H. E. "The Mission as a Frontier Institution in the Spanish American Colonies." In *Bolton and the Spanish Borderlands,* ed. Francis Bannon, 188–211. Norman: University of Oklahoma Press, 1964.

Borges Morán, Pedro. *El envío de misioneros a América durante la época española.* Salamanca: Universidad Pontífica, 1977.

Bowden, Henry Warner. *American Indians and Christian Missions.* Chicago: University of Chicago Press, 1981.

Brown, C. Barrington, and William Lidstone. *Fifteen Thousand Miles on the Amazon and Its Tributaries.* London: Edward Stanford, 1878.

Brown, Kendall W. "Jesuit Wealth and Economic Activity within the Peruvian Economy: The Case of Colonial Southern Peru." *The Americas* 44, no.1 (July 1987): 23–43.

Bueno, Cosme. *Descripción del Peru.* [Lima, 1771?].

Buschiazzo, Mario J. *Architectura en las misiones de Mojos y Chiquitos.* La Paz: Imprenta de la Universidad Mayor de San Andres, 1972.

Bushnell, Amy Turner. "Ruling 'the Republic of Indians' in Seventeenth-Century Florida." In *Powhatan's Mantle,* ed. Peter H. Wood et al., 134–50. Lincoln: University of Nebraska Press, 1989.

Caraman, Philip. *The Lost Paradise: The Jesuit Republic in South America.* New York: Seabury Press, 1976.

"Carta del Padre Niel, misionero de la compañía de Jesus." In *Cartas edificantes y curiosas escritas de las misiones estranjeras, y de levante por algunos misioneros de la Compañia de Jésus,* 5:133–44.

Cartas e informes de misioneros jesuitas extranjeros en hispanoamérica. Ed. Mauro Matthei. 3 vols. Santiago: Universidad Católica de Chile, 1968–72.

Cartas edificantes y curiosas escritas de las misiones estranjeras, y de levante por algunos misioneros de la Compañia de Jésus. Ed. Diego Davin. 16 vols. Madrid: Imprenta de la viuda de Manuel Fernández, 1755.

Carvalho Urey, Antonio. *Beni ensayo de interpretación histórica.* Trinidad: n.p., 1983.

———. *Pedro Ignacio Muiba: el héroe.* Trinidad: n.p., 1977.

———. "Síntesis histórica del Beni." In *Monografía de Bolivia,* 4 vols., 4:15–70. La Paz: Biblioteca del Sesquicentenario de la República, 1975.

Castillo, Joseph del. "Relacíon de la provincia de Mojos." In *Documentos para la historia geográfica de la República de Bolivia.*

"Centro de Documentación e Información de la Universidad del Beni." In *Simposio sobre las misiones jesuitas en Bolivia,* 215–36.

Chávez Suárez, José. *Historia de Moxos.* 2d ed. La Paz: Editorial Don Bosco, 1986.

Church, George Earl. *Explorations Made in the Valley of the River Madeira from 1749 to 1868.* n.p.: Published for the National Bolivia Navigation Company, 1875.

Claro, Samuel. "La música en las misiones de Moxos." *Revista musical chilena* 22, no.108 (July/Sept. 1969): 7–31.

"Consultas hechas a S.M. por Don Juan de Lizarazu presidente de Charcas sobre su entrada a Moxos o Toros." In *Juicio de límites entre el Perú y Bolivia,* 9:121–216.

Cook, Sherburne F. *Population Trends among the California Mission Indians.* Berkeley and Los Angeles: University of California Press, 1940.

Cortesão, Jaime. *Rapóso Tavares e a formação territorial do Brasil.* Rio de Janeiro: Ministerio da Educação e Cultura, 1958.

Cronistas cruceños del Alto Perú virreinal. Santa Cruz: Universidad Gabriel René Moreno, 1961.

Cushner, Nicholas P. *Farm and Factory.* Albany: State University of New York Press, 1982.

———. *Jesuit Ranches and the Agrarian Development of Colonial Argentina, 1650–1767.* Albany: State University of New York Press, 1983.

———. *Lords of the Land.* Albany: State University of New York Press, 1980.

Dalence, José María. *Bosquejo estadístico de Bolivia.* La Paz: n.p., 1975.

Das reduções latino-americanas às lutas indígenas atuais. São Paulo: Edições Paulinas, 1982.

Davidson, David M. "Rivers and Empire: The Madeira Route and the Incorporation of the Brazilian Far West, 1737–1808." Ph.D. diss., Yale University, 1970.

Decorme, Gerard. *La obra de los Jesuitas mexicanos durante la época colonial.* 2 vols. México: Antigua Librería Robredo de José Porrua, 1941.

Denevan, William M. *The Aboriginal Cultural Geography of the Llanos de Mojos of Bolivia.* Berkeley and Los Angeles: University of California Press, 1966.

———. *La geografía cultural aborigen de los Llanos de Mojos.* La Paz: Editorial Juventud, 1980.

Díaz de Guzmán, Rui. *La Argentina.* Buenos Aires: Librería Huemel, 1974.

Documentos que comprueban la conducta nada honrosa de D. Damón Barberi Prefecto del Beni. Santa Cruz: Imprenta del Cayetano R. Daza, 1872.

Documentos para la historia geográfica de la República de Bolivia. Ed. M. V. Ballivián. 2 vols. La Paz: J. M. Gamarra, 1906.

Dougherty, Bernard, and Joracio A. Calandra, "Prehispanic Human Settlement in the Llanos de Moxos, Bolivia." In *Quarentary of South America and Antarctic Peninsula*, ed. Jorge Rabassa, 2 vols., 2:163–99. Rotterdam: A. A. Balkema, 1983.

Eder, Francisco J. *Breve descripción de las reducciones de Mojos*. Trans. and ed. Josep M. Barnadas. Cochabamba: Historia Boliviana, 1985.

Egaña, Antonio de. *Historia de la iglesia en la América española*. 2 vols. Madrid: Biblioteca de Autores Cristianos, 1966.

Eguiguren, Luís Antonio. *Las huellas de la Compañía de Jesús en el Perú*. Lima: Librería y Imprenta Gil, 1956.

Eguiluz, Diego de. *Historia de la misión de Mojos*. Lima: Imprenta del Universo de C. Prince, 1884.

Erickson, Clark L. "Sistemas agrícolas prehispánicos en los Llanos de Mojos." *América indígena* 40, no.4 (Oct.–Dec. 1980): 731–55.

Fifer, J. Valerie. "The Empire Builders: A History of the Bolivian Rubber Boom and the Rise of the House of Suárez." *Journal of Latin American Studies* 2, no.2 (1970): 113–46.

Fisher, Robin. *Contact and Conflict: Indian European Relations in British Columbia, 1744–1890*. Vancouver: University of British Columbia Press, 1977.

Furlong Cardiff, Guillermo. *Cartografía histórica argentina*. Buenos Aires: Comisión Nacional Ejecutiva de Homenaje al 150 Aniversario de la Revolución de Mayo, 1963.

——. "Lázaro de Ribera y su cartilla real." *Humanidades* 34 (1954): 15–69.

——. *Misiones y sus pueblos de Guaraníes*. Buenos Aires: Imprenta Balmes, 1962.

García Recio, José María. *Análisis de una sociedad de frontera: Santa Cruz de la Sierra en los siglos XVI y XVII*. Sevilla: Publicaciones de la Exema, Diputación Provincial de Sevilla, 1988.

Garriga, Antonio de. "Linderos de los pueblos de las misiones de Mojos." In *Juicio de límites entre el Perú y Bolivia*, 34–42.

Geiger, Maynard. "Biographical Data on the California Missionaries." *California Historical Society Quarterly* 44, no.4 (Dec. 1965): 291–310.

Gómez Canedo, Lino. *Evangelización y conquista*. Mexico: Porrúa, 1977.

Gonçalves da Fonseca, José. "Primeira exploração dos rios Madeira e Guaporé em 1749." In *Memorias para a historia do extincto estado do Maranhão*, 2:267–418.

Graham, R. B. Cunninghame. *A Vanished Arcadia: Being Some Account of the Jesuits in Paraguay, 1607 to 1767*. London: Heinemann, 1901.

Greever, Janet Groff. *José Ballivián y el oriente boliviano*. La Paz: Empresa Editora Siglo Ltda., 1987.

Hamnett, Brian. "Church Wealth in Peru: Estates and Loans in the Archdiocesis of

Lima in the Seventeenth Century." *Jahrbuch für geschichte von staat, wirtschaft und gesellschaft lateinamerikas* 10 (1973): 113–32.

Hanisch Espíndola, Walter. *Historia de la Compañía de Jesús en Chile, 1593–1955.* Buenos Aires: Editorial Francisco de Aguirre, 1974.

Heath, Eduardo. *Informe sobre los estudios hechos en el departamento del Beni.* La Paz: Imp. de "La Libertad," 1882.

Hemming, John. *Amazon Frontier.* Cambridge, Mass.: Harvard University Press, 1987.

Hernández, Pablo. *El extrañamiento de los jesuitas del Rio de la Plata y de las misiones del Paraguay por decreto de Carlos III.* Madrid: V. Suárez, 1908.

———. *Organización social de las doctrinas guaraníes de la Compañía de Jesús.* 2 vols. Barcelona: Gustavo Gili, 1913.

Herndon, William Lewis, and Lardner Gibbon. *Exploration of the Valley of the Amazon.* 2 vols. Washington, D.C.: A.O.P. Nicholson, Public Printer, 1854.

Hervás y Panduro, Lorenzo. *Catálogo de las lenguas de las naciones conocidas.* 2 vols. Madrid: Imprenta del Real Arbitro de Beneficiencia, 1800.

Historia de la Compañía de Jesús en la provincia de Paraguay (Argentina, Paraguay, Uruguay, Peru, Bolivia, y Brasil). Ed. Pablo Pastells. 9 vols. Madrid: V. Suárez, 1912–49.

Hu de Hart, Evelyn. *Missionaries, Miners and Indians.* Tucson: University of Arizona Press, 1981.

Hurtado, Albert L. *Indian Survival on the California Frontier.* New Haven: Conn.: Yale University Press, 1988.

"Informação sôbre as missões dos moxos, dos jesuitas espanhóis mandada tomar por ordem do Ouvidor de Cuiabá, João Gonçalves Pereira, entre os sertanistas alidos 20 de setembro de 1743." In *Alexandre de Gusmão e o tratado de Madrid,* 2:64–80.

Itinerario y pensamientao de los jesuitas expulsados de Chile, 1767–1815. [Santiago]: Editorial Andrés Bello, [1972].

Jones, James C. "Conflict between Whites and Indians on the Llanos de Moxos, Beni Department: A Case Study in Development from the Cattle Regions of the Bolivian Oriente." Ph.D. diss., University of Florida, 1980.

Juicio de límites entre el Perú y Bolivia. Ed. Victor M. Maurtua. 12 vols. and case of maps. Barcelona: Imprenta de Henrich y Compañía, 1906.

Keller, Franz. *The Amazon and Madeira Rivers.* Philadelphia: J. B. Lippincott and Co., 1875.

———. "Report of José and Francisco Keller, Made to the Imperial Government of

Brazil." In George Earl Church, *Explorations Made in the Valley of the Rivera Madeira from 1749 to 1868,* 3–71.

Konrad, Herman W. *A Jesuit Hacienda in Colonial Mexico: Santa Lucía, 1576–1767.* Stanford, Calif.: Stanford University Press, 1980.

Lacerda e Almeida, Francisco José de. "Memoria a respecto dos Rios Baures, Branco, da Conceição, de S. Joaquim, Itonamas e Maxupo." *Revista do Instituto Historico e Geográfico Brasileiro* 12 (1849): 106–19.

Langer, Erik D., and Robert H. Jackson. "Colonial and Republican Missions Compared: The Cases of Alta California and Southeastern Bolivia." *Comparative Studies in Society and History* 20, no.2 (Apr. 1988): 286–311.

Langmore, Diane. *Missionary Lives, Papua 1874–1914.* Honolulu: University of Hawaii Press, 1989.

Larreta, Francisco de. "Estado temporal de la Provincia del Perú." *Revista de archivos y bibliotecas nacionales* [Lima] 3, no.5 (1990): 33–140.

Lathrap, Donald W. *The Upper Amazon.* New York: Praeger, 1970.

Lehm Ardaya, Zulema. "Diagnostico de la situación actual de los indígenas de Trinidad y areas cercanas." In *Simposio sobre las misiones jesuitas en Bolivia,* 205–13.

Lehnertz, Jay F. "Lands of the Infidels: The Franciscans in the Central Montaña of Peru, 1709–1824." Ph.D. diss., University of Wisconsin, 1974.

"Lettre du Pere Nyel, missionnaire de la Compagnie de Jesus au Pere Dez." In *Lettres édifiantes et curieuses écrite des missions étrangères,* 8:138–54.

Lettres édifiantes et curieuses écrites des missions étrangères. 26 vols. Paris: Chez J. G. Merigot, 1780–83.

Lettres édifiantes et curieuses écrites par des missionaires de la Compagnie de Jésus. 34 vols. Paris: Chez N. Le Clerc, 1702–76.

Limpias Saucedo, Manuel. *Los gobernadores de Mojos.* La Paz: Escuela Tipográfica Salesiana, 1942.

"Linderos de los pueblos de Mojos, declarados y confirmados por el Padre Provincial Antonio Garriga en su visita de 10 de Octubre de 1715." In *Juicio de límites entre el Perú y Bolivia,* 10:34–42.

Lofstrom, William Lee. *El Mariscal Sucre en Bolivia.* La Paz: Editorial e Imprenta Alenkar Ltda., 1983.

Maccheti, Jesualdo. *Diario del viaje fluvial del padre Fray Jesualdo Maccheti.* [La Paz]: Imprenta El Siglo Industrial, 1869.

MacCormack, Sabine. "'The Heart Has Its Reasons': Predicaments of Missionary Christianity in Early Colonial Peru." *Hispanic American Historical Review* 65, no.3 (Oct. 1985): 443–66.

Macera, Pablo. *Bolivia, tierra y población, 1825–1936.* Lima: Biblioteca Andina, 1978.

Magalhães, Basilio de. *Expansão geográfico do Brasil colonial.* São Paulo: Companhia Editorial Nacional, 1935.

Maggio, Antonio. *Arte de la lengua de los indios baures de la Provincia de los Moxos.* Paris: Maisonneuve y Cia., 1880.

Marbán, Pedro. *Arte y vocabulario de la lengua Moxa.* Lima: Imprimase El Conde, 1701.

Markham, Clements. *Travels in Peru and India.* London: John Murray, 1862.

Mateos, Francisco. "Avances portugueses y misiones españolas en la America del Sur." *Misionalia Hispánica* 5, no.15 (1948): 459–504.

Mathews, Edward D. *Up the Amazon and Madeira Rivers, through Bolivia and Peru.* London: Sampson Low, Marston, Searle and Rivington, 1879.

Medina, José Toribio. *Noticias bio-bibliográficas de los jesuitas expulsos de América en 1767.* Santiago: Imprenta de Elzeviriana, 1914.

Meireles, Denise Maldi. *Guardiães da fronteira Río Guaporé, século XVIII.* Petrópolis: Vozes, 1989.

Memorias para a historia do extincto estado do Maranhão. Ed. Candido Mendez de Almeida. 2 vols. Rio de Janeiro: n.p., 1874.

Mesa, José de, and Teresa Gisbert. *Bolivia: monumentos historicós y arqueológicos.* Mexico: Instituto Panamericano de Geografía y Historia, 1970.

Métraux, Alfred. "The Revolution of the Ax." *Diogenes* 25 (Spring 1959): 28–40.

——. "Tribes of Eastern Bolivia and the Madeira Headwaters." In *Handbook of South American Indians.* Ed. Julian Steward, 8 vols., 3:351–454. Washington, D.C.: U.S. Government Printing Office, 1948.

Mojos y Chiquitos. 2 vols. Lima: Biblioteca Andina, 1988.

Monumenta Peruana. Ed. Antonio de Egaña. Rome: APUD Institutum Historicum Societatis Iesu, 1954–.

Mörner, Magnus. *The Political and Economic Activities of the Jesuits in the Rio de la Plata Region: The Hapsburg Era.* Stockholm: Victor Petersens Bokindustri, 1953.

Moxos descripciones exactas e historia fiel de los indios, animales y plantas de la provincia de Moxos en el virreinato del Perú por Lázaro de Ribera 1786–1794. Madrid: Ministerio de Agricultura Pesca y Alimentación, Ediciones el Viso [1989].

The Native Populations of the Americas in 1492. Ed. William M. Denevan. Madison: University of Wisconsin Press, 1976.

Neill, Stephen. *A History of Christian Missions.* Harmondsworth: Penguin Books, 1964.

Nordenskiöld, Erland. *L'archéologie du bassin de l'Amazone.* Paris: Les Editions G. van Oest, 1930.

Nunes, José Maria de Souza. *Real forte Príncipe da Beira*. Rio de Janeiro: Fundação Emílio Odebrecht, 1985.

Orbigny, Alcide Dessalines d'. *Descripción geográfica, histórica y estadística de Bolivia*. Paris: Librería de los Señores Guide y Compañía, 1845.

———. *El hombre americano*. Buenos Aires: Editorial Futuro, 1944.

———. *L'homme americain*. Paris: Chez Pitois-Levrault, et Cie., 1839.

———. *Viaje a la América meridional*. Trans. Alfredo Cepeda. 4 vols. Buenos Aires: Editorial Futuro, 1945.

Orellana, P. Antonio de. "Carta del Padre Antonio de Orellana, sobre el origen de las missiones de Mojos." In *Juicio de límites entre el Perú y Bolivia*, 10:1–24.

Owens, David James. "A Historical Geography of the Indian Missions in the Jesuit Province of Paraguay: 1609–1768." Ph.D. diss., University of Kansas, 1977.

Palacios, José Agustín. *Exploraciones de don José Agustín Palacios realizados en los ríos Beni, Mamoré y Madera y en el lago Rogo-aquado, durante los años 1844 al 47*. La Paz: Editorial del Estado, 1944.

Parejas, Alcides. *Historia de Moxos y Chiquitos a fines del siglo XVIII*. La Paz: Instituto Boliviano de Cultura, 1976.

Pentland, Joseph Barclay. "Report on Bolivia, 1827." In *Camden Miscellany*, ed. J. Valerie Fifer, 4th ser. vol.13, 169–267. London: Offices of the Royal Historical Society, 1974.

Phelan, John Leddy. *The Hispanization of the Philippines, Spanish Aims and Filipino Responses 1565–1700*. Madison: University of Wisconsin Press, 1967.

Porras P., María Elena. *La gobernación y el obispado de Mainas*. Quito: Ediciones Abya-Yala, 1987.

Quevedo, Quintín. *Pequeño bosquejo de la provincia de Mojos en el Departamento del Beni*. La Paz: Imprenta Paceña, 1861.

Radding, Cynthia. *Las estructuras socio-económicas de las misiones de la Pimería Alta 1768–1850*. Hermosillo: Instituto Nacional de Antropología e Historia, Centro Regional del Noroeste, 1979.

Reis, Artur C. F. *Límites e demarcações na Amazonia brasileira*. 2 vols. Rio de Janeiro: Imprenta Nacional, 1947.

"Relación de la provincia de los Mojos." In *Documentos para la historia geográfica de la República de Bolivia*, 1:294–395.

"Relación de los casos en que el Capitán Nufrio de Chavez a servido a Su Magestad desde el año de quinientos quarenta." In *Colección de documentos relativos a la historia de América y particularmente a la historia del Paraguay*, ed. Blas Garay, 2 vols, 1:336–40. Asunción: Talleres Nacionales de H. Kraus, 1899.

René-Moreno, Gabriel. *Catálogo del Archivo de Mojos y Chiquitos.* 2d ed. La Paz: Librería Editorial "Juventud," 1973.

Reyes Ortiz, Felix. *Anuario administrativo y político de Bolivia, 1856.* La Paz: Imprenta del Vapor, 1856.

Río, Ignacio del. *Conquista y aculturación en la California jesuítica 1697–1768.* Mexico: Universidad Nacional Autónoma de México, 1984.

Rippy, J. Fred, and Jean Thomas Nelson. *Crusaders of the Jungle.* Chapel Hill: University of North Carolina Press, 1936.

Sá, Joseph Barboza de. *Relaçaó das povoaçoens do Cuyabá e Mato Groso de seos principios thé os prezentes tempos.* [Cuiabá]: Universidade Federal de Mato Grosso, 1975.

Saeger, James Schofield. "Another View of the Mission as a Frontier Institution: The Guaycuruan Reductions of Santa Fe, 1743–1810." *Hispanic American Historical Review* 65, no.3 (1985): 493–517.

Salinas, Manuel Macedonio. *Navegación de los ríos de Bolivia confluentes del Madera y Amazonas y colonización.* Cochabamba: Imprenta de Gutierrez, 1871.

Sanabria Fernández, Fernando. *En busca de el dorado: la colonización del oriente boliviano por los cruceños.* Buenos Aires: Imprenta Lopez, 1958.

Santamaría, Daniel J. "La economía de las misiones de Moxos y Chiquitos (1675–1810)." *Ibero-Amerikanisches archiv* n.s. 13, no.2 (1987): 255–95.

Schuetz, Mardith Keithly. "The Indians of the San Antonio Missions." Ph.D. diss., University of Texas, 1980.

Sierra, Vicente D. *Los jesuitas germanos en la conquista espiritual de hispanoamerica.* Buenos Aires: Institución Cultural Argentino-Germano, 1944.

Simposio sobre las misiones jesuitas en Bolivia. La Paz: Ministerio de Relaciones Exteriores y Culto, 1987.

Southey, Robert. *History of Brazil.* 2d ed. 3 vols. New York: Greenwood Press, 1969.

Storni, Hugo. *Catálogo de los Jesuitas de la provincia del Paraguay (Cuenca de la Plata) 1585–1768.* Rome: Institutum Historicum, S.I., 1980.

Suppan, Leo. "Three Centuries of Cinchona." In *Proceedings of the Celebration of the Three Hundredth Anniversary of the First Recognized Use of Cinchona,* 29–138. St. Louis: [Missouri Botanical Garden], 1931.

Sweet, David G. "A Rich Realm of Nature Destroyed: The Middle Amazon Valley 1640–1750." Ph.D. diss., University of Wisconsin, 1974.

Tibesar, Antonine. "The Alternativa: A Study in the Spanish-Creole Relations in 17th Century Peru." *The Americas* 11 (Jan. 1955): 229–83.

Tormo Sanz, Leandro. "Una biblioteca perdida entre los llanos del Mamoré." *Missionalia hispánica* 17 (1960): 367–71.

———. "La campaña de Moxos contra los Portugueses del Brasil." *Revista de la Universidad Autónoma "Gabriel René Moreno"* 9, no.18 (July–Dec. 1962): 6–28.

———. "Historia demográfica de las misiones de Mojos." *Missionalia hispánica* 35–36, no.103–108 (1978–79): 285–309; 38, no.114 (1981): 257–303.

———. "El Padre Julián de Aller y su relación de Mojos." *Missionalia hispánica* 13, no.38 (1956): 371–80.

———. "El sistema comunalista indiano en la región comunera de Mojos-Chiquitos." *Comunidades* 1, no.1 (Jan.–April 1966): 96–140, and 1, no.2 (May–Aug. 1966): 89–117.

———. "Situación y población de los Mojos en 1679." *Revista española de antropología americana* 7, no.2 (1972): 151–59.

Torrez Saldamando, Enrique. "El Padre Antonio Garriga." *Revista de artes y letras* [Santiago de Chile] 17 (1890): 412–24.

Travels of the Jesuits into Various Parts of the World: Compiled from Their Letters by Mr. Lockman. 2 vols. London: J. Noon, 1743.

Treutlein, Theodore Edward. "Jesuit Travel to America (1678–1756) as Recorded in the Travel Diaries of German Jesuits." Ph.D. diss., University of California, 1934.

Vaca Díez, Antonio. *Memorial que presenta al Delegado Nacional en el Madre de Dios, Acre y Purús.* La Paz: Imprenta y Litografía de "El Nacional" de Isaac V. Vila, 1894.

Vargas Ugarte, Rubén. *Historia de la Compañía de Jesús en el Perú.* 4 vols. Burgos: Imprenta de Aldecoa, 1963–65.

———. *Jesuitas peruanos desterrados a Italia.* Lima: n.p., 1934.

"Verdadeira noticia que deu Francisco Leme do Prádo, do que passou, vio, e experimentou na viagem que fez destas Minas de Mato Grosso pelo Rio abaixo as missoenz dos Padres da Companhia do Rno de Castella a q Chamão Mogos." In *Alexandre de Gusmão e o Tratrado de Madrid,* 2:57–63.

Viedma, Francisco de. *Descripción geográfica y estadística de la provincia de Santa Cruz de la Sierra.* 3d ed. Cochabamba: Editorial "Los Amigos del Libro," 1969.

Weber, Francis J. *A Select Bibliography: The California Missions, 1765–1972.* Los Angeles: Dawson's Book Shop, 1972.

Weddell, Hughes Algernon. *Histoire naturelle des quinquinas, ou, monographie du genre Cinchona.* Paris: V. Masson, 1849.

———. *Voyages dans le nord de la Bolivie et dans les parties voisines de Pérou.* Paris: P. Bertrand, 1853.

Zapata, Agustín. "Carta del Padre Agustín Zapata al Padre Joseph de Buendía, en la que da noticias del Partiti." In *Juicio de límites entre el Perú y Bolivia,* 10:25–28.

Zelis, Rafael de. *Catálogo de los sugetos de la Compañía de Jesús que formaban la Provincia de Mexico en el día del arresto, 25 de junio de 1767.* México: Imprenta de I. Escalante y Cia, 1871.

Zubillaga, Félix. "Métodos misionales de la primera instrucción de San Francisco de Borja para la América Española (1567)." *Archivum historicum Societatis Iesu* 12, no.1–11 (Jan.–Dec. 1943): 58–88.

INDEX

Barace, Cipriano, 20, 26, 35, 37, 114; first Jesuit martyr in Moxos, 109; founding father of missions, 38; martyrdom of, 43, 109, 124; biography of, 109

Barberi, Damón, 170

Barnadas, Josep M., 4, 115

Barro Nuebo, Don Juan de, 70

Baurano Indians, 117

Baure Indians, 16, 18, 38, 78, 153, 163; agriculture of, 23; armed campaign against, 43; chiefs of, 27, 88; demographics of in mission period, 84–85; Father Cipriano Barace killed by, 109; fishing of, 24; handicrafts, 25; hunting of, 24; language of, 16, 118; missions founded in country of, 43–44; pacification of, 43; population statistics of, 83–84; stations in country of, 115, 134; villages of, 26

Beans, 23, 52

Beccera Casanovos, Rogers (Bolivian scholar), 3, 96

Beef, price of, 163

Beeswax, 68, 158

Belém do Pará, 48, 51, 161, 163

Belgian Colonization Company, 154

Bells, 96; church, 90

Beni (natives of Beni region), decline of population of, 166

Beni Department of Bolivia, 6, 11, 55, 154, 155, 170; creation of, 3, 9, 152; prefects of, 155, 157–58, 163, 170

Beni River, 11, 18, 39, 60, 100, 157, 160–61; drainage, 15; Jesuit outpost on, 40

Benites, Juan José (administrator of Exaltación), 130

Bible, 35, 93, 109, 117

Biological systems, evolution of, 1–2

Biological warfare, speculated use of, 52

Birds, 13

Bishop of Santa Cruz, 151

Bitterli, Urs, 124

Blacks, as slaves in Chalguani vineyards, 71

Blacksmithing, skills taught to Indians, 41

Bleeding, as medical treatment, 121

Boats: routes for, 157; rowing styles of Indians, 164

Bolivar, Simon, 150

Bolivia, Republic of, 1, 8–9, 11, 22, 106, 149–73; administration of, 150–53;

cinchona collection in, 159; colonization schemes, 154; Constituent Assembly of, 151; creation of, 149; economic activities of, 153–56; epidemics in, 165; homicides of officials of, 172; Indian caciques' diminished role in, 168; Indian demographics in, 163–66; Indian labor in, 169–73; Indian revolt in, 171–72; Indian rubber collectors in, 170–71; Indian rubber collectors in, 170–71; Indian society in, 166–69; land acquisition by whites in, 155; museum holdings in, 68; products and goods produced in, 169; revenues of, 155; rubber extraction in, 161–66; settlements of, 164; textile production in, 158–59; treasury officials of, 154; white immigration to Moxos, 153–55. See also Beni Department of Bolivia

Bolton, Herbert E. (mission researcher), 176

Books, collected in Moxos' missions, 64, 193

Boots, 138

Borah, Woodrow, 78–79

Borda, Rafael de la Prefect, 157, 170

Borges Morán, Pedro, 111

Borgia, General Francisco de, 116

Borja. See San Borja

Bourbon period, 128, 133, 149–50, 177. See also Spanish Crown; Spanish Empire

Brazil, 47, 49, 143, 162, 170; as border of Moxos, 11; expansion of Portuguese empire from, 47; rubber patrons from, 163

British Asia, 160, 163

British colonies, 120

Brown, C. Barrington, 162

Buenos Aires, 111, 127–28, 131

Burns, E. Bradford, 173

Buschiazzo, Mario, 63

Bushnell, Amy, 102

Cabildo, 144, 145; officers of the, 94; offices of the, 86

Cabredo, Hernando, 37, 116

Cacao, 57, 98, 135, 136, 138, 146, 147, 151, 156, 158, 168, 169, 177, 179; illegally sold, 130

Caciques, 86, 94, 130–32, 144, 164, 168, 169

Cadiz, 66–67

Calaba oil, 59, 158

Caldrons, 96

California: comparison with Moxos, 106; gold rush, 181; Indians, 166; missions of, 68, 80, 85, 111–13

Callao (port of Lima), 106

Callejas la Baja (vineyard deeded to missions), 70

Câmara, João Pedro da, 51

Cañacure Indians, 18, 19; missions established among, 38; villages of, 31

Canada, far west region, 181

Candles, 60, 136

Cane. *See* Sugarcane

Canesí Indians, 18–19; map of region of, 17

Canisiana Indians, 16, 18, 83, 100, 117, 142, 146, 162; and axes, as enticement to convert, 101–2; fishing of, 24; hunting of, 24; initial missionary contact with, 101; map of region of, 17; missions established among, 38; physical description of, 23

Cannons, 96

Canoes, 23, 25, 46, 138; armed, 51; rowing styles of Indians, 164

Capitalism, effects on Moxos, 173

Caribbean, 111

Carmen, 172

Carpentry, 60, 86, 95, 99; skills taught to Indians, 41

Carrasco, Matias, 169

Cartagena, 54

Carvers, 60, 94–95

Carving, 63, 156

Cascarilla, 158

Castillo, José del (Jesuit missionary and surgeon), 35, 37, 105

Catholic calendar, 93

Catholicism, 67

Cattle, 41, 44, 57, 99, 136, 146, 151, 155, 157, 163, 169, 178; driven by Indian cowboys, 93; ranching, 156; slaughtered in Loreto, 134

Caupolicán region, 160

Cayman, 13

Censos (mortgages), 71, 194 n. 30

Censuses, 19, 80, 86–88, 94–95, 99; of Bolivian Moxos, 164–68; of occupations, 169. *See also* Demographics

Ceramics, 25

Chaco, 28

Chairs, 63

Chalguani, hacienda of, 71

Chané Indians, 33–34

Chapacura Indians, 19

Chapare River, 22

Charcas, 9, 44, 49, 106, 151; audencia of, 19, 47, 131; judges of, 142; removal of native people to, 189; Spanish centers in, 126; troops assembled in, 51

Charles III: ascension to Spanish throne, 49; decree of Jesuit exile, 177; Gallicanist advisors to, 108; reign of, 128

Chávez, Lorenzo, 134

Chávez, Nuflo de, 28

Chávez, Ricardo (exporter of rubber seeds), 163

Chávez Suarez, José (Moxos researcher), 3

Chenesí River, 22

Chickens, 41

Children, Indian, 81–82, 85; as gatherers, 146; left behind by men, 150; as mission students, 119; statistics on, 141

Chile, 54, 127

Chiquito Indians, 34, 47, 63, 128, 157

Chiquitos Uplands, 11

Chiriguano Indians, 31

Christianity, 12, 37, 114, 119; Bible, 35, 93, 117; morality in, 121. *See also* Conversion to Christianity

Churches, 45–46, 159, 179; architecture of, 56, 59–63; at Concepción, 59–63; industry of, 46, 60, 159; of Magdalena, 61, 63; maintenance of, 99; ornaments of, 63–64; of Paraguay, 63; as part of Spanish mission colony, 6; at San Ignacio, 60; of San José, 44; of San Pedro, 44, 60, 64; of San Ramón, 61, 63; Te Deum mass in, 112

Cigarettes, 138

Cinchona, 8, 149, 159; Bolivian sales of, 160; collection, 159, 173; plantation production in British Asia, 160; quinine from, 120; research on chemical properties of, 159

Citizenship: granted to neophytes, 126; rights granted in Bolivian Moxos, 152

Citrus, 57

Clarinets, played by Indians, 112

Cloth. *See* Textiles

Clothing: illustration of, 92; Indian, 90, 162; mission, 90; Spanish, 94, 121, 144; undergarments, 137

Education, of Indians, 42, 44, 104–5, 110–11, 118–20, 175. *See also* Jesuit college(s)

Effigies, burning of, 93

Eggs: cayman, 24; chicken, 41; rhea, 24; turtle, 24

El Dorado, 1, 16, 18, 29, 32, 133, 155

Elite Indians. *See* Familia

Encinas, Gabriel, Don, 70

Enlightenment view of natural man, 115

Epidemics. *See* Disease(s)

Espinosa, Joaquín, Colonel, 53

Esteban, 143

Europe, war in, 50

European(s), 1, 23, 33, 44, 46, 78, 86, 105, 108, 110–11, 121, 148, 174–75, 202 n. 44; as allies with Indians in war, 100; as bearers of disease, 6–7, 18, 31; as Bolivian administrators, 168; culture, 179; first to reach Moxos, 15; immigration to Moxos, 9, 149, 153–55, 165, 173, 178, 181; introducing domestic animals to Moxos, 57; perspective on mission culture, 9; supplies, 44; views on mission wealth, 65; violence against, 172. *See also* Jesuit missionaries: Belgian, German, Hungarian, Italian, Portugal; Spanish; Spaniards

Exaltación (mission), 44, 83, 88, 127, 130–31, 153, 172, 206 n. 56; armed expedition into, 48; church of, 63

Exiles, 154. *See also* Jesuit exile

Expeditions, 28–32, 34, 44, 47–48, 113, 134; Portuguese, 47

Exports, 68, 147–48; agricultural products, 68, 149, 156; beeswax, 68, 158; feathers, 95; mission, 138. *See also* Cacao; Cotton; Sugar; Textiles

Familia (elite Indians), 88, 89, 96, 99, 130, 144, 164, 166–67, 179–80; and use of Spanish language, 94, 119

Far East, Jesuit experience in, 116

Farming, 23, 65, 87, 98, 167. *See also* Agriculture; Crops

Faron, Louis, 22

Feasts, 93–94

Feather: headdresses, 25; painting, 25; weaving, 25, 95, 177

Felix, Manoel, de Lima (commander of Portuguese expedition), 48, 57, 60, 63, 86, 100; visit to Magdalena, 56

Fertility, Indian, 80–82, 84–85

Fertilizer, wood pulp, 23

Fevers, 165

Fiesta cycle, 93

Fifer, J. Valerie, 9

Figueroa, Nicolás de (procurador for Moxos missions), 72–74, 77

Firearms, 48

First Provincial Congregation, 115, 119

Fish, 13

Fishing, 7, 24

Fitzcarraldo (film), 171

Flags, 47

Flooding, 12, 14, 26, 30, 46, 52, 58, 83, 142; Indians and, 23, 54, 56–57

Flour, 169; manioc, 117

Flutes, played by Indians, 112; illustration of, 97

Food, 23–25, 146; cookery, 25; distribution of, 94, 121; feasts, 93–94; fruits, 57, 137, 147; gifts of, 94; grains, 71–72; shortages, 46; wild game, 24. *See also* Crops

Forests, 14; Andean rain, 152; horticulture of, 23; Madeira, 161; preservation of, 61; rain, 160; rubber, 162; sub-Andean, 60, 120, 150; Yungas, 160

Foundries, 60, 120

Franciscans, 33, 41, 82, 107, 112, 177

Franco, José, (interim governor of Moxos), 133

Fraser, Valerie, 65

Fritz, Samuel, 35, 175

Fruits, 57, 137, 147

Furniture, 95, 64–65; making, 156

Game, wild, 24

Gardens, communal, 153, 179

Garriga, Antonio de, 44, 70, 59, 114, 121

Gems, 47, 64

General Congregation in Rome, 66

Genoa, 110

Ghost towns, 9

Gloves, 137, 138

Gold: fields in Cuiabá, 47–48; rush, 181; in missions, 64

Gongora, Mario, 30

Goodyear, Charles, 161

Gorotoqui Indians, 33–34
Governors: of Moxos, 129, 131–33, 144, 151; rivalries with curas, 130, 148; of Santa Cruz, 29–30, 43, 48, 117, 126. *See also* Ribera, Lázaro de
Grains, provided to missions by haciendas, 71–72
Gran Moxo: legendary, 16, 28; failure of expeditions to discover, 30; vision of, 133; waning pursuit of, 33
Grasses, 12
Guapay River, 28
Guaporé (region), 49, 51, 143; defense of, 100; Portuguese occupation of, 82–83
Guaporé River, 11, 43, 47, 82, 100; route through, 51
Guaraní Indians, 33, 86, 98; missions among, 128; neophytes, 82, 102; and War of 1750–51, 53
Guarayo Indians, 43; map of region of, 17
Gutiérrez, Michaela, Doña, 68

Habana, La (hacienda), supplier of grains to Moxos, 71
Haciendas, 71–75; Royal Hacienda, 52
Haircutting, as punishment, 95
Hair styles, Indian, 90
Handicrafts, 24, 46; displacement of industry of, 165; feather weaving, 25, 95, 177; production of, 94–95, 138, 155–56
Hats, 138
Havana, 54
Heath, Edwin, 161
Herboso, Francisco Ramon de, 126–27
Herbs, 121
Hervas y Panduro, Lorenzo, 16; treatise on Indian languages, 101–2
Herzog, Werner (filmmaker), 171
Hirscko, Carlos (manager of Moxos real estate holdings), 72
Holidays, 93, 121
Holy Saturday, 93
Holy vows, 105
Holy Week, 93, 94
Horses, 57, 157; breeding of, 158; racing of, 93. *See also* Livestock
Horticulture, forest, 23
Huarochirí, 116
Huarura (hacienda), 74–75

Humay (Umay) vineyard, 75
Hunting, 24
Hurtado, Albert L., 166

Iberia/Iberian: intra-Iberian conflicts in South America, 47–52, 77–79, 104, 145. *See also* Portugal; Spain; Spaniards; Spanish; Spanish Crown; Spanish Empire; Spanish language; Spanish period
Ignatius Loyola, writings of, 109
Incas, 24; fall of, 16
Incense, 138
India, 176
Indian(s), 1–2, 9, 24, 31, 206; American, 101, 166; annual floods and, 23, 54, 56–57; Baurano, 17, 117; Canesí, 17–19; Chané, 33–34; Chapacura, 19; Chiriguano, 31; clothing of, 90, 92, 144, 162; Cosseremono, 19; cowboys (vaqueros), 58, 93, 94, 99, 137; diet of, 23–24; emigration to European settlements, 143; family groupings of, 26; Gorotoqui, 33–34; Guarayo, 43; hispanized warriors against Baure, 43; labor, 10, 52, 55, 59, 63, 138, 169–73; languages of, 19, 42–43, 101–2, 113, 116, 118; and legacy of missions, 179–81; map of regions of, 17; and marriage, 86–88, 167; mission, during Spanish period, 141–48; mission, militia, 99; mission, police forces, 86; mission, political leaders, 94; mission, property rights, 98; orchestras, 96; of Peru, 115; physical descriptions of, 23; rebellions of, 39, 41, 131–32, 147–48, 180; skills taught to, 41; prehistory of, 14–16; Spanish-speaking, 28, 94; resettlement programs for, 19; sociopolitical structure of, 9; surnames of, 88; Tapacura, 17–19, 38; version of Jesuit-century history, 100–102; views on European changes to daily lives, 89. *See also* Baure Indians; Cañacure Indians; Canisiana Indians; Children, Indian; Chiquito Indians; Conversion to Christianity; Education: of Indians; Familia; Guarani Indians; Itonama Indians; Kayubaba Indians; Mobimo Indians; Moxo Indians; Handicrafts; Neophytes; Population; Pueblos. *See under* Bolivia, Republic of; Demographics; Disease(s)

Indigo, 158
Infanticide, practice of, 81–82
Infrared satellite imagery, 14
Insects, 113
Iron, 169; ironworkers, 96; tools, 40, 65, 101–2
Itenez River. *See* Guaporé River
Itonama Indians, 16, 18, 23, 78, 118, 142, 147, 164; demographic trends during mission period, 84–85; foundation of missions among, 44; map of region of, 17; physical description of, 23
Itonamas River, 50

Javier. *See* San Javier
Javier, San Francisco, statue of, 63
Jesuit Black Legend, 76
Jesuit college(s): archives of, 76; in Cochabamba, 70; in Cuzco, 33; in Durango, 107; European model of, 108; for Indian nobility, 115; in La Paz, 33; in La Plata, 68, 107; in Lima, 72–73; Peruvian, 76; at San Pablo, 114
Jesuit Colegio Maximo de San Pablo (Lima), 72–73
Jesuit exile, 1, 51–54, 57, 60, 84, 123, 125–26, 130; decree of, 177
Jesuit missionaries, 1–2, 6, 124; arrival of in Lima, 33; arrival of in Moxos, 16; Belgian, 107; Castillo, José del, 35, 37, 105; censuses taken by, 80, 86, 167; Creole, 105–6; demographics of, 103–6; drownings of, on *Venezia*, 110; education and training, 104–5, 110, 111; expenses of, 65, 111; foreign recruitment, 107–8; German, 107, 110–13; hierarchy of Indians, 16; Hungarian, 107, 114; initial encounters with Moxos, 27, 34; Italian, 107, 110, 162; Kino, Eusebio, 35, 175; lay brothers, 104–5, 176, 181; letters and essays of, 109; Ligardo, Jorge, 60, 120; literature portraying, 109; and language, 19, 36, 42, 110, 116; medical practice of, 120–21; Marterer, Alberto, 120; Mendoza, Alvaro de, 38; Messia, Alonso, 115; national origins of, 105–6; novices, 111–12; recruitment of, 108–11; replaced by secular leaders, 125; salaries, 65; service records, 111–15, 124; Spanish, 105; statistics on, 104–5;

sufferings of, 36–37, 113; suppression of (1767), 52–53; technical expertise of, 55; Urbe, Diego, 120. *See also* Conversion to Christianity; Jesuit exile; Jesuit missions; Jesuit priests
Jesuit mission income, 6, 33, 44–45, 65–77, 107, 133, 138, 150–51, 175, 177; from censos, 71, 194. *See also* Jesuit missions: financial support of
Jesuit missions (of Moxos), 2–4, 9–10, 77, 176; called towns, 8; central administration of, in Peru, 35–36; consolidations of, 127, 146; decline of, 9, 149–73; diseases in, 46, 52, 83, 85, 113, 120, 125; dwellings in, 56, 59; expenses, 67–68; export operations, 68–69; as farms and factories, 46, 57–60, 65; financial support of, 65, 67, 70–76, 111, 175; foundation of, 37–43; furniture and fixtures of, 64–65; haciendas in support of, 71–75; hegemony of, on western savanna, 41; history of, 7, 33, 121, 181; holidays of, 93–94, 121; inventories of possessions of, 63–66; Juli station, 116; landscape of, 57; libraries of, 64, 66, 93; locations of, 39–40, 50; and Luso-Spanish conflicts, 47–52, 77–79, 104, 145; Mamoré region, 83–84, 127; material culture of, 21, 103, 175; natural disasters, 46; secular policy toward, 7, 125–41, 176–78; supplies depleted, 83, 145, 177; transportation routes to, 100, 110–11; wealth of, 8, 24, 55, 64–65, 155. *See also* Architecture; Education; Exaltación; Jesuit exile; Jesuit missionaries; Jesuit mission income. *See under* Indians; Livestock; Loreto; Magdalena; Missions; Paraguay; Reyes; San Borja; San Ignacio; San Javier; San Joaquín; San Luís; San Martín; San Miguel; Santa Ana; Trinidad
Jesuit priests, 52, 103, 121, 176, 181; Aller, Julian de, 35–36; Bermudo, José, 35; Cárdenas, Diego de, 73; and death, 114, 124; España, Gabriel de, 71; Espejo, Juan de, 38; Espinosa, Balthasar de, 124; Fernández, Ignacio, 43; Fritz, Samuel, 35, 175; Legarda, Lorenzo, 38; Martínez, Diego, 33; Monitola, Angelo, 33; Montenegro, Juan de, 38; Orellana, Antonio de, 37–38, 113–14; Ortiz Ortuño, Andrés,

Magalhaes, Basilio de (Brazilian historian), 48

Magdalena (San Magdalena mission), 44, 84–86, 99, 146, 153; church of, 61, 63; Indians of, 56–57; lands sold, 155; Portuguese visit to, 48

Maggio, Antonio, 118

Maia da Gama, João da (governor of Belém), 48

Mainas, 54

Maize, 52, 98, 117, 179

Majieno (parcialidad of Reyes), 87–88

Malaria, 113

Mamoré-Madeira-Amazon river route, 157

Mamoré (region), 127, 130; maps of, 17, 21; populations of, 83–84. *See also* Exaltación; Loreto; Mamoré River; San Javier; San Pedro; Santa Ana; Trinidad

Mamoré River, 11, 15–16, 18, 20, 25, 29–30, 35–37, 42, 44, 49, 53, 60, 100, 157, 160–61

Manatee, 13

Manaus, 162–63

Manioc, 23, 98, 117, 146, 147, 177, 179; flour, 117; pots for processing, 25

Maniquí River, 43, 51, 172

Marasa, Juan (cacique of San Pedro), 130–32

Marbán, Pedro, 20, 25–26, 35, 42, 93, 95, 109, 118–19; arrival on the Mamoré, 36; and discomforts of mission life in Moxos, 113; requests grant money from Crown, 65

Marques de Pombal (Lisbon priest), 49

Marriage: Indian, 25, 86–88; Indian, of infants, 87, 164; Bolivian incentive to, 153

Martín. *See* San Martín

Masonry, skills taught to Indians, 41

Mathews, Edward, 162, 166, 172

Mato Grosso, 47–49, 51, 53

Mats, 138

Mazareono Indians, 31

Medals, 144

Melgarejo, Mariano (Bolivian president), 155

Mello Palheta, Francisco de, 48

Mendoza, Alvaro de (Jesuit missionary), 38

Mendoza, Juan de (governor of Santa Cruz), 30

Mercado, Antonio, 144

Mercedarians, 33

Mestizos, immigration into Moxos, 9, 155

Metraux, Alfred, 3, 102

Mexican Reforma, 173

Mexico, 74, 110

Missiology, understanding of, 123

Mission (film), The, 1, 10

Missions: Augustinian, 33, 177; of Baja California, 178; of California, 68, 80, 85, 106–7, 111–13; Capuchin, 177; Dominican, 33, 41, 134, 177; Franciscan, 82, 107, 177, 199 n. 7; Franciscan Apolobamba mission, 41; Mercedarian, 33; of New Guinea, 118; of North America, 68, 126, 176; of Paraguay, 1–2, 82, 102; Protestant, 180; and stipends from Spain, 175; Spanish, research on, 2, 176. *See also* Jesuit missions

Mobima Indians, 16, 18, 43, 83, 146; initial contact with by missionaries, 117; map of region of, 17; religious tracts in language of, 118–19; at Reyes, 43; at Santa Rosa, 43; physical description of, 23

Mocato palm fruit, 137

Mojos/Mojas. *See* Moxo Indians

Montevideo, 128

Mopeciano Indians, 117; map of region of, 17

Morner, Magnus (mission researcher), 2

Mosquitos, 113

Moura, Antonio Rolim de, 49–51; as captain general of Mato Grosso, 49, 51; knighthood of, 51; as Viceroy of Brazil, 51

Moxa (language), 118–19

Moxo Indians, 16, 19, 31, 162–63; chiefs of, 27; gods of, 27; language of, 16, 22, 42, 118–19; map of region of, 17; missions founded among, 36–39; physical description of, 23; scouts, 31; villages of, 20, 26, 86. *See also* Indians

Moxos (region), 179; arrival of Jesuit missionaries in, 16; becomes military governorship, 128; boundary of Spanish territory, 48; climate of, 12, 36; cultural geography of, 15; decline of expeditions to, 34; defined, 5–6; ecology of, 12–14, 58–59; established as theater of war, 177; expeditions into, 44; first Spanish exploration of, 28–29; forests of, 14; isolation of, 6–7, 154; landscape of, 11–13; location of,

Moxos (region) (*cont.*)
11, 188 n. 39; natural resources strained by mission culture, 58; Peruvian jurisdiction of, 28; pre-Columbian era, 20; prehistory of, 14–16; river systems of, 6; savanna of, 14; vegetation of, 12, 14; wildlife of, 12–14. *See under* Bolivia, Republic of; Jesuit missions
Moysuti Indians, 39–41
Muiba, Pedro Ignacio (cacique of San Javier), 131–32
Mules, 57; mule trains, 100, 138
Mure Indians, 146; map of regions of, 17
Murga, Juan de (mission benefactor), 70
Music(al), 45, 90; instruments, 96, 98, 124; instruments, of missions, 64–65; in mission services, 119; scores, 98
Musicians, 94, 96, 98, 167; illustration of, 97

Napkins, 137
Native peoples. *See* Indian(s)
Neophytes (new converts), 49, 55, 78; accounts of mission life, 52; armed for battle, 43; as artisans, 59; and citizenship, 126; Guarani Indian, 82, 102; labor of, 52, 59, 63; move to San Pedro, 50; and Portuguese war, 48, 52, 145. *See also* Conversion to Christianity
New Guinea, missions of, 118
New Plan, 129, 132, 136, 141, 146, 148, 177
Niza, Marco de, Fray, 35
Nordenskiöld, Baron Erland, 24; excavations conducted by, 15
Nossa Senhora da Conceição. *See* Santa Rosa
North America, 78, 120, 170; colonial period, 174; Florida, 102; Jesuits in, 68, 126; southwest region, 176. *See also* California
Nuestra Señora de Loreto. *See* Loreto
Nueva Asuncion. *See* Santa Cruz de la Sierra
Nueva Granada, 41, 82

Occupations, 95; archers, 49, 100; census of, 167; carpenters, 41, 86, 95, 99; carvers, 60, 94–95; cinchona collectors, 159, 173; cooks, 95; copyists, 95; construction workers, 59; doctors, 154; farmers, 23, 167; ironworkers, 96; masons, 41; paint-

ers, 95; postal employees, 154; rubber collectors, 162, 170–73; shoemakers, 167; spinners, 167; tallow-makers, 86; traders, 35; weavers, 60, 86, 95; woodworkers, 95. *See also* Handicrafts; Indians: labor of; Indians: cowboys; Musicians; Singers
Orbigny, Alcide Dessalines d', 167, 169; as ethnologist, 164; visit to Moxos, 163–64
Orellana, Antonio de (Jesuit missionary), 26, 37–38, 44, 113–14; architect-builder, 60
Oruro, 111; Jesuit travel to, 54
Osorio, José Luís (Bolivian corregidor of Loreto), 168
Owens, David, 82

Pacaguara Indians, 172
Pageants, 93
Painters, 95
Paintings, 156; fresco of church, 63; painted with feathers, 25; for religious instruction to Indians, 119
Paititi (Kayubaba chief), 18
Palacios, José Agustin, 172
Palca, 71
Palm Sunday, 93
Palm trees, 12
Pampas del Tigre, 71
Pampas missions, 85; population statistics of, 83–84
Panama, 66; Isthmus of, 111; missionaries bound for, 54; study of, 30
Papal agreement (Patronato Real), 67, 108, 177
Paper, 169
Pará. *See* Belém do Pará
Parades, 93
Paraguay, 41, 82, 107, 129, 165; comparison with Moxos, 1, 106; Jesuit churches in, 63; missionaries of, 1–2, 82, 102; takeover by Portuguese, 53
Parcialidades (groups of Pueblo), 87–88; linguistic groups, 167–69
Parejas Moreno, Alcides, 135, 141; research on Bourbon period in the missions, 3
Parry, J. H., 123
Passports, issued by Beni Prefects, 153
Pastures, 57–58
Paternalism, 102, 123

Patico (Indian interpreter), 31
Patronato Real (papal agreement), 67, 108, 177
Pax Jesuitica, 180
Peanuts, 23, 52
Peccary, 24
Peñalosa, Antonio de (Dominican priest and cura), 134
Pentland, Joseph Barclay (British diplomat), 156
Peppers, 23
Peru, 30, 33, 41, 44, 55, 63, 70–77, 103, 109–10, 150, 175; and administration of missions, 1, 35–36, 66–67, 70–71, 75, 116; colleges of, 72–73, 76; Creoles of, 176; earthquake of 1687, 71; European goods shipped from, 121; Indians of, 115; Province of, 103, 106, 108, 175; Viceroyalty of, 28, 51. See also Lima
Pestaña, Juan de, 52, 134; assembled troops in Charcas and Potosí, 51
Pharmaceutical industry, 149. See also Quinine
Pharmacies, 120
Philippines: Jesuits in, 126; Spanish spoken by natives of, 198 n. 33
Pillows, 138
Pinkas, Julio, 171
Pinto Parada, Rodolfo (Bolivian scholar), 3
Pizarro, Gonzalo, rebellion of, 28
Plantation, 98
Police officers, 154
Polygamy, prohibited, 87
Ponchos, 158
Population, Indian, 46, 142, 166, 196 n. 4
Population statistics. See Censuses; Demographics
Portugal, 47–51; conflicts with Spain, 47–52, 77–79, 104, 145; defenses against, 96, 100; expansions into Moxos, 47–49, 82–84, 99; expeditions against, 7, 47–48, 134; Luso-Spanish frontier, 77; presence in South America, 7; San Miguel captured by, 50; settlements in Moxos, 47; takeover of Paraguay, 53. See also Felix, Manoel, de Lima
Postal employees, 154
Potosí, 33, 111; mines of, 74, 138; troops assembled in, 51

Pottery, 25
Priests, Jesuit. See Jesuit priests
Principe da Beira, 143
Prisoners, native, 31
Procuradores, 70, 77, 109
Prostitution, 166
Pueblo (common Indians), 87–89, 94, 98–99, 144, 164, 166–67
Puerto Bello, 111
Pulpits, 63
Punishments, 95, 145, 156
Punuana Indians, missions established among, 38

Quechua (Indian language), 43
Quinine, 159–60; known as Jesuit Bark, 120; cinchona, 8, 120, 149, 159–60, 173

Rain, 12, 28, 46; rainy season, 51, 53. See also Flooding
Rapôso Tavares, Antonio, 47
Rausch, Jane, 82
Rebellions. See Indians: rebellions of
Religious observances, 90
Religious tracts in native languages, 118–19
René-Moreno, Gabriel, 172; research on Moxos, 3
Republic of Bolivia. See Bolivia, Republic of
Reyes (Los Santos Reyes mission), 68, 160, 161; census of, 167; founded by Fernández, 43; Mobima Indians in, 43
Ribadeneira, Juan de (procurador), 109
Ribera, Lázaro de (governor of Moxos), 127–36, 141–43, 146, 148, 177; administration of, 127–130, 135
Riberalta, 11
Rice, 41, 52, 57, 98
Río de la Plata, 28, 49, 99, 128
Río Grande, 29
Río Matos, 19
Risco, Juan, 70–71
Rivera y Quiroga, Benito (governor of Santa Cruz de la Sierra), 43; military campaigns of, 43
River culture, 23, 26, 178
Rivers, 6, 11–12; Amazon-Madeira-Guaporé route, 51; Apere River, 15; Chapare, 22; Chenesí, 22; Cuiabá, 47–48; Guapay (Grande), 28; Itonamas, 50; Ma-

Shamans, 27, 43, 197 n. 18; conversion of, 86

Sheets, 138

Shoemakers, 167

Silver, 24; discoveries in Charcas, 47; in missions, 64

Singers, 86, 96

Sivapaire, José (cacique of Loreto), 144

Slavery, 7, 19, 36, 47, 71, 73, 82, 169, 171, 178–79; raids for slaves, 6, 30–31, 38; slavers, 32

Smallpox, 142, 165

Smiths, 95–96

Soap, 169; from tallow, 136

Society of Jesus. *See* Jesuit missionaries; Jesuit missions

Soto, Juan de (Jesuit missionary and surgeon), 34–35

South America, 17, 28, 47; intra-Iberian conflicts in, 47–52, 77–79, 104, 145; trade in, 160

Spain: Jesuits embarking from, 111; Jesuits exiled back to, 54. *See also* Spaniards; Spanish; Spanish Crown; Spanish Empire; Spanish language; Spanish period

Spaniards, 6, 16, 28, 41, 51, 107, 176; prohibited from entering missions, 116

Spanish: army, 30–31, 43, 50–52, 83, 117, 132, 150; explorations, 28–29; family alliances, 89; markets, 95; intrusion as cause of native population decline, 78; missionaries, 105; model of government, 9, 115–16; relations with Moxos natives, 31; settlements, 27. *See also* Spaniards; Spanish Crown; Spanish language; Spanish period

Spanish Crown, 12, 54, 77, 108, 123, 127, 138, 177; Charles III, 49, 108, 128, 177; confiscation of Jesuit estates by, 8; inventories taken by, 57, 64; and mission support, 65, 67, 111, 175; Moxos governors as representatives of, 133; Portugal, conflicts with, 47–52, 77–79, 104, 145; unable to maintain authority in Moxos, 131

Spanish Empire, 8, 56; neophytes as citizens in, 177

Spanish Florida, 102

Spanish language: learned by natives, 28, 94, 119, 125; in Philippines, 198 n. 33

Spanish period (in Moxos), 125–48, 180; intramission rivalries during, 146; rebellion during, 8, 145, 147–48; administration during, 126–32; economic activities during, 132–41; mission Indians during, 141–48

Spinners, 167

Squash, 23

Steward, Julian, 22

Stucco, 59

Suárez, José Manuel, 163

Suárez de Figueroa, Lorenzo (governor of Santa Cruz), 29–30, 34

Sucre, Antonio José de (first president of Bolivia), 150–51

Sucre, collection of wood furnishings in, 96

Sugarcane, 57, 98, 138, 146–47, 156, 169; cane alcohol, 169; cultivation of, 41; mills, 60, 73–74; produced on haciendas, 73

Surnames: Indian, 88; Spanish, 153

Sweet, David, 31

Swords, 144

Tablecloths, 137, 158

Tacna, Jesuit travel to, 54

Tajibo, 12

Tallow, 60, 86, 135–36, 156

Tallow-makers, 86

Tamarinds, 138, 156, 158

Tamucu, 146

Tapacura Indians, 18, 38; map of region of, 17

Tapir, 24

Taxes, 150–53, 166

Texas, mission profits of, 68

Textiles, 120; cotton, 24–25, 48, 138, 158, 177–78; production of, 94–95, 155, 158; tablecloths, 137, 158; woolen, 146, 169

Tiahuanaco, 24

Tilici, Estanislao (cacique of Loreto), 131

Timber, 14, 60

Tobacco, 158

Todos Santos, 12

Tools, 96, 175; axes, 23–24, 101–2, 124; iron, 40, 65, 101–2

Tormo Sanz, Leandro, 20, 85, 90; research on Moxos, 3–4

Town planning, 56

Trade, 48, 160; between mission Indians and Europeans, 25, 101–2, 148; networks, 24; rubber, 163. *See also* Exports

Trade goods, distribution of, 121

Traders, 35